Mobile telephony constitutes a new challenge to philosophy, and indeed to the humanities in general. For the mobile telephone is not just the most successful machine ever invented, spreading with unheard-of speed; it is also a machine which corresponds to deep, primordial human communicational urges. Indeed the term "mobile information society" needs to be reconsidered. Mobile communications point to a future which offers a wealth of knowledge, not just of information, and promises to re-establish, within the life of modern society, some of the features formerly enjoyed by genuine local communities.

Kristóf Nyíri has published widely on Wittgenstein, Austrian intellectual history, and the philosophy of communication. He directs the interdisciplinary research program COMMUNICATIONS IN THE 21ST CENTURY, conducted jointly by the Institute for Philosophical Research of the Hungarian Academy of Sciences and Westel Mobile Telecommunications, Budapest.

MOBILE COMMUNICATION

PASSAGEN VERLAG

Communications in the 21st Century

Edited by
Kristóf Nyíri

Kristóf Nyíri (ed.)
Mobile Communication

Essays on Cognition and Community

Passagen Verlag

First English edition, 2003
Originally published in German under the title
Allzeit zuhanden. Gemeinschaft und Erkenntnis im Mobilzeitalter

We are grateful to Westel Mobile Telecommunications (Hungary)
for providing us with financial assistance in meeting publishing costs.

Bibliographic information published by Die Deutsche Bibliothek

Die Deutsche Bibliothek lists this publication in the Deutsche
Nationalbibliografie; detailed bibliographic
data are available on the Internet at http://dnb.ddb.de.

All rights reserved
ISBN 3-85165-602-4
© 2003 by Passagen Verlag Ges.m.b.H., Vienna
© of the German version 2002 by Passagen Verlag Ges.m.b.H., Vienna
© of the Hungarian version 2002 by Westel and the authors
Graphic concept: Ecke Bonk and ART 1st Design Studio Budapest
Typeset by ART 1st Design Studio Budapest
Printed by ART Photo

Contents

Kristóf Nyíri
Introduction: From the Information Society
to Knowledge Communities   11

Péter Gedeon
Market and Trust
in the Mobile Information Society   25

Nicola Green
Community Redefined:
Privacy and Accountability   43

R. I. M. Dunbar
Are There Cognitive Constraints on an E-World?   57

Klára Sándor
The Fall of Linguistic Aristocratism   71

Wolfgang Coy
Text and Voice – The Changing Role
of Computing in Communication   83

Péter György
Virtual Distance   97

Herbert Hrachovec
Mediated Presence   105

Valéria Csépe
Children in the Mobile Information Society:
Cognitive Costs and Benefits   117

Csaba Pléh
Communication Patterns
and Cognitive Architectures   127

Barbara Tversky
Some Ways Graphics Communicate   143

Kristóf Nyíri
Pictorial Meaning and Mobile Communication   157

János Laki - Gábor Palló
New Communication Media and Scientific Change   185

Endre Dányi - Miklós Sükösd
M-Politics in the Making: SMS and E-mail
in the 2002 Hungarian Election Campaign   211

Notes on Contributors   235

Index   241

Kristóf Nyíri: Introduction

From the Information Society
to Knowledge Communities

One of the leading philosophers of the twentieth century, Martin Heidegger, introduced in his major work *Being and Time* the concept of "readiness-to-hand" (*Zuhandenheit*). The things that surround us in a serviceable and manipulable manner, things to which we relate "by using them and manipulating them" – Heidegger calls them *equipment* – are "ready-to-hand".[1] Readiness-to-hand means unobtrusive usability; equipment – say a damaged tool – becomes conspicuous only when it ceases to be "handy", or indeed is not "to hand" at all.[2] Mobile phones are at hand to an ever-increasing degree. (Colloquial German, curiously, uses the imported English term *Handy* to refer to mobiles.) One can however hardly assume that Heidegger would have found them to his liking.[3] For, first, the mobile telephone is a machine, a product of high technology, and Heidegger posits a sharp opposition between tools and crafts on the one hand (good), and machines and technology on the other (bad). He has reservations even about the typewriter, "which is not quite a machine in the strict sense of machine technology, but rather something 'in between' a tool and a machine, a mechanism". Word, writing, and the hand, stresses Heidegger, stand in an "original essential relationship" to each other, which is "veiled by the type-writer".[4] Secondly, Heidegger had no time for mobility, especially for the mobile scientist accommodating himself to the technological age. "The scholar disappears", writes

---

[1] Martin Heidegger, *Sein und Zeit* (1927). I am quoting from the English translation by John Macquarrie and Edward Robinson, Oxford: Basil Blackwell, 1962, pp. 97 f.

[2] *Being and Time*, p. 103.

[3] See the excellent analyses by Alexander Roesler, in his essay "Das Telefon in der Philosophie: Sokrates, Heidegger, Derrida", in Stefan Münker and Alexander Roesler (eds.), *Telefonbuch: Beiträge zu einer Kulturgeschichte des Telefons* (Frankfurt/M.: Suhrkamp, 2000). George Myerson's booklet *Heidegger, Habermas and the Mobile Phone* (Cambridge: Icon Books, 2001) is informative on some aspects of German philosophy, but unperceptive when it comes to the miracle of mobile telephony.

[4] Martin Heidegger, *Parmenides*, Frankfurt/M.: Vittorio Klostermann, 1982, pp. 127 and 125 f.

Heidegger. "He is succeeded by the research man who is engaged in research projects. The research man no longer needs a library at home. Moreover, he is constantly on the move. He negotiates at meetings and collects information at congresses."[5]

Still, the mobile telephone need not necessarily be anathema to the spirit of Heideggerian romanticism. For the mobile phone is not just the most successful machine ever invented, spreading with unheard-of speed;[6] it is also a machine which corresponds to deep, primordial human communicational urges. The phenomenon of the mobile phone constitutes an obvious challenge to philosophy, and indeed to the humanities.[7] In Hungary the interdisciplinary research program "Communications in the 21st Century" was launched in January 2001. The program is conducted, in collaboration with Westel Mobile Telecommunications (Hungary), by the Institute for Philosophical Research of the Hungarian Academy of Sciences.[8] The first results of the program were published in two volumes in 2001.[9] In May 2002 there followed an international conference in Budapest; the papers in the present volume originate in the talks given at this conference.[10]

---

[5] Martin Heidegger, "The Age of the World Picture" (1938), in Heidegger, *The Question Concerning Technology and Other Essays*, New York: Garland Publishing, 1977, p. 125.

[6] Cf. esp. pp. 2–6 of the editors' introduction in James E. Katz and Mark Aakhus (eds.), *Perpetual Contact: Mobile Communication, Private Talk, Public Performance*, Cambridge: Cambridge University Press, 2002.

[7] For some first responses to this challenge see, besides the outstanding volume edited by Katz and Aakhus, Roesler's essay mentioned above; further James E. Katz, *Connections: Social and Cultural Studies of the Telephone in American Life*, New Brunswick, NJ: Transaction Publishers, 1999; Timo Kopomaa, *The City in Your Pocket: Birth of the Mobile Information Society*, Helsinki: Gaudeamus, 2000; Barry Brown, Nicola Green and Richard Harper (eds.), *Wireless World: Social and Interactional Aspects of the Mobile Age*, London: Springer, 2002. Howard Rheingold's *Smart Mobs*, Cambridge, MA: Perseus, 2002, published at the time the present volume was about to go to press, represents a useful compilation of quotes and interviews.

[8] For a regularly updated overview of the program see the website http://21st.century.phil-inst.hu.

[9] See Kristóf Nyíri (ed.), *Mobil információs társadalom: Tanulmányok* [The Mobile Information Society: Essays], Budapest: MTA Filozófiai Kutatóintézete, 2001, and Kristóf Nyíri (ed.), *A 21. századi kommunikáció új útjai: Tanulmányok* [New Perspectives on 21st-Century Communications: Essays], Budapest: MTA Filozófiai Kutatóintézete, 2001.

[10] The German translation of the present volume was published as Kristóf Nyíri (ed.), *Allzeit zuhanden: Gemeinschaft und Erkenntnis im Mobilzeitalter* (Vienna: Passagen Verlag, 2002). An extended Hungarian version appeared as Kristóf Nyíri (ed.), *Mobilközösség – mobilmegismerés: Tanulmányok*, Budapest: MTA Filozófiai Kutatóintézete, 2002. I am indebted to Warwick Luttrell for his assistance in revising the text of the present volume.

Communication and Community

The early phase of the research program went under the title "The Mobile Information Society", a phrase that has been current since 1999 or so. The phrase still figures on our project website; but we have increasingly come to realize that it is somewhat misleading. Mobile communications point to a future which offers a wealth of knowledge, not just of information, and promises to re-establish, within the life of modern society, some of the features formerly enjoyed by genuine local communities. "Community" on the one hand, "society" on the other, clearly differ in their connotations; and it was Tönnies who, towards the end of the nineteenth century, crystallized this difference into a conceptual contrast.[11] As Tönnies sees it, community involves "real", "organic", *continuous* associations. While the members of societies "are essentially separated in spite of all connecting factors", the members of a community "remain essentially connected in spite of all separating factors". As Tönnies of course states, "community is old, society is new, as a phenomenon and as a name";[12] however, the striking observation in the recent literature on mobile telephony is that through constant communicative connectedness a kind of turning back to the living, personal interactions of earlier communities is brought about.[13] In the present volume Tönnies' notion of a community is discussed by Nicola Green. Green pleads

---

[11] Ferdinand Tönnies, *Gemeinschaft und Gesellschaft*, 1887.

[12] Compare Ferdinand Tönnies, *Community and Society*, East Lansing, MI: Michigan State University Press, 1957, pp. 33 ff. and 65. I had to modify the Loomis translation at a number of points.

[13] Certainly this is the message of the formula "perpetual contact" in the Katz––Aakhus volume. The "socio-logic", indeed the "ontologies", of perpetual contact receive here (*op. cit.*, pp. 305–309) – not without a sidelong glance at Heidegger, incidentally – an especially profound analysis in the editors' closing essay: "Conclusion: Making Meaning of Mobiles – a Theory of *Apparatgeist*". Writing about fixed line telephone networks Claude S. Fischer had already in 1994 marshalled arguments against the view that "the telephone is yet another of modernity's blows against local *Gemeinschaft*, the close community" (Fischer, *America Calling: A Social History of the Telephone to 1940*, Berkeley: University of California Press, 1994, p. 25). Barry Wellman advocates in a series of publications the thesis that as a consequence of the internet and especially of the mobile telephone the nature of communities changes "from door-to-door and place-to-place communities to person-to-person and role-to-role communities... ... mobile phones afford a fundamental liberation from place... Their use shifts community ties from linking people-in-places to linking people wherever they are." (Barry Wellman, "Physical Place and CyberPlace", *International Journal of Urban and Regional Research*, 25, 2001.)

for a new view of community, in which the significance of localities recedes to the benefit of *symbolic processes*, in particular the negotiation of reciprocal *trust relations*. The concept of trust is at the centre also of Péter Gedeon's paper on issues of the mobile market economy, the first chapter of this volume.

Cleaving to a fundamental idea of the German Romantic philosophy of language, Tönnies propounds the view that it is not individual consciousness, but rather *communication within the commmunity*, that is the agent of human thinking. "Mental life", writes Tönnies, "manifests itself through communication, that is through the effect on kindred beings through signs, especially words pronounced by the use of vocal organs. From this develops thinking, i.e., the communication to oneself through audible or inaudible speech."[14] In the introductory chapter "The Theory of Community" Tönnies emphasizes that language, which "by means of gestures and sounds, enables expressions", is not "a means and tool by which one *makes* oneself understood", but it is "itself the living understanding".[15] The same idea of course plays a major role also in Heidegger's views, for whom "understanding" and "being together" (*Mitsein*) are intrinsically related to each other. As he puts it in the famous § 34 of *Being and Time*, making assertions or giving information is just a special case of "communication". In its most general sense, communication is the relationship in which "being with one another is understandingly constituted"; "communication is never anything like a conveying of experiences ... from the interior of one subject into the interior of another."

John Dewey already in 1915 formulated the thesis that social life is not just maintained by communication, but indeed constituted by it. As his oft-quoted lines run:

> Society not only continues to exist *by* transmission, *by* communication, but it may fairly be said to exist *in* transmission, *in* communication. There is more than a verbal tie between the words common, community, and communication. Men live in a community in virtue of the things they have in common; and communication is the way in which they come to possess things in common.[16]

Dewey's thesis is corroborated by contemporary research in evolutionary psychology. The essay by Robin Dunbar in the present volume

---

[14] *Op. cit.*, p. 107.
[15] *Ibid.*, p. 47.
[16] John Dewey, *Democracy and Education*, New York: Macmillan Co., 1915, p. 4.

propounds the view that language emerged in order to ensure social cohesion within primate groups at a stage where pre-verbal means of mutual attention had ceased to be effective due to growing group size. However, not even the potentials of verbal – and hence of digital, networked – communication will allow, according to Dunbar, a significant increase in the number of those with whom one can entertain cognitively transparent relationships. Dunbar's thesis is taken up by Klára Sándor's paper. Language creates social cohesion and group identity; linguistic differences serve the isolating of groups from each other. With the increasing influence of *literacy* however there arises a functional disorder: written language appears as the "correct" one in contrast to the merely spoken dialects. The new technologies of communication – the rise of *secondary orality*,[17] especially in the form of mobile telephony – now promise to heal that disorder.

There is an occasion here to refer once more to Heidegger. For Heidegger was – just like Wittgenstein by the way – a philosopher of secondary orality.[18] Language, for Heidegger, is always "discourse or talk", *Rede*; the spoken, *resounding*, heard language constitutes the primary environment of the individual human being. "Hearing", writes Heidegger, "is constitutive for discourse." Language is "intonation, modulation, the tempo of talk".[19] This view goes back at least to Rousseau and Herder – and receives a particularly impressive formulation in Richard Wagner's famous essay "Beethoven", published in 1870. "If we would conjure up a paradise of the human spirit's productivity", he writes,

> we must transfer ourselves to the days before the invention of Writing and its preservation on parchment or paper. We cannot but hold that here was born the whole of [our inherited] Culture... Here Poesis was nothing other than the actual invention of Myths... This faculty we see innate in every Folk of noble blood, down to the point when the use of written letters reached it. From then it loses its poetic force; Speech, theretofore in a living flux of natural evolution, now falls into the crystallising stage and stiffens..."[20]

---

[17] The term "secondary orality" was coined by Walter J. Ong, on whose work I shall touch upon later in this introduction.

[18] See my papers "Heidegger and Wittgenstein" (in J. C. Nyíri, *Tradition and Individuality: Essays*, Dordrecht: Kluwer, 1992) and "Wittgenstein as a Philosopher of Secondary Orality", *Grazer Philosophische Studien* 52 (1996/97), also acessible digitally: http://www.fil.hu/uniworld/nyiri/gps97/gps.htm.

[19] Heidegger, *Being and Time*, pp. 205 f.

[20] *Richard Wagner's Prose Works*, vol. 5 (1896), transl. by William Ashton Ellis, here quoted from the webpage http://users.belgacom.net/wagnerlibrary/prose/wlpr0133.htm.

Similar views were then of course held by Nietzsche. "The German does not read aloud, he does not read for the ear", runs an oft-quoted passage from *Beyond Good and Evil,*

> but only with his eyes... In antiquity when a man read – which was seldom enough – he read something to himself, and in a loud voice... In a loud voice: that is to say, with all the swellings, inflections, and variations of key and changes of TEMPO, in which the ancient PUBLIC world took delight. The laws of the written style were then the same as those of the spoken style.[21]

Nietzsche, who had very weak eyes and later became almost blind, liked to draw special attention to the pitfalls of written – visible – language. His short-sightedness soon drove him to limit himself to jotting down aphorisms, which he thought up by reciting to himself during long walks and then tried to memorize. He curses this imposed "telegraphic style"[22], he hates the way written language becomes abridged and flat through the telegraph, but at the same time he quite clearly feels a sense of liberation at the idea that the rise of telegraphic culture could spell the end of the age of the book. Nietzsche had no high regard for the logic and the world of abstract concepts made possible by written language – an attitude which today is of course widely shared in philosophical discourses on communication, and is taken issue with by Wolfgang Coy in the present volume.

Everyday communication in Nietzsche's age was already strongly dependent on telegraphy – by the early 1870s there was hardly a big city not wired. And the invention of the telegraph led to almost chiliastic expectations. Samuel Morse himself opened in 1844 the first telegraph line between Baltimore and Washington with the biblical words *What hath God wrought* (Num 23:23). An invention of such significance, he presumably wanted to indicate, could only have been engineered by divine providence. Soon, he wrote, the whole surface of America "would be channelled for those nerves which are to diffuse, with the speed of thought, a knowledge of all that is occurring throughout the land; making, in fact, one *neighborhood* of the whole country".[23] Innumerable com-

---

[21] Transl. by Helen Zimmern, as published in *The Complete Works of Friedrich Nietzsche* (1909–1913), here quoted from the webpage http://ibiblio.org/gutenberg/etext03/bygdv10.txt.

[22] Letter to Köselitz, Nov. 5, 1879.

[23] Quoted from Daniel J. Czitrom, *Media and the American Mind: From Morse to McLuhan*, Chapel Hill: University of North Carolina Press, 1982, pp. 11 f.

mentaries by his fellow-countrymen spoke of the promise of "a unity of interest, men linked by a single mind, and the worldwide victory of Christianity", of the coming of universal peace and harmony.[24] Expectations – and disappointments – the echoes of which are still resounding today. Their background and contemporary variations are discussed in the present volume by Péter György.

After the spread of the telegraph there followed that of the telephone beginning in the 1880s, radio broadcasting in the 1920s, and television in the 1940s – events that of course profoundly changed the meanings of direct communication and personal presence, topics analyzed by Herbert Hrachovec in this volume.[25] Philosophical reflection on changes in communications technology in the late-nineteenth century began with Dewey and his circle. It was Dewey's student Charles Horton Cooley who introduced the concept of *primary groups*, which is to say groups characterized by intimate face-to-face association and cooperation. Cooley's hypothesis was that what gesture and speech ensured in primary groups, modern means of communication would guarantee for the whole of society.[26] Dewey was rather skeptical of this hypothesis. He doubted if the face-to-face intimacy of smaller communities could be transplanted to the broader society. As he put it: "The Great Community, in the sense of free and full intercommunication, is conceivable. But it can never possess all the qualities which mark the local community."[27] It is local neighbourhoods that constitute those sorts of environments in which direct spoken intercourse coalesces with social communication as mediated via

---

[24] Cf. Czitrom, *op. cit.*, p. 10. See also Carolyn Marvin, *When Old Technologies Were New: Thinking About Electric Communication in the Late Nineteenth Century*, New York: Oxford University Press, 1988.

[25] On these issues see also Kenneth J. Gergen, "The challenge of absent presence", in Katz and Aakhus (eds.), *Perpetual Contact*. The phenomenon of "absent presence", as Gergen stresses, emerged already with printing: "the development of print technology harbors the potential for pandemic revolution: myriad voices from far-flung locales may enter without detection at any time to challenge the cherished realities of one's imediate community. ... In print, the absent voices are now present and, as they are absorbed, the claims of the local community are diminished" (*op. cit.*, p. 228). Gergen's contention is that while the development of communications technology brings ever stronger intrusions of "absent presence" into the life of face-to-face communities, by the rise of telephony, and especially of mobile telephony, this tendency is reversed: "The realities and moralities of the face-to-face relationship are revitalized", *ibid.*, p. 237.

[26] I am here following Czitrom, *Media and the American Mind*, pp. 93 ff.

[27] John Dewey, *The Public and Its Problems*, here quoted from Dewey, *The Later Works*, vol. 2, ed. by J. A. Boydston, Carbondale: Southern Illinois University Press, 1988, p. 367.

newspapers and books.

A different strand in philosophical reflexion on the effects of communications technologies emerged in Vienna after the first world war. It was here that Robert Musil in 1923 published his review of Spengler's *The Decline of the West*. Spengler proposed a contrast between the two concepts of what he called culture and civilisation; this contrast formed a parallel to the earlier distinction between community and society. Musil thought that when seen from the perspective of communications technology the contrast between culture and civilisation was not a sharp one. As he put it:

> The increase in the numbers of people participating in the process is the main reason for the transition from culture to civilization. It is clear that reaching hundreds of millions of people poses very different tasks from reaching a hundred thousand. The negative sides of civilization in the main hang together with the fact that the volume of the social body has become too immense; thus its susceptibility to influences no longer survives. ... Intellectual organization does not keep pace with the increase in numbers... No initiative is able to penetrate the body of society across broad fronts, and to receive feedback from its totality.[28]

Musil's circle included the Hungarian poet and playwright Béla Balázs, whose influential book *Der sichtbare Mensch* ("The visible person"), a book dealing with the aesthetics of the film, was published in 1924. For Balázs film was the *folk art* of the 20th century. He believed that it is actually "the language of gestures" that is the "mother tongue of mankind", and, as he wrote:

> It is not the same spirit that is expressed now in words, now in gestures. ... For the possibility of expressing ourselves conditions in advance our thoughts and feelings. ... Psychological and logical analyses have proven that our words are not subsequent representations of our thoughts, but forms which will from the beginning determine the latter.[29]

---

[28] Robert Musil, "Geist und Erfahrung. Anmerkungen für Leser, welche dem Untergang des Abendlandes entronnen sind", in Musil, *Gesammelte Werke in neun Bänden*, Reinbek bei Hamburg: Rowohlt, 1978, vol. 8, pp. 1057 f.

[29] Béla Balázs, *Schriften zum Film I–II*, vol. I: *Der sichtbare Mensch. Kritiken und Aufsätze 1922–1926*, Budapest: Akadémiai Kiadó, 1982, pp. 46 ff.

Balázs associates the view that words are mere carriers of thoughts from person to person with the emergence of *printing*; and he observes that as a consequence of printing all forms of communication other than reading and writing have receded into the background.

Balázs's work exerted an influence, among others, on Marshall McLuhan and his Toronto circle. This was the circle from which, in the 1950s and 1960s, the great attack on the printed book was launched. In 1963 the ground-breaking study "The Consequences of Literacy" by Goody and Watt appeared.[30] Here the authors could point out that it is of course no longer the book, but rather, and ever-increasingly, the new communications media – they mention radio, film, and television – by which our age is dominated. These, Goody and Watt stress, "do not have the abstract and solitary quality of reading and writing", but on the contrary bring back, to some extent, the "direct personal interaction which obtains in oral cultures". As Goody and Watt write:

> It may even be that these new modes of communicating sight and sound without any limit of time or place will lead to a new kind of culture: less inward and individualistic than literate culture, probably, and sharing some of the relative homogeneity, though not the mutuality, of oral society.[31]

McLuhan, Goody–Watt, Parry[32] (and Lord[33], who continued Parry's endeavours), as well as the classic scholar Eric Havelock[34] form the background, finally, of the work of Walter J. Ong. It is Ong's merit to have created a *synthesis* between the theories of post-literary, literary, and pre-literary communication. As he writes:

> with telephone, radio, television and various kinds of sound tape, electronic technology has brought us into the age of "secondary orality". This new orality has striking resemblances to the old in its participatory mystique, its fostering of a communal sense, its concentration on the

---

[30] Jack Goody and Ian Watt, "The Consequences of Literacy", *Comparative Studies in Society and History* 5/3 (April 1963).

[31] Jack Goody (ed.), *Literacy in Traditional Societies*, Cambridge: Cambridge University Press, 1968, p. 63.

[32] Milman Parry, "Studies in the Epic Technique of Oral Verse-making", I–II, *Harvard Stud. in Class. Phil.* 41 and 43 (1930 and 1932).

[33] Albert B. Lord, *The Singer of Tales*, Cambridge, MA: Harvard University Press, 1960.

[34] See especially Eric A. Havelock, *Preface to Plato*, Cambridge, MA: Harvard University Press, 1963.

present moment... But it is essentially a more deliberate and self-conscious orality, based permanently on the use of writing and print, which are essential for the manufacture and operation of the equipment and for its use as well. ... secondary orality generates a sense for groups immeasurably larger than those of primary oral culture..."[35]

Even the most cursory survey of the topic of communication and community would be one-sided without a reference to the book *Nationalism and Social Communication* by Karl W. Deutsch,[36] a book it is imperative for contemporary philosophical research on communication to rediscover. Like Tönnies, Deutsch postulates a conceptual contrast between community and society, but in his case the dimension of communication plays a rather more explicit role than it did in Tönnies' work.[37] Deutsch applies the notion of *complementarity*, originally a concept in communications theory, to the issues of social communication, and defines communities as characterized by patterns of communication that display a high level of complementarity between information conveyed through various channels.[38] It is because of the drive to *multimedia* inherent in networked and mobile communication that the approach of Deutsch today again appears as especially timely.

Information and Knowledge

Echoing T.S. Eliot's famous lines from the early 1930s – "Where is the wisdom we have lost in knowledge? Where is the knowledge we have lost in information?" – John Naisbitt in his popular book *Megatrends*, published in 1982, bemoans the phenomenon that the world is "drown-

---

[35] Walter J. Ong, *Orality and Literacy: The Technologizing of the Word*, London: Methuen, 1982, p. 136.

[36] Karl W. Deutsch, *Nationalism and Social Communication: An Inquiry into the Foundations of Nationality*, New York: John Wiley & Sons, 1953.

[37] As a third element Deutsch here introduces the concept of *culture*. As he writes: "'Culture' and 'community' can be used interchangeably because they describe a single complex of processes. When we say 'culture', we stress the configuration of preferences or values; when we say 'community' we stress the aspects of communication... ... There is no community nor culture without society. And there can be no society, no division of labour, without a minimum of transfer of information, without communication. Yet the difference between society and community is crucial." (*Nationalism and Social Communication*, pp. 63 and 69.)

[38] *Ibid.*, pp. 69 ff.

ing in information, but is starved for knowledge". Naisbitt's formulation is taken up by Vartan Gregorian among many others, in an address given in 1992.[39] Gregorian – at that time President of Brown University – there also refers to Carlos Fuentes as saying that "one of the greatest challenges facing modern society and contemporary civilization is how to transform information into knowledge". The conclusion Gregorian reaches is that today's educational institutions must be careful to "provide not just information, but its distillation, namely knowledge".

The notion that "information" is somehow inferior to "knowledge" is not of recent origin. Although the Latin word *informare*, meaning the action of forming matter, such as stone, wood, leather, etc., also took on the senses "to instruct", "to educate", "to form an idea"[40] – Cicero's *informare deos coniectura* was explained as "imaginer en son esprit et conjecturer quels sont les dieux" by Robert Estienne in his *Dictionarium Latinogallicum* (1552) – "informare" in Italian, "informer" in French, and "to inform" in English from the beginning had the connotation of conveying knowledge that is merely particular. Perhaps another Latin word, *informis* – meaning unshapen, formless – had, with its French and English derivatives ("informe", "inform"), a certain coincidental effect here. To have information amounted to knowing details, possibly unconnected. Hence the use of the word "information" in the contexts of criminal accusation, charge, legal process. John Locke, in his *Essay Concerning Human Understanding* (1690), might have thought that "information" had to do with "truth and real knowledge";[41] however, what the OED refers to as the "prevailing mod. sense" of *inform*, namely "to impart knowledge of some particular fact or occurrence", or the *Larousse* phrase "informer quel-qu'un de quelque chose", indeed appear to capture the essentials of the concept.

Thus Roszak can correctly point out, in his *The Cult of Information* (1986), that in the days of his childhood, shortly before the outbreak of World War II, "information" was a dull word, referring to answers to concrete questions, having the form of names, numbers, dates, etc. With Shannon's and Weaver's technical concept of information, put forward in *The Mathematical Theory of Communication* (1949), and with the emergence of computers, it also became a misleading – and glorious – word. Attempts at clarification of course abound. Daniel Bell made such an

---

[39] See http://www.cni.org/docs/tsh/Keynote.html.

[40] Recall, also, the original meaning of the Greek words *eidos* or *idea*: "pattern", "visual form".

[41] Cf. book 3, chapter 10, sect. 34.

attempt in 1979, writing: "By information I mean data processing in the broadest sense; the storage, retrieval, and processing of data becomes the essential resource for all economic and social exchanges. ... By knowledge, I mean an organized set of statements of facts or ideas, presenting a reasoned judgment or an experimental result, which is transmitted to others through some communication medium in some systematic form."[42]

Let me sum up the foregoing by saying that knowledge can be usefully regarded as information in context.[43] Now it is a standard observation that information sought through mobile phones is, characteristically, location-specific and situation-specific. It seems, then, that mobile communication tends to engender not just information, but information in context: that is, knowledge per se. Five papers in the present volume focus on issues of cognition and knowledge. Valéria Csépe examines the way *children* handle mobile phones, and shows that in their case *procedural* – practical – learning and memory play the major role, in contrast to adults, who learn and apply excplicit rules. Csépe's argument relates not just to some particular divergence as regards the mode of knowledge processing of the different generations, but also to the fundamental question whether there is to be expected, in the near future, a general mod-

---

[42] Daniel Bell, "The Social Framework of the Information Society", in M. L. Dertouzos and Joel Moses, eds., *The Computer Age: A Twenty-Year View*, Cambridge, MA: MIT Press, 1979, p. 168. – Compare Alvin Toffler, *Powershift: Knowledge, Wealth, and Violence at the Edge of the 21st Century*, New York: Bantam Books, 1990: "There are, of course, as many definitions of knowledge as there are people who regard themselves as knowledgeable. Matters grow worse when words like *signs*, *symbols*, and *imagery* are given highly technical meanings. And the confusion is heightened when we discover that the famous definition of *information* by Claude Shannon and Warren Weaver, who helped found information science, while useful for technological purposes, has no bearing on semantic meaning or the 'content' of communication. – In general, in the pages ahead, *data* will mean more or less unconnected 'facts'; *information* will refer to data that have been fitted into categories and classification schemes or other patterns; and *knowledge* will mean information that has been further refined into more general statements. But to avoid tedious repetition, all three terms may sometimes be used interchangeably" (p. 18). – Less useful, for our present purposes, is Dretske's well-known distinction: "Roughly speaking, information is that commodity capable of yielding knowledge, and what information a signal carries is what we can learn from it" (Fred I. Dretske, *Knowledge and the Flow of Information*, Oxford: Basil Blackwell, 1981, p. 44).

[43] For inspiring discussions on the topic of information and knowledge I am indebted to Dr. Ferenc Tompa, Executive Director for Telecom Policy, Westel Mobile Telecommunications.

ification in learning and recalling patterns. Pléh's paper, taking its point of departure from Merlin Donald's theory of an *external memory*, formulates the hypothesis that the new cognitive environment created by mobile communication might well lead to changes in our mental architecture, introducing, as it were, a new phase in human cognitive evolution. Barbara Tversky analyzes the fascinating interactions, within our mental architecture, between verbal and graphic communication, and refers to the role graphics play as cognitive instruments in the collective thinking of communities. The paper of the present editor accepts the assumption that human cognition is initially of a markedly pictorial character, and examines the question to what extent pictorial thinking can be mediated in a multimedia and mobile communication environment. János Laki and Gábor Palló in their contribution investigate a crucial issue in the philosophy of science, namely the connection between technologies of communication on the one hand, and scientific content on the other. They conclude that with the emergence of mobile telephony in scientific communication, a revision of some basic views in the philosophy of science, too, will become inevitable.

The volume ends with a paper on some recent developments in the domains of *political communities* and *political insight*. The Hungarian parliamentary election campaign in 2002 has for the first time shown that with mobile telephony becoming widespread, the European political scene will experience some very new phenomena. The study by Miklós Sükösd and Endre Dányi is both empirical and theoretical, and provides a subtly nuanced and essential contribution to the picture we here attempted to draw of the coming mobile knowledge communities.

Péter Gedeon: # Market and Trust in the Mobile Information Society

Trust in a Complex Economy

Within the framework of a traditional society the coordination of individual economic activities is carried out by the community. The uncertainties inherent in the individuals' economic activities may be reduced owing to the trust engendered by personal relationships among members of the community. However, there is a price to be paid for the successful coordination of individual activities: personal trust among individuals is able to reduce the complexity arising from the uncertainties of economic transactions only if it also reduces the complexity of the economic order arising from the same transactions.[1] Modern societies, in their turn, having spawned market coordination, can create a complex economic system based on *impersonal* relationships among individuals. It is market coordination that makes it possible to reduce the uncertainties of economic transactions without reducing the complexity of the economic system. These economic transactions built on impersonal contacts among individuals make personal trust as a means for

---

[1] "The security of the conduct of life transcending trust in other people was achieved, if at all, in primitive social orders through religiously based assumptions about true existence, nature and supernature, and through myth, language and natural law. That is, the lawful order was normatively given and taken for granted. Insofar as the world was deprived of human disposition, its complexity had already been presumed in a reduced form. Impersonal forms of trust were not required. Where the mediation and interpretation of this world order was needed, there it was done through the authority of those gods, saints or that of those knowledgeable interpreters who could be trusted like a person. In contrast, differentiated social orders enhance their problem-solving capacity and therefore are able to see the world in a more complex way. They themselves become much more complex, in order to be able to grasp and sort more possibilities. Consequently, the processes of internal differentiation and critical reflection will be activated and the development will be pushed further on." (Niklas Luhmann, *Vertrauen. Ein Mechanismus der Reduktion sozialer Komplexität*, Stuttgart: Ferdinand Enke Verlag, 1968, p. 44.)

reducing uncertainty superfluous. In a modern economy the trust in money has evolved as a substitute for personal trust among members of a community. Within a market economy it is the impersonal trust in money that assumes the function of stabilizing economic transactions among individuals.[2]

However, the assumption that there is an impersonal relationship among buyers and sellers is closer to a theoretical postulate than to empirical reality. The social connections of individuals, the social embeddedness of economic activities should not be neglected in the study of the everyday functioning of markets.[3] If one takes into consideration that market transactions incur costs, the economic effects of the social conditions of markets may be brought into the economic analysis: the specific characteristics of the social embeddedness of the market may increase or decrease the transaction costs of economic exchange.

Mass Customization

In the capitalist economy the material content and the institutional form of production and regulation undergo changes, and so does the market. The transformation of an industrial society into an information society has been the latest important change in the production and regulation regime of capitalism to date.[4] From the point of view of the economy, the emergence of an information society is equal to the penetration of information technology into the process of production and regulation. The application of information technology enables the economic actors to supersede the regime of mass production. Mass production built on industrial technology and corporate hierarchy resembles the theoretical model that described the market as a system of impersonal relationships of economic actors – especially when we contrast it to the technology of

---

[2] "Money makes it possible to give the complexity of the whole economic system literally into the hands of the individuals... However, for its functioning the mechanism presumes that money itself is being trusted." (Luhmann, *op. cit.*, pp. 45–46.) – "Those who possess money do not have to trust others. The generalized trust in the institution of money replaces those numerous individual and diffficult ways of authentication that were necessary to provide for subsistence in a cooperative society through a global act." (Luhmann, *op. cit.*, p. 48.)

[3] See Mark Granovetter, "Economic Action and Social Structure: The Problem of Embeddedness", *American Journal of Sociology*, vol. 91, no. 3 (Nov. 1985), pp. 481–510.

[4] See Manuel Castells, *The Information Age: Economy, Society and Culture*, vols. I–III, Oxford: Blackwell, 1996, 1997, 1998.

flexible specialization.[5] Mass production standardized products and homogenized labor. It made the individual units of products, labor and even consumers substitutable with each other. The words of Henry Ford aptly characterize the spirit of mass production:

> The way to make automobiles is to make one automobile like another, to make them all alike, to make them come through the factory just alike – just like one pin is like another pin when it comes from the pin factory and one match is like another match when it comes from the match factory.[6]

The market of mass production appears to lack personal relationships and personal trust among the economic actors. However, the emergence of oligopolies in mass production introduced certain elements of personal trust into the sphere of market competition. If the products of competing producers do not differ from one another and the information cost of product comparison is relatively small for the consumers, producers may be compelled to compete for customers by reducing their prices, which in turn will diminish their profits. For this reason and in order to counterbalance this effect, large corporations have tried to differentiate their products through the introduction of trademarks. The impersonal competition of atomistic economic actors was transformed into a monopolistic competition of sellers personified by trademarks. This process of personification takes on a series of new dimensions with the emergence of mass customization.

Mass production created global markets. The economic success of mass producing corporations was dependent on the size of their markets: competitiveness tied to the application of economics of scale demanded large production series and consumer markets. Mass production created global markets transcending national borders and local communities. At the same time, these new global markets resting on the impersonal relationships of economic actors were created not on the ruins of, but above, local communities, in another dimension, not threatening their existence. Localism built on personal contacts was not endangered by the globalism of mass production, partly because the different centers of

---

[5] For this contrast see Michael J. Piore and Charles F. Sabel, *The Second Industrial Divide*, New York: Basic Books, 1984.

[6] The words of Henry Ford are cited in Alfred D. Chandler, Jr. (ed.), *Giant Enterprise: Ford, General Motors, and the Automobile Industry*, New York: Harcourt, Brace, and World, 1964, p. 28.

mass production also belonged to certain localities.

The emergence of the information society, the penetration of information technology into the production has made mass production different in both aspects discussed above. Information technology made the customization of mass products possible. In the process of market competition producers try to satisfy the specific individual preferences of customers and to gain market advantage and larger market share through the customization of their products. The spirit of this new epoch is expressed by Jeff Bezos:

> If I have 3 million customers on the Web, I should have 3 million stores on the Web.[7]

In the new production and market regime the mass consumer has become an individualized personal consumer, with whom the seller has to build up a personal relationship under the pressure of market competition. The importance of personal trust between seller and buyer has been appreciated. The tendency of personalization created by the customization of mass products has supplemented the impersonal trust in money with personal trust among market players. As a result of this, the market has been following the new principle of "impersonal intimacy", the principle of the "impersonal-personal".

Electronic Commerce (E-Commerce)

E-commerce enables a buyer to substantially reduce the costs of acquiring information about the supply side. On the other hand, sellers may also gain, at a very low cost, information about the individual preferences of buyers. For instance, consumers may search for the least expensive product they want to purchase by utilizing internet search engines. Sellers may also run computer programs to collect and filter information provided by would-be buyers during their search operations, in order to analyse the personal preferences and shopping habits of their customers.[8]

---

[7] Jeff Bezos is the CEO of Amazon.com. His words are cited in Ben J. Schafer, Joseph A. Konstan, and John Riedl, "Electronic Commerce Recommender Applications", *Journal of Data Mining and Knowledge Discovery*, vol. 5, nos. 1–2, p. 115, http://www.cs.umn.edu/Research/GroupLens/papers/pdf/ec-99.pdf.

[8] See Corinna Schulze and Jeffrey Baumgartner, "Don't Panic! Do E-Commerce. A Beginner's Guide to European Law Affecting E-Commerce". Published by the European

Electronic commerce is expected to increase efficiency by decreasing the transaction costs of search and exchange, improving product information for buyers, and increasing the pressure of competition on the supply side.[9] As buyers become better informed, the prices of identical goods will tend toward the lowest price to be found in the market. This will result in a consumer surplus increase that is advantageous to the welfare of the buyer. However, information technology increases not only the information of buyers about sellers but also contributes to the knowledge of the sellers about buyers. Consequently, the anticipated increase in consumer welfare becomes uncertain. The seller may be able to quote different prices to different buyers (price discrimination) by utilizing the information collected on the individual preferences of buyers. Sellers also may follow the strategy of product differentiation and individual customization, making more difficult for the buyers to compare products, thereby reducing transparency of the market.[10] While electronic commerce intensifies the sellers' competition for buyers, they are not completely helpless in this situation. Sellers may in turn try to create and maintain their own secure and profitable market segments by means of product customization and price discrimination.[11] To summarize, elec-

---

Commission's Electronic Commerce Team (Information Society Directorate General), 2000–2001, p. 10., http://europa.eu.int/ISPO/ecommerce/books/dont_panic. pdf. – "To target advertisements, sellers are no longer limited to using crude demographic data. Instead, cybercommunities and online interest groups segment consumers into finer groups than ever before." (Soon-Yong Choi, Dale O. Stahl and Andrew B. Whinston, *Electronic Payments and the Future of Electronic Commerce*, The Center for Research in Electronic Commerce, The University of Texas at Austin, 1997, http://cism.bus. utexas.edu/works/articles/cyberpayments.html.)

[9] See Varun Grover and Pradipkumar Ramanlal, "Six Myths of Information and Markets: Information Technology Networks, Electronic Commerce, and the Battle for Consumer Surplus", *MIS Quarterly*, vol. 23, no. 4 (Dec. 1999), pp. 465–495, and Jonathan Coppel, "E-Commerce: Impacts and Policy Challenges", Working Papers No. 252, 2000, Economics Department, Graduate School of Business, The University of Texas at Austin, p. 14, http://www.olis.oecd.org/olis/2000doc.nsf/linkto/eco-wkp(2000)25.

[10] Yannis Bakos, "The Emerging Role of Electronic Marketplaces on the Internet", *Communications of the ACM*, vol. 41, no. 8 (Aug. 1998), p. 9. – Varun Grover and Pradipkumar Ramanlal, "Playing the E-Commerce Game", *Business & Economic Review*, vol. 47, no. 1 (Oct.–Nov. 2000), pp. 9–14.

[11] "This perspective of markets describes the two extremes of a spectrum: perfect price discrimination, where suppliers extract the entire consumer surplus and markets are least effective; and perfect competition, where markets are most effective because the surplus in its entirety accrues to consumers. Given the reality of opposing motives of suppliers and consumers, however, most markets fall between these two extremes. The

tronic commerce will not necessarily lead to frictionless, perfect markets.[12]

On the supply side the market compels the competing economic actors to develop personal contacts with the actors on the demand side, to personalize mass products, and to adjust to the new market principle of supplementing the impersonal contacts between market actors with personal elements. This mix of the personal and the impersonal burdens the trust between market players with a new element: buyers have to trust sellers that they do not use the information gathered about buyers as they please. As a result of the application of information technology in economic transactions the relationships between sellers and buyers have become more than a simple economic contract. In economic transactions sellers may get hold of personal information about buyers.[13] The use of this information should be regulated in the framework of a social contract concluded by sellers and buyers.[14] The personalization of

---

conflicting forces at play will determine the eventual market structure. For example, commoditization enhances product substitutability and lower search costs permit comparative shopping, which results in more effective markets. Conversely, information asymmetries between suppliers and customers and cost differentials between them for acquiring information about products and prices result in less effective markets. In the latter case, some of the consumer surplus will be expropriated from customers as suppliers set prices based on decisions made within the corporate hierarchy rather than as a consequence of market forces." (Varun Grover and Pradipkumar Ramanlal, "Six Myths of Information and Markets", *op. cit.*)

[12] Mark Kvamme, the president of USWeb/CKS seems to show an inordinate optimism about the use of internet in economic transactions: "To paraphrase Dell Computer founder Michael Dell, the Internet results in 'zero variable cost transactions, the only thing better would be mental telepathy'." (John W. Cioffi, "Analytical Summary and Report", *The Digital Economy in International Perspective: Common Construction or Regional Rivalry. A Conference of the University of California E-conomy Project*, Washington, D.C., May 27, 1999, http://e-conomy.berkeley.edu/events/deip/summary.htm.)

[13] "...commercial institutions gather information about their customers, compiling extensive databases of information about consumer preferences and habits, as well as exhaustive lists of personal details. These practices have also become taken for granted, and often employ the active collaboration of those under scrutiny to maintain and update the information in a form of self-surveillance." (Nicola Green, "Who's Watching Whom? Monitoring and Accountability in Mobile Relations", in Barry Brown, Nicola Green and Richard Harper (eds.), *Wireless World. Social and Interactional Aspects of the Mobile Age*, London: Springer, 2001, p. 36.)

[14] "It seems obvious that relationship exchanges over the Web involve both an economic and a social contract. The economic contract with the seller is characterized by an exchange of goods or services for money. Because the seller may capture personal information from the consumer without the consumer's notice or consent, this infor-

market relationships may encounter barriers purposely set up by buyers aspiring to depersonalize their contacts with sellers.

Mobile Commerce (M-Commerce)

Mobile commerce is a variant of electronic commerce. The mobile phone may become a special device for mass customization creating the new mix of impersonal-personal contacts in market processes. On the one hand, the mobile phone allows for a personalized communication between buyer and seller. The mobile phone offers market players a more direct and more personal contact than the internet.[15] On the other hand, economic actors of the supply side may utilize a specific feature of the mobile phone that makes it possible to determine the current local position of the bearer of the mobile device. With the help of the mobile phone sellers will be able to customize mass products along the dimension of locality.[16]

---

mation exchange is not included in the quid pro quo and is thus comprised within a social contract. In the current commercial Web environment, this social contract dictates how commercial Web providers handle consumer information. A consumer engaging in an online transaction implicitly trusts the seller not to compromise his or her information privacy. Yet in current practice, the exact nature of this future return is rarely stipulated in advance, and not regulated by law. We believe that many consumers avoid relationship exchanges on the Web primarily because they do not trust commercial Web providers. We believe this lack of trust arises from consumers' belief that commercial Web providers do not share their values about information privacy in online commercial environments, and that commercial Web providers are likely to engage in opportunistic behaviors. This may likely lead to a lessened commitment to the relationship, which in turn generates higher decision-making uncertainty, less cooperation, and higher propensity to leave." (Donna L. Hoffman, Thomas P. Novak and Marcos A. Peralta, "Information Privacy in the Marketspace: Implications for the Commercial Uses of Anonymity on the Web", *Information Society*, vol. 15, no. 2 [April–June 1999], p. 133.)

[15] M. Rao cites a manager: "Some learnings from the Internet world can be applied to the wireless world as well, but the wireless user environment is more immediate, personal and impatient..." (Madanmohan Rao, "Internet Ushers in Fourth Wave of Banking and Finance Innovation", *EM-Wire*, March 27, 2001.)

[16] Experts and mobile service providers equally draw attention to the possible use of mobile appliances in providing services tied to locality. "The networks know who you are and where you are. This has enormous leverage potential..." (Madanmohan Rao, "Asia Leads World in Wireless Internet Technology Markets", *EM-Wire*, April 5 2001.) – "Retailers must look beyond transactions. For example, mobile phones reach consumers anywhere. They can cultivate loyalty through personalized alerts, create opportunities for location-based services that advance consumers toward purchases, and build

Funk treats this feature of m-commerce in terms of reach and richness. Services dependent on locality as opposed to those provided by the fixed internet create a tradeoff between reach and richness. The information provided by spatially fixed terminals is richer in content than that provided by mobile phones, but the accessibility of the information supplied by the internet is narrower than that received by the mobile phone. One can receive information and purchase goods and services through the mobile phone any time, anywhere, and according to changing needs, that may have altered precisely due to a change in the spatial position of the actor.[17]

Potential buyers may be reached by potential sellers through the mobile phone everywhere and all the time. This connectivity of mobile phone owners attracts the application of new marketing strategies that adapt their messages to the change in the spatial position of mobile phone owners. However, mobile marketing, too, has its limitations: constantly attacking the potential buyer on his mobile phone with information linked to local purchasing opportunities might violate the buyer's personal sphere. The buyer will defend his sphere of intimacy against

---

brand awareness through opt-in ads." (Michael Pastore, "M-Commerce? Maybe M-Games? Yes", *M-Commerce Times*, Sept. 17, 2000, http://www.mcommercetimes.com/Marketing/58.) – "Advertisers can reach the exact people they want to reach ... in the exact spot where they want to reach them – and they can often get an immediate response." (*The Economist*, "Ring In the New", Oct. 9, 1999, pp. 28–29. – "A mobile Internet device ... will thus become a convenient way to probe local information and services. Location will, in effect, be used as a search parameter, to narrow down the information presented to the user. Mobile devices ... 'reassert geography on the Internet'." ("Geography and the Net. Putting It in Its Place", *The Economist*, Aug. 24, 2001, www.economist.com/printedition/displayStory.cfm?Story_ID=729808.)

[17] "The tradeoff between 'reach' and 'richness' is a critical aspect of location-dependent services. Location-specific information can be just as easily acquired from the fixed-line Internet as from the mobile Internet. Airline tickets, hotels, and rental cars can be reserved using a desktop computer and information on local bars, restaurants, stores, and trains can be obtained from a desktop computer. The difference between these types of reservations and information and other types of information is that your plans often change while you are in the specific location. Therefore, a high reach device such as a mobile phone is needed to acquire new information or make new reservations. Thus, the unique aspect of location-specific information is that it requires high reach." (Jeffrey L. Funk, "The Mobile Internet Market: Lessons from Japan's i-Mode System", Sept. 26–27, 2000, Washington D.C., p. 6, http://e-conomy.berkeley.edu/conferences/9-2000/EC-conference2000_papers/Funk.pdf.)

[18] "...mobile e-commerce has interesting possibilities, but it could also be a very powerful tool for alienating customers. However, beware of using location technology to

the intrusion of the seller who tries to inject personal aspects into the impersonal relationship between them. Consequently, the only sellers that will be able to rely on the tools of mobile marketing will be those authorized by the buyer, and then only within spatial and temporal limitations also imposed by each individual consumer.[18] The use of mobile devices may multiply the attacks on the privacy of economic actors as consumers, however, if those consumers object to this invasion they will rigourously defend their sphere of privacy.[19]

The marketing strategy of mass customization linked to the dimension of locality will also inevitably be affected by the constraint of information overload. Networked individuals connected through mobile tools will be forced to apply selection mechanisms in order to reduce the complexity arising from information overload.[20]

Electronic Money

Electronic commerce creates its own medium called electronic money.[21] White points out that the use of money in the form of spendable balances represented solely by digits on a bank's balance sheet is

---

target people for sales calls. Nobody wants to hear sales pitches in the middle of dinner. It doesn't matter how accurately you target marketing messages if you deliver them at the wrong time. Wireless devices make this possible. There is some potential in m-commerce. But as with other new technologies, using it properly can be the difference between pleasing customers and making them angry." (Grant Buckler, "Mobile Users Want Service, Not Pitches", *Computing Canada*, vol. 27, no. 3, Febr. 9, 2001, p. 21.)

[19] "...the monitoring activities [about the geographical whereabouts of individuals] can come to be taken for granted, and become 'normalised' as an aspect of social life to be accepted and integrated into everyday interaction. There are therefore ways in which these devices can be used to (either 'publicly' or 'privately') institutionally monitor individuals, and for individuals to resist that monitoring through their use of the very same devices." (Nicola Green, "Who's Watching Whom? Monitoring and Accountability in Mobile Relations", *loc. cit.*, p. 37.)

[20] Sørensen discusses individual strategies aiming at the reduction of information overload. See Carsten Sørensen, "Don't Call Us, We'll Call You", *LSE Magazine*, Summer 2001.

[21] "Electronic money (also variously labelled digital currency, computer money, or e-cash) presently comes in two basic forms, *smart cards* and *network money*. Both are based on encrypted strings of digits – information coded into series of zeros and ones – that can be transmitted and processed electronically." (Benjamin J. Cohen, "Electronic Money: New Day or False Dawn?", *Review of International Political Economy*, vol. 8, no. 2, Summer 2001, pp. 199–200.)

33

not new, it was already possible in the 13th century.[22] What has changed is the method of authorizing the transfer of money in the form of balances from one account to another. In the thirteenth century, payments intended for transfer between accounts were only permitted when the individuals participating in the transaction met personally with the banker and gave their oral consent for the transaction to be concluded. In the 1300s a written form of authorization – the paper check – became the accepted substitute for the earlier method of oral authorization. As the levels of literacy became more widespread, the need for personal contact as a form of authorization in concluding monetary transactions declined; this led to a substantial reduction in the costs of money transfers. The spread of the electric telegraph in the second half of the nineteenth century quickly made possible the remote, paperless and instantaneous authorization of money transfers. As White points out, the use of electronic money on the basis of information technology further broadens the possibility for transfers, further reducing transaction costs.

The evolution of money from gold, a commodity, to electronic money, an electronically created symbol, was possible only because the different forms of money were able to rely on the impersonal trust generated by the individuals taking part in economic transactions. From an economic point of view the driving force behind the evolution of money in all its forms is the reduction of the transaction costs tied to its use. Electronic money may ultimately become a substitute or supplementary form of paper money because its use is cheaper and generally more convenient.[23] Electronic money will continue to gain acceptance and continue to spread only if economic actors trust in it, that is they are going to accept it as a form of payment, and if the actors

---

[22] Lawrence H. White, "The Technology Revolution and Monetary Evolution", paper prepared for the Cato Institute's 14th Annual Monetary Conference, May 23, 1996, Washington, D.C. (http://www.cato.org/moneyconf/14mc-7.html).

[23] "Existing paper money, to be sure, is inconvenient (physically cumbersome, difficult to transport and process, easy to steal) and it has been steadily losing 'market share' to other payment systems (checks, credit cards, electronic funds transfer) that seem better suited to the needs of the modern world of electronic commerce. But shorn of these disadvantages, cash is pretty wonderful stuff: portable, instantly recognizable, instantly accepted by everyone without any of the overhead associated with the other payment systems, and entirely anonymous. And any form of cash that can retain these features and be utilized in the world of electronic commerce is going to prove extremely attractive. It also will likely earn its developers significant amounts of money, digital or otherwise." (David G Post, "E-Cash: Can't Live With It, Can't Live Without It", *American Lawyer*, February 1995, http://www.eff.org/Publications/David_Post/e-cash_post.article.)

of the transaction may preserve their anonymity if they want to.

The emergence of electronic money is a spontaneous process that may question the role of the state in the creation of money. Electronic money can be created by private banks, private persons, and private businesses. For this reason some experts think that with the spread of electronic money Hayek's proposition about the competition of private monies crowding out state created money may come true.

> Money in the 21st century will surely prove to be as different from the money of the current century as our money is from that of the previous century. Just as fiat money replaced specie-backed paper currencies, electronically initiated debits and credits will become the dominant payment modes, creating the potential for private money to compete with government-issued currencies.[24]

If electronic money assumes the form of private money emancipating itself from state control, the borders of the national state will not set limits to its movement. This electronic money will then become a global, transnational money breaking away from localities.[25]

---

[24] Jerry L. Jordan (President and CEO, Federal Reserve Bank of Cleveland) is cited by Turk (Geoffrey Turk, "Money and Currency in the 21st Century", July 1997, http://www.goldmoney.com/futuremoney.html.) – Similarly: "Modern societies have long adjusted to the fact that money is created by government fiat and has no intrinsic redeemable value other than that by law a creditor must accept it in settlement of any outstanding claims by her or his debtors. The emergence of electronic commerce may be leading to a further evolutionary stage, a monetary system in which convertibility into legal tender ceases to be a condition for electronic money. Some electronic money might be backed by governments, others by private issuers which enjoy the absolute confidence of the market. Such private issuers could be viewed as more secure than many governments (as is already the case in the international bond securities markets). The ultimate electronic money would be a currency without a country which is infinitely exchangeable at defined rates with other more traditional currencies. It may constitute itself as a wholly new currency with its own denomination – the 'cyber- thaler', harking back to early trans-European currencies and the forerunner of the US dollar." (Andreas Crede, "Electronic Commerce and the Banking Industry: The Requirement and Opportunities for New Payment Systems Using the Internet", *JCMC*, vol. 1, no. 3, Dec. 1995, http://www.goldmoney.com/futuremoney.html.) – Also: "With the arrival of electronic money, money creation will become increasingly privatized. Hayek's vision of a world of unrestricted currency competition could, for better or for worse, soon become reality." (Benjamin J. Cohen, "Electronic Money: New Day or False Dawn?", *op. cit.*, p. 221.)

[25] "The result is likely to be the creation of a new global commercial market place which permits goods to be ordered and paid for electronically irrespective of location.

The emergence of electronic cash and a digitally networked global economy pose direct threats to the very basis of the territorial state... Digitalization is cutting money and finance loose from its geographic moorings. The framework of regulation that governs financial institutions assumes that customers and institutions are linked by geography – that spatial proximity matters. E-cash and e-commerce snap that link. What remains are systems of economic and political governance that are rooted in geography and are trying nonetheless to deal with e-cash and markets that exist in cyberspace. The obvious disconnect here will only worsen over time... E-cash and e-commerce are symptoms, albeit important ones, of an increasing asymmetry between economics and politics, between an electronically integrated world economy and territorial nation-states, and between cyberspace and geographic space. How this asymmetry will be resolved and how economic and political relations will be reconstructed are two of the critical questions of our time.[26]

At the same time, market competition among the various forms of money creates a new challenge for national states as they endeavour to regulate this process.[27]

However, electronic money may also be considered not as a means of transcending local limitations but as a means of exchange that is strongly tied to localities and adapted to the process of mass customization along the dimension of locality. Electronic money may also become the tool of micro transactions because of its suitability and cost effective-

---

This will require new institutional structures to be formed as well as changes to existing outdated legal and commercial systems." (Andreas Crede, *op. cit.*) – "...digital cash is not constrained by national borders. First, people using digital cash are transnational because they can purchase service and goods from every site on the Internet. Second, banks issuing digital cash are transnational because not only the US bank but also all other banks can issue dollar-term digital cash. To put this another way, as far as digital cash is concerned, both the demand side and the supply side has no national borders." (Tatsuo Tanaka, "Possible Economic Consequences of Digital-Cash", *First Monday*, March 1996, http://www.firstmonday.dk/issues/issue2/digital_cash/index.html.)

[26] Stephen J. Kobrin, "Electronic Cash and the End of National Markets", *Foreign Policy*, Summer 1997, Issue 107, pp. 65–77.

[27] The states interested in increasing their revenues will try to control and regulate the circulation of electronic money. An interesting problem will be to what extent state intervention will threaten the private sphere of individuals, the secrecy of economic transactions. See Post, *op. cit.*

ness for this function when compared to the traditional forms of money.[28]

> Digital cash is ideal for what is known as micro payments, or transactions of less than US$10 in value. Micropayments are generally not economical with credit cards or electronic fund transfers, primarily because of the high overhead costs in processing those transactions. Digital cash makes small payments of just a few cents possible and profitable for both the merchant receiving the payment and the issuer of the digital cash. One of the interesting features of digital cash is that it allows for relative degrees of privacy in monetary transactions. DigiCash's ecash only provides privacy (anonymity) for the payer in the transaction. The payee reveals himself when he verifies the authenticity of the ecash with the issuer. Other types of digital cash involve anonymity for both parties or neither party. Ideally, individuals will be able to choose between these different systems to decide the level of privacy they wish to maintain in any transaction.[29]

The mobile phone is also appropriate for mediating micro transactions tied to the locality as it is able to function as an electronic purse executing micro payments. It is unlikely that m-money will crowd out other forms of money in the short run, but it makes sense to assume that the mobile form of money will increasingly spread in the sphere of micro payments.[30]

> For the foreseeable future I predict these new payment media will have major economic effects only in the part of the economy that uses small and micro-transactions. Unless legal rules change significantly, con-

---

[28] "The major attraction for consumers is convenience: using the card for small-ticket purchases such as newspapers, coffee, and various vending machine items would reduce the need to carry loose change and would speed transactions because consumers would always have 'exact change'. The electronic purse would also be more convenient than checks or debit cards for smaller transactions. Because it functions independently of a bank account, the electronic purse would afford users both greater privacy and freedom from the need to record expenditures in a checkbook. The electronic purse could even promote budgeting because a user can spend only the amount on the card." (John Wenninger and David Laster, "The Electronic Purse", *Current Issues in Economics and Finance*, vol. 1, no. 1, April 1995, p. 2, http://www.ny.frb.org/rmaghome/curr_iss/ci1-1.html.)

[29] Geoffrey Turk, *op. cit.*

[30] "...electronic purses are only likely to displace a fraction of the smaller denomination currency and coins used in routine transactions, at least for the foreseeable future." (John Wenninger and David Laster, *op. cit.*, p. 5.)

sumers who live in jurisdictions that provide legal protections for debit or credit cards transactions will tend to use them for larger payments. After all, why use e-cash when you can use a credit card and cancel the payment if the seller fails to deliver what was promised? Thus, e-cash will have relatively modest overall effects on commerce, the money supply, and the economy. And e-cash will have equally modest effects on taxes and social mores.[31]

To summarize, information technology contributes not only to the customization of mass products, but also to the customization of money mediating the exchange of goods and services. Market competition also means competition among the forms of money.[32]

Local versus Global

The new information technology has contributed to the formation of global virtual communities that could endanger personal relationships linked to localities. Global networks may emerge that will function not above localities, but will intrude into the life of local communities and will change them. The internet is able to enrich the impersonal relationship of market players with a personal dimension. Networked individuals now find themselves connected to one another by personal-impersonal relationships. Some authors think that these contacts may compete with the personal relationships nurtured in local communities, and may be able to decrease their importance for the individuals. The personal-impersonal network of global virtual communities seems to endanger local communities built on personal connections. Is it really the case?

Alstyne and Brynjolfsson argue that information technology reduces the transaction costs of establishing global contacts to a great extent. In

---

[31] Michael Froomkin, "The Unintended Consequences of E-Cash", position paper for the panel on "Governmental and Social Implications of Digital Money", *Computers, Freedom & Privacy Conference* (CFP '97), Burlingame, California, USA, March 12, 1997, http://www.law.miami.edu/~froomkin/articles/cfp97.htm.

[32] "Unlike today's national currencies and payment methods which operate in spatially-delineated markets, digital currencies and payment systems will be customized for specific products or services and for online communities and markets concerning them. Monetary policies and regulations based on territorial boundaries have little meaning in this worldwide virtual economy. As with any digital product, the future of digital currency will be determined by the market demand and supply." (Soon-Yong Choi, Dale O. Stahl and Andrew B. Whinston, "Electronic Payments and the Future of Electronic Commerce", *loc. cit.*)

this way information technology may contribute to the enrichment of global, and to the impoverishment of local contacts.

Thus local heterogeneity can give way to virtual homogeneity as communities coalesce across geographic boundaries.[33]

This conclusion assumes as its precondition the scarcity of resources available to be mobilized for establishing and maintaining personal contacts. On this basis the liberation of individuals from the local, spatial limits of communication may result in rolling back local contacts.[34] Homogeneous virtual communities may improve the economic performance of their members, although the weakening of personal contacts bridging local heterogeneity may also impose losses on local communities, argue the authors. Only changes in the players' preferences may limit this process of balkanization, as they call it. If individuals prefer heterogeneity to the homogeneity of goals, the heterogeneity of locality may increase in value in comparison with the homogeneous goals of the global and virtual community.[35]

However, this analysis assumes not only the scarcity of resources necessary for establishing and maintaining contacts, but also takes the trust for global contacts as given, and presumes that the connections enabled by the internet are external to the locality. Against these assumptions one could argue that the connections enabled by information technology can be used and are being used not only for the strengthening of global but also local communities.[36] Information tech-

---

[33] Marshall V. Alstyne and Erik Brynjolfsson, "Electronic Communities: Global Village or Cyberbalkans?", March 1997, http://web.mit.edu/marshall/www/papers/CyberBalkans.pdf, p. 4.

[34] "When geography no longer narrows interaction, people are able to select their acquaintances by other criteria such as common interests, status, economic class, academic discipline, or ethnic group. The result can easily be a greater balkanization along dimensions which matter far more than geography." (Van Alstyne and Brynjolfsson, *op. cit.*, p. 5.) – "The Internet can also facilitate the de facto secession of individuals or groups from their geographic neighborhoods. Because time is limited, spending more time interacting with online communities necessarily means spending less time interacting with geographic communities or even family members" (*ibid.*).

[35] "With greater connectivity, a taste for randomness or diversity unbalkanizes interaction." (Alstyne and Brynjolfsson, *op. cit.*, p. 17.)

[36] In a number of essays Wellman makes the argument that the internet may strengthen personal connections tied to localities. See for instance Barry Wellman, "Computer Networks As Social Networks", *Science* 293, Sept. 14, 2001, pp. 2031–2034;

39

nology fixed to localities may also sustain the dispersed local connections of individuals. The mobile phone can also contribute to the strengthening of the openness toward locality by stimulating local and personal relationships at a low cost, while additionally maintaining global contacts. E-mail may also encourage the maintenance of local and personal contacts. On the other hand, the mobile phone cannot compete with e-mail in the perpetuation of global and virtual ties, because while the costs of using the latter are not sensitive to the change of distance, usage costs of the former are. At the same time the mobile phone may strengthen local networks built on personal connections by utilizing the personal effects of the living voice. This effect has less importance for the maintenance of global networks of virtual communities. The mobile phone is also able to strengthen personal connections through the use of SMS, essentially because SMS messages are more limited in their content than e-mail messages that have no limitations at all. The function of SMS is less the communication of important contents and more the gesture of upkeeping personal contacts. The mobile phone can also contribute to a reduction in the scarcity of resources necessary for maintaining connections. In the process of moving from one place to another the mobile actor is able to effectively use the amount of time required for moving for reaffirming local personal connections that would not otherwise be utilized.[37]

Conclusion

The use of information technology in market transactions based on the impersonal trust in money allows for the personalization of impersonal contacts. The resulting "impersonal intimacy" – the impersonal as personal – fits well into the new market regime of mass customization. Mass customization invokes personal trust as a complementary factor to the impersonal trust in money in order to stabilize the market position

---

Barry Wellman and Keith Hampton, "Living Networked in a Wired World", *Contemporary Sociology*, vol. 28, no. 6, Nov. 1999, pp. 648–654; Keith N. Hampton and Barry Wellman, "Long Distance Community in the Network Society. Contact and Support Beyond Netville", *American Behavioral Scientist*, vol. 45, no. 3, Nov. 2001, pp. 477–496.

[37] Laki and Palló analyze in their essay the possibilities of the utilization of fraction time by mobile devices in scientific activities. See János Laki and Gábor Palló, "A tudományos kommunikáció átalakulása" [The Transformation of Scientific Communication], in Kristóf Nyíri (ed.), *Mobil információs társadalom: Tanulmányok* [The Mobile Information Society: Essays], Budapest: MTA Filozófiai Kutatóintézete 2001, p. 108.

of the seller. In this market regime the actors on the demand side are not treated as substitutable impersonal consuming automats but individuals with specific preferences that should be satisfied in a way that matches their different personalities. The mobile phone as a special tool could also contribute to the personalization of impersonal contacts among market players. On the one hand, the mobile phone allows for "personal" communication between the seller and buyer. On the other hand, by using the mobile phone sellers are able to customize mass products along the dimension of locality. Electronic commerce begets electronic money that in turn contributes to the development of global markets. In contrast, the mobile phone, as a specific and possible form of electronic money, is tied to locality and to the world of micro transactions. In contemporary markets not only different goods but also different monies will compete with each other. Relying on the achievements of information technology the mass customization of products will be supplemented with the customization of money. While information technology contributes to a new relationship between the local and global, threatening former personal contacts built on local heterogeneity, mobile devices are able to effectively contribute towards the maintenance of local and personal contacts in the era of new global communication networks.

Nicola Green: Community Redefined: Privacy and Accountability

From the telephone to the internet, technologies have historically transformed what is meant by community, and how communities are lived. What happens to the notion of community when our interpersonal and institutional relationships are not only increasingly "virtual", but also increasingly "mobile"?

It seems that in a social world increasingly mediated through mobile technologies, individuals are becoming more visible, more transparent and more accountable to others – firstly through the permanent communicative connections mobiles create, and secondly through the capacities of the technology to generate information about individuals. Drawing on qualitative and ethnographic research in the UK, this paper discusses the implications of mobile visibility and accountability for how we understand community. The paper argues that community relations should be understood as networks of trust that are established contextually, the most important factor in forming trust being *reciprocity* in visibility and knowledge, and thus reciprocity in the power relation implicit in that knowledge.

Introduction

This paper is a preliminary attempt to analyse and deconstruct the relationship between self and community in the mediated relations constructed via mobile technologies. It seems, at first glance, that mobile devices are a rather curious way to begin a discussion about emerging "communities", when our common-sense understandings of the technologies cast them as highly *individualized* communicative commodities in the consumption economies of late modernity.

In one sense, of course, mobiles are individualized and personalized commodity-objects, associated so closely with the individual, and individual bodies, that their material properties and information traces become – or stand in for – "person" and "personhood" within discourses about, and material practices of, communicative consumption.[1] These material and discursive practices of individualization with regard to traditional sociological understandings of "community", imply a shift from a definition of personhood embedded in reciprocal, embodied and co-located relations of mutual obligation and interdependency (personhood as social relation in community), to an understanding of persons as "disjointed", interpellated as alienated subjects within the organization of late modern social relations and commodity consumption (personhood as individualized selfhood).[2]

As is the case with other information technologies however, mobile technologies are extremely ambiguous, being both objects to consume, as well as media through which social relations are instantiated and performed.[3] While personalized commodity-objects, they are also, of course, communicative *media*, linking interpersonal networks of individuals at a distance. Again, in traditional sociological approaches to community the very fact that these technologies *allow* or *promote* communication at a distance implies that the individuals they are linking have been "de-territorialised", and spatially displaced from the "communities" of which they are a part.

---

[1] There are indications that the very *replacement* of the person by the mobile object and its communicative traces is becoming more extensive. In a recent murder trial in the UK, the mainstay of the defense argument for two accused relied on mobile network traffic data, which recorded calls made on a mobile phone owned by the accused – away from the scene, but at the same time, as the alleged murder took place. The defence attorney stated of the accused, that "The bottom line is this: if they were using those phones at 16.47, they could not have committed these offences and the only verdict you can return is not guilty. That is hard, cold evidence" (http://news.bbc.co.uk/hi/english /uk/england/newsid_1908000/1908648.stm). In his critical ruling at the end of the trial, the judge stated that "Whoever used those telephones could not have been involved in the death of Damilola Taylor", clearly implying that the use of the device, and the person of the accused, were inextricably connected (http://www.tiscali.co.uk/cgi-bin/ news/newswire.cgi/news/telegraph/2002/04/12/news/77_.html&template=/news /telegraph/templates/main.html). This data replacement of the person shifts across relations of consumption and communication in everyday life to socio-legal realms, in much the same way that the "data-subject" of fixed-network organizational databases replaces the embodied subject in social relation. See D. Lyon, *Surveillance Society*, Milton Keynes: Open University Press, 2001, pp. 15 ff.

[2] See also D. Nafus and K. Tracey, "Mobile Phone Consumption and Concepts of Personhood", in James E. Katz and Mark Aakhus (eds.), *Perpetual Contact: Mobile Communication, Private Talk, Public Performance*, Cambridge: Cambridge University Press, 2002.

[3] E. Hirsch and R. Silverstone (eds.), *Consuming Technologies: Media and Information in Domestic Spaces*, London: Routledge, 1992.

Both of these characterizations deploy a kind of nostalgia for sociability and commonality that ignore the ambiguities inherent in attempting to define the boundaries, meanings, and lived relations of "communities". It is exactly these more traditional and problematic sociological understandings of "community" and their relation to concepts of "the individual" that I would like to interrogate here, by focusing on aspects of visibility, accountability, risk and trust, in the networks of communicative relationships implied by emerging mobile technologies. These networks include not only reciprocal interpersonal relationships, but also the organizational and regulatory frameworks within which those interpersonal relations are situated.

Uncertainties

Mobile technologies present particular kinds of interpersonal and organizational *uncertainties* that are both connected to, but also differentiated from, related technologies such as the fixed-line telephone, or the internet.

Historically, these latter technologies have been positioned as technical resources deployed in social relations to enable access to communication with others across newly globalised time and space,[4] in the face of what Giddens refers to as "time-space distanciation".[5] Many authors have since considered the ways that internet technologies in particular reconfigure the relation between self and others via computer-mediated communication (CMC). Beyond a purely mechanical "sender-receiver" model of communication, the relation between self and other here is fundamentally organized around the *ambiguities* surrounding meaning, identity and lived relation in communicative information spaces. These ambiguities are generated by the potential for anonymity, the potential to construct multiple selves and identities, and the multiple "spaces" that internet communication provides. In some early nostalgic fantasies, these ambiguities were celebrated as the opportunity to leave our bodies behind, to construct our "personhood" from mind alone, the information traces constituting flexible, multiple and shifting selves and relations, unhindered by the norms, rituals and prejudices associated with face-to-

---

[4] I have argued elsewhere that notions of place and locale are more useful than time-space to understand mobile relations, acknowledging as they do multiple and overlapping situated rhythms and embodied activities in everyday life. See N. Green, "On the Move: Technology, Mobility, and the Mediation of Social Time and Space", *The Information Society*, vol. 18, no. 4 (2002).

[5] Anthony Giddens, *The Consequences of Modernity*, Cambridge: Polity, 1990.

face communication. The argument that "(t)he social construction of the reality that exists on-line is ... not constituted by the networks CMC users utilize, it is constituted in the networks"[6] underlines the notion that in a reality mediated via communication technologies, the *symbolic* plays a highly salient role in constructing the lived relations of personhood and community, a relation without necessary reference to the "grounding" of personhood in relations of embodied presence.

The construction of information personhood *purely* as data (in the realm of the symbolic) is, however, highly problematic, and a number of authors have stressed that CMC requires an embodiment that cannot ever be eradicated, and that online and offline selves and spaces are inextricably connected. There remains significant uncertainty and ambiguity in CMC relations however, because the self, already constituted symbolically as well as materially in relation, becomes "doubled". On the one hand, the self, to others, is constituted through the subjective positioning and performance of "personhood" in *interpersonal* relation over time via symbolic means. On the other hand, the self is also articulated through the positioning and performance of "data subjecthood" with respect to the information generated as both a constitutive element and effect of that exchange. The traces of this "data subjecthood" endure beyond reciprocal interpersonal exchange: as Lyon argues, one compelling feature of communicative information technologies is their capacity to record and trace aspects of symbolic electronic behaviour (although this is not to argue the embodied individual is thereby identified in any way, nor does it imply that any organizational use of residual data, beyond interpersonal communicative exchange, constitutes knowledge of those individuals).[7]

The ambiguities and uncertainties presented by the capacities of fixed line information and communication networks are echoed in the networks made possible via mobile information and communicative exchange, although the ambiguities surrounding meaning, identity and lived relation are also different in several crucial ways. On the one hand, in an organizational sense, the residual traces of personhood preserved in mobile technologies (consitituted via traffic data, via contractual service and commodity relations) no more guarantee the identity of the individual than they do in fixed line network technologies. The "real"

---

[6] S. Jones, "Information, Internet and Community: Notes Toward an Understanding of Community in the Information Age", in S. Jones (ed.), *Cybersociety 2.0: Revisiting Computer-Mediated Communication and Community*, Thousand Oaks, CA: Sage, 1998.

[7] D. Lyon, *Surveillance Society*, passim.

of the embodied individual in situated action remains opaque: only device data is routinely monitored on a significant scale. On the other hand, however, interpersonal and communicative relations via the mobile are complicated by the connections forged between the technology and the embodied individual. This is achieved firstly via the mobile as a prosthetic device, carrying stronger material (as well as symbolic) traces of the body, such as voice and speech, and implying the complicating factor of the body and its relation to space within any communicative interaction. While it is certainly the case that the locales through which *internet* connection takes place are salient, their relevance does not extend to the communicative space itself. With mobile technologies, the salience of the connective locale carries through into the "space" created by the communication, because the connection point is not divorced from the embodied individual. As in other information spaces, the self, to others, is constituted through the subjective positioning and performance of "personhood" in *interpersonal* relation over time via symbolic means.

Mobile communicative relations are also complicated by the "doubling" of the subject relation to the technology not only as media, but also as object-commodity, situated within the commodity consumption system. Mobiles as object-commodities, at least in the west, are framed via meanings of those commodities as personalized prosthetics, securing the technology to the body as the ground of identity (however precarious), and the person to the service via neo-liberal notions of contractual obligation in law.

Different kinds of uncertainties are thereby generated. On the one hand, the connections between mobile technologies and the individual carry the potential to render that embodied individual more visible to both interpersonal and organizational others, rendering the self and behaviour more transparent. Mobiles are assumed to be permanent connective devices, "always-on" technology, which imply that the individual is always available to interpersonal others, and symbolically obligated to engage in reciprocal communicative relations. This permanent communicative capacity also renders the subject potentially more visible to organizational others, corporate bodies such as the business corporation or the state, through the capacities of the technology to generate information about individuals, and for the capacity of that information to be shared.

On the other hand however, the connection between the technology and the body remains uncertain. An interpersonal communicative relation via mobile technology no more guarantees identity and personhood than do symbolic relations in internet spaces. The material echoes of the embodied individual are stronger, but do not guarantee the authenticity of, or knowledge about, the person and their situated action. Similarly, the symbolic traces of device operation (as is constituted in, for example, traffic data), do not guarantee the physical connection between a body and a technology.

As Lyon notes, "(i)ndirect communication ... [in] a world that is unstable, uncertain and deterritorializing raises questions about conventional conceptions of subjectivities, bodies, and places. In contemporary surveillance situations, the digital persona seems to pass as a representation of the subject for some purposes ... and places are only fleetingly occupied. Thus traces rather than tradition are what connects body with place."[8]

The doubling of the subject as both material and symbolic "trace" renders uncertain and unstable both interpersonal and organizational relationships. These uncertainties imply certain constructions of "risk" for individuals and their interpersonal others, as they are situated within community relations.

Risks

In the operation of mobile systems, a number of social institutions and agencies intersect to enable communicative interaction, including not only the interpersonal communicative partners (or traces of them), but also any number of corporate organizations from business to the state, hardware and software technologies, regulatory and policy frameworks and the informational bodies they generate. How individuals and their traces are positioned (and position themselves) within these matrices of relation, depends crucially on the character of the risks constructed by different subject positions with respect to the uncertainties accompanying mobile technologies.

So far, organizational responses to the uncertainties surrounding identity and meaning in mobile technologies have been to attempt ever more rationalized means of binding bodies, personhood and technologies together. There are two distinct discourses in operation here, as the corporate bodies of the state, and the corporate bodies of industry organizations hold different powers, knowledges and responsibilities with respect to mobile individuals. On the one hand, the state (at least in the UK) constructs risks as calculable systemic phenomena, generated via the technologies that produce aggregated "data subjects". Regulatory frameworks assume a correspondence (at least in part) between symbol-

---

[8] D. Lyon, *op. cit.*, p. 19.

ic, information traces, and embodied, liberal subjects. The risks presented to individuals are constructed as those of the "risk society",[9] wherein the structural technologisation and rationalization of late modernity threaten the constitution of the (ideologically defined) sovereign and private individual of liberal democracies. The state, as systemic citizen-body, therefore has a regulatory role to play in the management of these calculable risks, i.e. the institution of policy and legal frameworks that define and regulate the production and protection of "data subjects" (and by implication the embodied individuals they are attached to), and codify the relations between individual and corporate bodies (whether those relations are material or symbolic). On the other hand, the organizations involved in mobile industries construct "risk" as those relations that lie outside those contractually defined via the markers of economic exchange, exchange that takes place between the enterprise and the "possessive individual". Here, the sovereign liberal subject is marked as an economic entity located in exchange relations of labour and commodity value – and it is this exchange value and the ideologies of ownership and consumption that "secure" the bonding between body, technology and person. It is the responsibility of the individual bodies and the contractually obligated organization to manage any risks they might face above and beyond the exchange relation (given indeed that this relation is predicated on the organizational, rather than individual, ownership and control of information).

Evidence from our research so far then, implies that organizational and state regulation of information and communication in mobile technologies operates with reference to "privacy", on the assumption that the individualization of mobile devices and communications *reflects* the pre-existing constitution of social subjects as rational, neo-liberal, and individual consumers, choosing not only their goods and services, but their social and community relations.

Neither these constructions of "risk", nor the strategic responses of agencies in the form of privacy legislation, address the doubled nature of the mobile subject, nor the doubled nature of mobile technologies. It is not at all clear, for example, that the interpersonal relations constructed via mobile technologies as objects and as media, in lived relation, construct "risks" as they are defined by the state or corporate enterprise. If "risks" are constructed as calculable (in a rationalized sense), individually located and contractually defined, risks are considered objective,

---

[9] Ulrich Beck, *Risk Society: Towards a New Modernity*, transl. by Mark Ritter, London: Sage, 1992.

rather than relational. Mary Douglas argued, however, that when a risk-taking behaviour could be observed (in the case of the formation of mobile relations in the face of uncertainties), there also, necessarily, exists a system of trust relations. As ongoing interpersonal communicative relations are formed via mobile technologies, the reciprocities implied by these situated actions over time suggest that trust, as much as risk, is at stake in mobile relations. Indeed, the reciprocity implied suggests that the boundaries of risk and trust (as well as the boundaries of person, meaning and identity) are being continually renegotiated in *lived* relation, in contrast to the fixity implied by objectively or contractually defined relations.

Trust and Community

If, as we have seen above, the individualized mobile subject is at once embodied subject, performed personhood and data trace, it is perhaps only when all these aspects of self are re-performed and re-configured over time that a *particular kind of* personalized configuration of mobile subjects comes to ground individuals in interpersonal relations of trust. This is not the liberal subject of state and capital exchange value, defined predominantly via the data traces of personalization and customization, but rather the subject of trust and reciprocity, produced through symbolic and material exchange, in relation, via the mutual "gift".[10]

The construction of the individual as sovereign liberal subject, simultaneously positioned economically through commodity consumption as described above, results in, as Gedeon has noted, a production and regulation paradigm in which the mass consumer has become an individualized and personalized consumer with whom the seller must build up personal contacts. The importance of trust will be enhanced in this new paradigm, the prevalence of impersonal trust in money is supplemented in market transaction with an aspiration to personal relationships. As a result of these two tendencies, the market is now governed by the principle of "impersonal intimacy" – the impersonal as personal.[11]

This model is an extension of the governmentality exercised by modern corporate bodies over the social subject. Although contractually based, it *extends* the governmental power of the state and corporation

---

[10] Marcel Mauss, "Techniques of the Body", *Economy and Society*, vol. 2, no. 1 (1973), pp. 70–88.

[11] Cf. Péter Gedeon, "Market and Trust in the Mobile Information Society", in the present volume.

over the individual through the use of knowledge about them – the data traces of embodied subjects retained in informational systems. As Lupton argues, "a huge network of expert knowledges has developed, accompanied by apparatuses and institutions built around the construction, reproduction, dissemination and practice of these knowledges. This is an outcome of the emergence of the modern system of liberal government, with its emphasis on rule and the maintenance of order through voluntary self-discipline... Risk is understood as one of the heterogeneous governmental strategies of disciplinary power by which populations and individuals are monitored and managed so as to best meet the goals of democratic humanism."[12] In conjunction with the consumption system, where individuals are monitored and managed to best meet the needs of commodity capital, individuals are therefore normalized as *personalised individuals*. In this model, "trust" itself, as a relation of "impersonal intimacy", becomes a commodity. Contractually based trust (in its guarantee of authenticity in liberal individualism, and its basis in the confidence of institutional enforcement) is extended via the exchange of symbols of knowledge about the individual (data traces, or in Lyon's terms, "symbolic tokens"[13]) such that *trust itself* becomes a commodity to be symbolically exchanged. In the commodification of trust, "trustworthiness", as a form of social capital, is signaled via both symbolic and material means (personal ownership of a mobile device, and the use of it).

Organisational "knowledge" of (or rather, information about) the ownership and use of a mobile device does not, however, ultimately secure trust relations, because the exchange of knowledge, and therefore power, is *unequal* in that relationship. If only the commodified symbols of trust are exchanged (whether contractually or voluntarily), it ignores the performed personhood and embodied subjectivity that equally constitute the mobile subject. Information gathered, the data traces, tell us nothing about the operation of desire (only its instantiation in consumption), or interpersonal motivation (only its behavioural outcomes), or values, or worldview and culture. Without these kinds of *reciprocally* maintained voluntary knowledge relations, trust, because commodified, is less stable.

Here, I am not attempting to argue that a form of collective reciprocal trust (linked, of course, to community) may exist *outside of* these conditions of governmentality. Instead, I am arguing that these different

---

[12] D. Lupton, "Introduction: Risk and Sociocultural Theory", in D. Lupton (ed.), *Risk and Sociocultural Theory*, Cambridge: Cambridge University Press, 1999.

[13] D. Lyon, *op. cit.*, p. 8.

modes of *ordering* social relations exist at the same time,[14] and overlap each other, such that individuals are positioned with regard to both impersonal and interpersonal intimacies and trust, at the same time. What this implies is that social subjects are relationally positioned with respect to each of these competing discourses. In this respect, the uncertainties presented by mobile devices offer individuals the opportunity to take up subject positions previously only available to corporate social bodies, in an extension of the governmental subject position beyond the organisations that have historically generated information about datasubjects. As I have argued elsewhere,[15] mobile technologies both allow and promote distributed means of monitoring. As the boundaries between organizational and interpersonal monitoring via mobile information and communication become more unstable, the ensuing relations present interpersonal "risks", as the (commodified) trust based on symbolic data gathered about the data subject might, in social relationships, override the trust based on the material and symbolic performed personhood, or embodied subjectivity, voluntarily negotiated by the subject. This implies the *unequal* (if not involuntary) exchange of *even interpersonal* knowledge between parties, in the same ways that the personalization and customization of organizational governmentality is based on unequal exchange of knowledge. It suggests a discourse of trust, but does not necessarily imply a reciprocal relation of "trustworthiness".

Trustworthiness, then, is not so much a response to objectively given risks and uncertainties, nor an overriding moral commitment based in contractual relation, nor necessarily generalisable, but is rather situated and relational with respect to configurations of risk and uncertainty within relevant social networks. It is the reciprocal ground for collectively negotiating what constitutes "uncertainty" or "risk" to self, meaning and identity in any given relation over time, an interpersonal and collective negotiation that must be actively maintained. The relevance of trustworthiness is always the possibility of its betrayal. Therefore, we don't so much enter social relations because we trust despite risk, but rather we trust because we maintain mutual relations that negotiate what those risks are. In mobile technologies, the negotiation of knowledge about the subject (and therefore a power relation) is crucial, and these knowledges include not only the data traces of interpersonal others in networks, but also performative and embodied *interactions* of self with other.

---

[14] S. Crook, "Ordering Risks", in D. Lupton (ed.), *Risk and Sociocultural Theory*.

[15] N. Green, "Who's Watching Whom? Monitoring and Accountability in Mobile Relations", in B. Brown, N. Green and R. Harper (eds.), *Wireless World: Social and Interactional Aspects of the Mobile Age*, London: Springer, 2002.

So what are the implications of these formulations of different kinds of trust relation for the constitution and negotiation of community? I want to argue that community relations, especially those emerging from informational, communicative and mobile media, should be understood as networks of trust that are established contextually, the most important factor in forming trust being *reciprocity* in visibility and knowledge, and thus reciprocity in the power relation implicit in that knowledge. This depends both on the capacity for "choice" (although not necessarily in its liberal and rational definition), and the capacity for commonality, broadly conceived.

Communities Redefined

So far, sociological challenges to the conceptualization of late modern subjectivity, especially analyses of the individualized subject of governmentality and commodity capital in its relation to community, have concentrated on struggles to maintain something called "community" relations *given* economically and technologically induced displacement, de-territorialisation, and alienation. This model of late modern relations assumes that trust relations involve the "trust of strangers" in Simmel's terms, trust that is abstract, individualized and contractually based, in relation to objective and calculable conditions of risk that emerge in post-industrial societies. One of the historical problems with these conceptualizations of "community" is that the terms have often been deployed as either negative, or residual categories: "community" is conceived as those relations that are either in opposition to, or "left over", when the economic, political and cultural organization of late modernity has been defined. "Community" has provided a model of social relations to contrast with the emergence of modern societies where cultural, economic and technological transformation has displaced tradition, and where complexity has created more rationalized and individualised social life, displacing mutual bonds of emotion and obligation. These negative and residual formulations have rendered "community" one of the most ambiguous concepts in sociology.

Perhaps the most widely cited conceptualization of community in this tradition is the Ferdinand Tönnies model of *gemeinschaft* and *gesellschaft* ("community" and "society"). Gemeinschaft, as an ideal type of relation corresponding to "natural will", is distinguished by an appeal to a totality of cultural history in the collective memory of tradition, is defined through common property, family, custom and fellowship, and is bound by consensus, language and ritual. Gesellschaft, as an ideal type of relation corresponding to "rational will" is, by contrast, characterized by an appeal to progress and individualism, permeated with relations that are fragmented, transitory, contractually based and rationally mechanized. Finding resonance both with Durkheim's "mechanical" and "organic" solidarity, as well as Weber's analyses of bureaucracy and the "iron cage", this characterization of changing social relations is nevertheless problematic for our purposes here – firstly because it concentrates on the structural dimensions of relation, to the neglect of the cultural and symbolic dimensions of social life, and secondly because implicit in this formulation is an assumption of spatial relationships as a mutually exclusive dichotomy between co-present and distant relations.[16] Simmel, by contrast, attempted to articulate the *contradictory* nature of social and community change in industrial societies by examining the experiences of affinity and commonality in an increasingly individualized modernity. He argued individuals were neither completely individualized, nor fully "unified" – but even this formulation continues to present us with the assumption of co-present relationships.

"Virtual" communities fully challenge these formulations, and Fernback argues convincingly that to account for the contemporary conditions of tele-present life online, we must turn to conceptualizations of community that acknowledge the central importance of the symbolic, and its role in creating commonalities beyond rationalistic definitions of "communities of interest". Focusing on the symbolic shifts the focus of enquiry such that the negotiation of meaning and identity become as important as structural and material relations in conceptualizing emergent communities. As Fernback notes, "if we embrace the *symbolic* form of community (... a community of substance and meaning), concerns of the 'real' juxtaposed against the 'virtual' are of less importance... Reality is socially constructed, and ... community exists in the minds of participants; it exists because participants define it and give it meaning. This doesn't mean that the community exists *solely* in the minds of participants but in the connection between what social constructs the user imagines (such as community) and the ... representations of those constructs."[17]

Alongside the material relations that position subjects simultaneously as the sovereign individuals of late commodity capitalism then, and

---

[16] J. Fernback, "There is a There There: Notes Towards a Definition of Cybercommunity", in S. Jones (ed.), *Doing Internet Research: Critical Issues and Methods for Examining the Net*, Thousand Oaks, CA: Sage, 1999.

[17] J. Fernback, *op. cit.*, p. 213.

subject to governmental disciplines that are becoming mobile and distributed, individuals are also positioned in interpersonal relation to each other through discourses *about* community, that derive from commonality of language, ritual, emotional investment, social experience, and mutual commitment. In this formulation, *personalization itself*, as an effect of body, data and performance in reciprocal and enduring relation, can therefore establish commonalities on which mutual trust is negotiated and maintained.

I want to argue here, then, that the particular kinds of personalization and individualisation surrounding mobile devices are explicit *effects* of (rather than causes of or reactions to) *collective trust relations*: the social effects of building trust networks in response to reciprocal and interpersonal uncertainties and risks constructed by mobile communications and the information they generate. This is not to argue that we build trust in the wake of its inevitable dissolution and the disintegration of community in late modernity, but rather that existing trust and community are based on the processual reconfiguration (rather than preservation) of "older" relations and collective means of materially and symbolically "grounding" personhood: older trust relations, and older uncertainties, are performed in new ways – in this case via mobile mediation.

As is the case with internet and "virtual" communities then,[18] understandings of mobile "communities" should move beyond the conceptualization of "communities-as-interest-groups" (secured via the authentication of the embodied liberal individual and their "right to privacy"), and indeed beyond a traditional sociological conceptualization of "communities-as-interpersonal-and-co-located" (secured via relations based on face-to-face interaction in kinship or social commonality). Rather, we should move towards a conceptualization of "communities-as-trust-processes" (secured via the mutual, reciprocal and multiple negotiation of mediated, interpersonal, and organizational uncertainty and risk).

A recognition of contextually established and reciprocally maintained networks of mediated uncertainty and trust take us beyond questions of "privacy", or indeed questions of late-modern "alienated" intimacy, to questions about how uncertainties, risk and trust are instantiated and performed in mobile networks of relation, both generating and depending upon the individualized mobile subject.

---

[18] N. Baym, "The Emergence of Online Community", in S. Jones (ed.), *Cybersociety* 2.0.

R. I. M. Dunbar: Are There Cognitive
                                        Constraints on an E-World?

The electronic revolution of the last decade of the twentieth century can genuinely be said to have revolutionised our way of life. Things can happen faster, further away and on a wider scale than anyone could ever have dreamed possible even in the preceding decade. In the end, the extent to which we can exploit the opportunities offered by the new technologies depends only on our ability to take advantage of them.

In this lecture, I want to pursue two themes in this respect. One is to illustrate ways in which we can find new ways to exploit these technologies for purposes which were wholly unintended. The other is that, despite our ingenuity in this respect, our ability to exploit these new technologies may nonetheless be limited. Our cognitive machinery – the design of our brains – did not evolve in a world characterised by twenty-first century electronic technology, and this may impose real limitations on what we can in fact do with it. But let me begin with a brief introduction to the evolution of the social brain.[1]

The Evolution of the Social Brain

Primates have unusually large brains for body size compared to all other vertebrate groups. This is primarily a consequence of the fact that primates have unusually large neocortices (essentially the thinking part of the brain). In primates, the neocortex represents in excess of 50% of total brain volume (ranging up to 80% in humans), whereas it never exceeds 50% in other non-primate mammals (and can be as low as 10%). The growing consensus is that the pressure to evolve large neocortices (and hence large brains) came from the fact that primates developed an intensely social style of life. So important was the careful management of the relationships that held their social groups together that primates

---

[1] For more detailed expositions see Robin I. M. Dunbar, *Grooming, Gossip, and the Evolution of Language*, Cambridge, MA: Harvard University Press, 1996, as well as Dunbar, "The Social Brain Hypothesis", *Evolutionary Anthropology* 6 (1998), pp. 178–190.

had to evolve the computing capacity needed to deal with the information processing required to keep track of the ever-changing nature of social relationships and to use that information in managing a way through the social complexities of life in a primate group.

Known as the Machiavellian Intelligence (or Social Brain) hypothesis, this view has received considerable support from analyses of the co-variation between neocortex volume of primates and various aspects of primate social behaviour, including social group size, grooming clique size, the use of subtle social strategies such as alliances and tactical deception and the levels of social play. There is, for example, a linear relationship between relative neocortex volume and social group size in primates. In a nutshell, if a primate species wants to live in a larger social group in order to be able to solve its ecological problems more effectively, then it first has to evolve a sufficiently large neocortex to be able to support the computations needed to allow it to do so.

Humans seem to fit rather neatly onto the end of the primate distribution in this respect. The regression line for primates suggests that, with a neocortex the size that humans have, we should live in groups of about 150. Surprisingly, this turns out to be well supported by the evidence. Although humans can obviously cope with very large urban environments and even nation-states, the number of people within those large population units with whom one can say that one has a direct personal relationship is very much smaller. Censuses of the population units of hunter-gatherers, the size of scientific sub-disciplines, the number of people to whom one sends Christmas cards and the number of people of whom one can ask a favour all turn out to be about 150 in number.

There is, however, considerable evidence from the study of primates to suggest that what is important here is not simply the number of individuals whom you can recognise. Rather the problem is more concerned with the kinds of relationships you can have with other individuals. It seems that how well a relationship works depends on the level of trust that exists between the two individuals, and that this in turn is related to the frequency of their interaction. Frequent affiliative social interactions build a level of emotional bonding between two individuals that allows the relationship to be the basis for commitment to future social support. Among primates, individuals who groom together support each other in future conflicts with a third party. They are more likely to come to each other's aid when attacked by a predator or a member of another group. That much is also surely familiar from our everyday experience of humans: we do not easily rush to the aid of strangers – when we do, it is apt to arouse comment and, indeed, approval in a way that would surely not be necessary if such behaviour were a prominent natural feature of human nature. Indeed, we know from our studies of human social networks that the intensity of a relationship is related to the frequency of contact involved (or, at least, that has been involved in the past).

We do not at this point really understand why there appears to be limits to the number of individuals we can hold in a particular relationship to ourselves. It seems likely that these are cognitive limitations on the number of individuals that can be held in a relationship of a given degree of intensity. There is some longstanding evidence, for example, that the number of individuals we can have a particularly close bond with is limited to around 12–15, and that within this there may be an inner circle of about 5 individuals with whom this relationship is especially strong. There is, in addition, evidence to suggest that there may in fact be a series of layers, with boundaries at around 35 and 80–100, each associated with a declining level of emotional intensity and closeness. It is as though each of us sits in the centre of a series of expanding circles at 5, 15, 35, 80 and 150 individuals.

Cognitive Constraints on Network Size

The social brain hypothesis has important implications for several aspects of the way our social relationships are structured. The evidence shows that there is a simple linear relationship between neocortex volume and group size at various levels. We seem only to be able to hold a certain number of individuals in a given degree of intensity of relationship. The intensity of that relationship, in any given case, reflects a combination of factors in the past history of those two individuals.

One important component is the knowledge that they share about each other (the way they behave, their likes and dislikes), but also aspects of their shared social history (how they are related to each other in genetic or affinal terms, shared worldviews and culture, shared experiences). This shared knowledge base provides each with the basis off which to interact in an effective way. The wheels of the relationship are oiled by this knowledge. They know just how much they can trust each other, how far they can push each other both in teasing and in making demands on each other.

In addition to this knowledge base, however, it is clear that there is a more fundamental emotional stream to that relationship. In the end, of course, shared knowledge and shared experiences come from having spent a lot of time together. You cannot simply be told that X holds certain relationship to you and then naturally behave in certain way towards them. We can use such knowledge as a stepping-stone to establishing a working relationship with someone, but ultimately the effectiveness of that relationship – and in particular the level of trust that we are prepared to put on that individual – comes from interacting with them. The relationships that we hold dear are those that involve individuals we have spent a lot of time with. Building a relationship requires a lot of time. It requires time sharing activities that give us pleasure; it requires time spent mining the mental world of that individual, building up a virtual simulation of that individual in the mind's eye as it were.

This combination of understanding and trust built on time spent interacting lies at the base of primate societies. For primates, the glue that binds individuals together is social grooming. Although in origin a mechanism for removing debris and ectoparasites from fur, the amount of time that many monkeys and apes devote to grooming each other far exceeds that required for hygiene. A gorilla, with the largest area of body fur to keep clean, copes quite adequately in this respect with just 1-2% of its day devoted to social grooming. Yet some species, such as baboons and macaques, can spend up to 20% of their day engaged in this activity. It hardly seems plausible to suggest that macaques with a quarter of the body surface of a gorilla should require ten times as much grooming to achieve an acceptable level of cleanliness. In fact, grooming has been coopted by the social primates as a mechanism for social bonding. It works because it is particularly effective at releasing endorphins (the brain's natural painkillers). The sense of relaxation, euphoria and contentedness that this induces creates a bond between those who groom each other regularly. The consequence of that bond is that those individuals are more willing to support each other against common enemies than individuals that do not groom. It is this that provides the social glue that welds primate societies together.

We humans are no less bound by these mechanisms. We too engage in this kind of grooming in a very primate-like way. We lack most of the fur that provides the excuse for grooming in primates, but we engage in the activity every bit as much as they do. In our case, the actions are reduced to forms of patting, rubbing, hugging and touching that produce the same mildly euphoric effects. But such pseudo-grooming occurs only in the context of our more intimate relationships. Physical stimulation of this kind is regarded as unacceptable among less closely acquainted individuals. Yet, we need to engage in that bonding process with all those who come within our social circle. For humans, that level of bonding is serviced by language – or, more precisely, by conversation mediated by language.

Among nonhuman primates, there is simple more or less linear relationship between time devoted to grooming and social group size. This is principally because the bigger the group, the better one's friendships have to work to provide defences against harassment by other group members. Inevitably, of course, time is a limiting factor. For animals that have to earn their living in the real world, the amount of time that can be spared for social interaction is constrained by the amount of time it takes them to find and extract food from their environment. In the limit, primates cannot afford to spend more than 20% of their total day time in social interaction. This sets an upper limit of group size at about 80-100 individuals. Since human groups are 150 in size, some mechanism is needed to bridge the gap between what is possible to bond by grooming and the group size that the species requires to survive successfully.

Language seems to have evolved to meet that need. Studies of time budgets in a wide range of modern humans suggests that, on average, we spend about 20% of our time is social interaction (principally, of course, conversation). This is exactly the limiting value seen in nonhuman primates. But language allows us to use that time more efficiently. It allows us to interact with more individuals at once (we can talk to several individuals simultaneously, but grooming – even in the form that we humans have it – is very much a one-on-one activity). Language also allows us to seek and exchange information about our social network. A nonhuman primate's knowledge about the state of its social network depends entirely on what it has seen for itself; in contrast, we can find out about what has happened in our absence, thereby allowing ourselves to keep track of the ever-changing social world even when we are not there in person.

However, language lacks one key feature that grooming provides – the opioid kick that seems to play so essential a role in social bonding. That gap appears to be filled by laughter. Laughter has the ability to produce the same kinds of opioid effects as grooming does: we feel relaxed, euphoric, at peace with the world and well disposed towards those with whom we laugh. It appears to play a very fundamental role in human social interaction.

These findings would seem to have a number of implications for the structure of social networks even in modern post-industrial environments. One is that no matter how good the technology, electronic media that are used to service individual's social networks need never be significantly larger than this value. Even the most social individual is unlikely to be contacting more than about 200 other individuals at any one time. A second implication is that the kinds of relationships we have are severely constrained. The fact that we can contact very large numbers of people does not mean that we can get to know them better. Our expanding circles of relationships remain where they have always been, and continue to be dependent on the same old-fashioned kinds of emotional intensity that can, in the final analysis, only be generated by direct intimate contact.

One obvious difference that electronic technology can make, however, is to allow us to extend the circle of relationships over a much greater geographical area than has previously been possible. The intimacy and intensity of a relationship needs to be constantly serviced – reinforced by frequent interaction at the appropriate level. Failure to reinforce the relationship causes it to fade away. The individual that once occupied one of the boxes in our circle disappears and is replaced by a new face whom we see more often, perhaps someone who occupied a box in a more distant circle of acquaintanceship, perhaps someone who has newly arrived in our social world. That constant turnover of identities was, in the past at least, terribly dependent on the physical proximity of the players. Someone who moved elsewhere faded gradually unless they were emotionally especially important. Letter-writing helped to slow the rate of fading, but could not prevent it altogether because letters travelled slowly and replies often arrived back months, perhaps years, after the initial letter had been sent.

Modern telecommunications technology allows that exchange to happen faster, so the rate with which old friends fade in our memories may be reduced if we so wish. But still, it cannot abolish the process altogether. The reason friends cease to be intimates and become mere acquaintances with separation is that we are unable to update our mental picture of them. They change with time, and we change with time, and gradually our old similarities, our once shared knowledge of each other and the social world in which we live, diverge too far to allow us to pick up the pieces when we meet again. We become strangers who need to start the process of getting to know each other all over again.

One example of how the design of our minds can impose limitations on the size of our social groups comes from the rather mundane example of conversations. In principle, we can get very large numbers of individuals into a conversation, as evidenced by what we manage to achieve during lectures or sermons. However, to do that, we have to impose very strict social rules on those present. Everyone must agree to remain silent and listen to the single speaker. Indeed, everyone must agree to give up the opportunity to intervene or ask questions. When an opportunity to make comments is provided – as at the end of a lecture – the process has to be stage-managed very carefully by a chairman who dictates who can ask questions and how long they can hold the floor for. If we do not act in this way, chaos ensues very quickly.

The reason for this is very simple. It seems that there is a natural limit to the number of people who can be involved in a free-flowing conversation, and this limit is set at four individuals – one speaker and three listeners. If more than four people join a conversation group, the group will split into two or more separate conversations within at most a minute. This effect is very robust and can be observed during any cocktail party or similar social gathering. There are two likely reasons for this. One is strictly psycho-acoustical: our ability to discriminate speech sounds decreases rapidly as the distance between speaker and hearer increases, and, once the group exceeds four individuals, the distance across the circle becomes too great. The other is social: since we only ever allow one person to hold the floor at a time during conversations (otherwise chaos intervenes), each individual's opportunity to contribute to a conversation declines rapidly with group size. With five people in a group, each can spend at most 20% of the time talking if everyone is to get an equal turn. Very quickly the group ceases to become an interaction and instead becomes a lecture. This constraint probably sets the limit on the number of people that can be involved in a multiway communication system.

At the same time, it is clear that modern telecommunications has unforeseen dangers for us. These are already familiar phenomena – flaming (the tendency to over-react on e-mail exchanges), stranger danger (our tendency to respond too intimately on e-mails). Most of these seem to arise because electronic communications currently lack the immediacy of face-to-face interaction. In everyday life, nonverbal signals play a crucially important role in allowing us to interpret the meaning and intentions of those with whom we interact. In e-mail – and even telephone – exchanges, we lack these cues and thus fail to interpret messages correctly. In face-to-face encounters, we make tentative forays into intimacy and watch very carefully to see how they are received; the feedback we get encourages or inhibits what we do next. The absence of these crucial cues in electronic communication (combined by the slowness of the response in e-mail) encourages us to go one step further than we would normally do. Premature declarations of eternal love are notorious in internet chatrooms for this reason. At the same time, we have few cues as to the honesty of the person we are interacting with. In real life, facial cues play a very prominent role in our assessment of individuals' suitability as partners or friends. When we lack those cues, we are apt to make assumptions about a person's honesty that aren't justified.

The Freerider Problem

I have suggested that relationships are based in large part on trust. Let me turn now to one of the central issues that underpins this, namely the problem of freeriders. Primate societies (and that includes human societies) are essentially cooperative solutions to the problems of survival and reproduction. In effect, individuals accept an implicit bargain whereby they forego some of their immediate objectives in order to obtain a greater longterm benefit. The problem that all such social systems face is that they are highly susceptible to freeriders – individuals who take the benefits that do not pay all the costs. This problem is ubiquitous in human societies. We find it in those who don't quite pay all the taxes they should, who park in the no parking zones (because it saves them a few moments of time); we find it on the grand scale in the so-called "Tragedy of the Commons", the over-fished oceans and the denuded landscapes once clothed in tropical forest. The problem is that, whenever there is a social bargain of this kind, it always pays some individuals to cheat – to allow others to bear the full cost of the communal benefit.

Human societies are especially susceptible to these kinds of problems because of their size. As social group size increases, so freeriders have more places to hide, more naïve individuals willing to allow them to join even after their anti-social behaviour has been uncovered elsewhere. Part of the problem here is the fact that freeriders can move faster than the information about their misdemeanours. They can always stay one step ahead of discovery.

Because the freerider problem is so intrusive in human societies, we have evolved a number of mechanisms for dealing with it. These include a particular sensitivity to social cheats, the use of language to exchange information about freeriders, verbal reprimands to make backsliders toe the social line and the use of dialects to identify members of our communities.

Language provides us with several important mechanisms whereby we can keep track of and police freeriders. One is the simple fact that we can use it to exchange information about what's been happening within our social circle while we have been engaged elsewhere. In one sense, this was probably the original function for which language evolved – a mechanism for monitoring the constantly changing state of a very dynamic system. Even today, 60–70% of conversation time in natural situations is devoted to social topics ("gossip" in its broadest sense). This is a phenomenal investment in time. Given that we devote 20% of our waking day to conversation, this means that we spend something like

15% of the waking day discussing the state of our social network. That's a very significant investment of our time. But ensuring that we know who is "in" and who is now "out", who has formed a partnership with who, and who has now broken up with who is crucial if we are to be able to negotiate our way through the complexities of everyday social life.

But language allows us to do more than that. It allows us to police the behaviour of our friends and colleagues – not just to catch up with their social misdemeanours but also to remonstrate with them when they offend against the communal code. There is nice experimental evidence of this from studies of cooperative games. In computerised investment markets where cooperation leads to significantly higher returns but lack of cooperation leads to very poor returns, the temptation to cheat is overwhelming: the problem is that if you don't cheat, you run a very high risk of doing very badly because someone else has cheated. So, in experiments in which individuals can observe the state of the market but not communicate directly with each other or see which individual is cheating, payouts can be as low as 20% of what full cooperation would yield, even when it is quite clear to everyone that cooperation would be a better strategy. However, allowing subjects to take a coffee break together midway through an experiment can result in a three- to fourfold increase in payouts, mainly because it provides the group with an opportunity to remonstrate with those who fail to adhere to the cooperative strategy. The effect works even if the subjects do not know which individual is responsible, but merely state their frustrations and irritations with whoever is responsible. Allowing the group to impose sanctions on the still anonymous freeriders improves payouts even further.

One other interesting feature of human languages is the speed with which they diversify to produce, first, local dialects and, later, distinct languages that are so different as to be mutually incomprehensible. We have modelled this issue as a problem in social badging. In other words, we suppose that dialects are really designed to allow you to identify people that come from your own very small local community, and in particular the community that you grew up in. The implication of the last point is that you share with them a significant level of genetic relatedness. Relatedness is important in the context of freeriders because it identifies individuals with whom you share sufficient common genetic interest that both of you will be willing to adhere to the communal agreement. More importantly, perhaps, genetic relatedness has one important consequence: it makes it less problematic if your partner cheats on the system because you will still benefit from their good fortune because you have a stake in that person's genetic success. This is one reason why alliances and agreements with relatives tend to be more open-ended and less demanding of strict reciprocation than similar contracts with unrelated individuals.

Innovative Exploitation

Finally, let me turn to the first of the two consequences of the social brain that I mentioned at the start of this talk. We humans are perhaps the most inventive species there has ever been, at least on Planet Earth. Our very survival as a species, our ability to colonise every continent with all their different habitats, even our less laudable ability to drive all other species to extinction – all these have been the consequence of our inventive minds. Religion, science and enterprise all share a common origin in our remarkable capacity to visualise new opportunities.

The example I want to offer here concerns uses to which electronic technology might be put which have absolutely no relationship with their intended function. The technology in question is cell phones, the use is as a mate-attraction device.

The origins of this particular study go back to some discussions I was having with Hewlett Packard's research staff while involved in a small project with them. They had noticed that teenage males (in particular) were fascinated with handsets during focus group discussions. They wanted to have them, even though they were in fact dummies. At the same time, we noticed a newspaper report from South America which said that one of the chic things to do on the dance floors of local clubs was to hold your mobile in your hand. However, the number of calls on these had become so irritating to everyone that some clubs had started to insist that clients hand in their mobiles at the door, rather in the way gunslingers were required to hand over their guns in the old Wild West saloons. The puzzle was that many people didn't bother to pick their phones up at the end of the evening: sometimes as many as a third of them were left behind on the concierge's shelves. Eventually, the clubs had to do something about them, and at that point they discovered that many of the phones were in fact dummies. The cell phone as fashion accessory had arrived.

These observations reminded me of something that I had noticed, but not paid much attention to. I spent a lot of time travelling on trains at that time, and I had become subconsciously aware of something odd: men almost always put their cell phones on the table beside them – often after taking them out of their briefcase or a pocket – but women didn't. Women clearly had phones, because every so often one would ring and the owner would search for it in her handbag or briefcase, take the call, and then carefully put it back again.

What could be going on, we wondered?

One obvious possibility suggested by this contrast in the behaviour of the two sexes is that it has something to do with sexual advertising. Men were using cell phones to display something that women were not especially interested in displaying for themselves. The obvious answer is that phones are cues of mate quality. In the study of human mate choice, it has become clear that a man's status or wealth (the two are often much the same thing) are an important consideration in women's evaluation of potential mates. It is not, of course, the *only* consideration, but it remains an important one nonetheless. A man's ability to provide the resources needed for successfully rearing children is just as important in modern society as it is in traditional societies. In more traditional societies, it was a man's ability to provide the land for agriculture or the products of his labours that made it possible for a woman to successfully feed her children. The only difference today is that the emphasis has now shifted into how wealth affects children's education and placement in a technological society. Rearing children successfully is now even more expensive than it has ever been, because there is so much more available both in terms of opportunity (careers in computing or communications that requires expensive training and/or equipment) and in terms of display (having the right kinds of trainers or clothes with the right labels).

To explore this in more detail, we set up a small study of what people do with their cell phones. We chose a pub in the centre of Liverpool, close to the Law Courts, where the clientele was likely to be up-market (lawyers, business executives) and then sampled various aspects of the behaviour of those who came into the pub during the early evening immediately after work (5–7 pm) on 23 separate days over a period of several months. Thirteen tables that were clearly visible from an upstairs balcony were sampled at regularly intervals, recording the number of cell phones on view, the frequencies with which phones were used (both to answer calls as well as being toyed with) and the number and sex of the people at each table.

As we had anticipated, men were significantly more likely to have their cell phones in view (for example, on the table) than women were, even when we take into account the fact that men owned slightly more cell phones than women did. (At the time of the study, around 59% of registered owners with one major UK provider were men.) More interestingly, however, men were more likely to expose their cell phones as both the number of men in the group round the table increased and as the sex ratio increased (more men per woman in the group). When there were more than four other men in the group, around 80–90% of all cell phones known to be owned by the men in the group were on display, compared to around 50–60% when there were four or fewer men present. More intriguingly, the proportion of known phones on view increased more or less linearly as the number of males per female at the table increased, from about 10% when the sex ratio was equal to around 80% when the sex ratio reached three men for every woman.

It seemed that, at least at the time of the study, men were using cell phones as signals of quality. The level of competition they faced from rivals over access to women apparently spurred them on to ever greater efforts of display. In this respect, cell phones were being used in exactly the same way that Rolex watches and Armani suits are used as signals of wealth. The message is: that I can afford to splash out on such a relatively useless item shows how wealthy I am. The important thing about such signals is that they are expensive and therefore rare. A general principle in evolutionary biology known as *Zahavi's Handicap Principle* reminds us that honest signals are costly: if cell phones (or Rolex watches) were cheap and abundant, they would lose their value as a signal.

We have not revisited this issue since we completed our study, but now that cell phones are both cheap and commonplace in the UK (their price was just starting to fall as we did our study), we can predict that their signal value will have been eroded and men no longer use them so conspicuously. Instead, they will have been replaced by another newer piece of technology or fashion accessory that carries the same message because it is new, expensive and rare. WAP phones or digital cameras are obvious examples, perhaps. This looks suspiciously like the phenomenon known in evolutionary biology as the *Red Queen Effect:* like the Red Queen in the children's book *Alice in Wonderland,* organisms have to keep running (in terms of changing their appearance) in order to stand still in the game of life. Animals that fail to do so are swept backwards to extinction by the tide of competition. Similarly, we humans are forced to seek for constant novelty in our displays in order to stay one step ahead of the opposition in the mating game.

Conclusions

I have tried to show how and why our ability to exploit the new technology of the e-world may ultimately be constrained by some very basic features of the way the human mind has evolved. Our task, in one sense, is not to try to exploit this technology to do the same tasks as we do with conversation but on a bigger scale, but to find innovative ways to exploit that technology to do things we cannot do naturally. I offered one example of this kind of unexpected use – the use of cell phones in mate advertising. Our task in the future is, perhaps, to understand how the human mind limits natural interaction, and to find ways to circumvent those limitations in ways that do not contravene the basic principles on which the human mind is built.

Klára Sándor: The Fall of Linguistic
Aristocratism

Introduction

One of the advantages of the world wide web mentioned very often in public discourse is that it makes the acquisition of knowledge more democratic. If the huge stores of knowledge are equally available for people living in small villages and for people who have access to large libraries, and if people who cannot get their education at expensive universities can still afford to use the internet, then the number of geographic and social factors that work against equal chances will decrease. When the access to the web becomes predominantly mobile, the advantages of the internet will be multiplied; the time we spend with traveling and other now long and boring activities would be utilized much better and we will be able to take with us all the information gathered in this huge external memory, and use it freely any time.

Sad, however, that the world is still far from this informational Paradise. The internet, in spite of its unbelievable richness of information, cannot compete with the Library of Congress, the British Library, or the Hungarian National Library. The access to the web is not general even in the highly developed countries, not to speak of countries of the third world. The expenses of the use of the mobile commons preclude its uninterrupted use today. New information technologies do nevertheless have the potential of moving the world toward a life of better quality spelled out above, and this not too far in the future.

Apparently, there is another, rarely mentioned effect of new technologies that will make our life more comforting. In my paper, I argue that the new channels and forms of communication will reduce linguistic discrimination. This would be a rather welcome consequence since equal chances in modern societies are hindered not only by social and economic factors but also by the linguistic differences that symbolize them.

I think it is reasonable to start with considering how the present situation that can be called "linguistic aristocratism" has emerged. For a better comprehension we should step back in time, at least to the so-called "Mitochondrial Eve".[1] Although the topic of the present volume is communications in the 21st century, we will spend some time in prehistoric ages, as I assume that modern technologies can help us get back – or forward – to a communicational environment that was – or will be – a more comfortable one. To one that fits better the biology of human beings and which used to be our natural surroundings for thousands of years. Leaving this nice starting-point behind, we set out on a short virtual tour whose stations are the birth, the development and the extension of linguistic aristocratism. Then I consider how in the 21st century new technologies can drive us to a friendly, natural, and human-like communicational environment, similar to the one we left.

The Original Social Functions of Language

Most theories about the evolution of language share the idea that language evolved in connection with the increased social needs of early humans. To mention only a few examples: according to Robin Dunbar's "gossip as grooming" theory, language played and still plays a similar role in human communities as grooming does for apes, namely, the building and maintaining of coalitions within the group, the strengthening of friendships and family ties, and the decreasing of ingroup aggression.[2] Drawing his arguments mostly upon anthropological data, Steven Mithen claims that linguistic intelligence became slowly separated from social intelligence that had originally been responsible for handling social situations in the primate brain.[3] Similarly, Robert Worden assumes that the internal representation of linguistic meaning derives from the representations of social situations in apes.[4] Merlin Donald's theory suggests that both transitions that prepared the evolution of vocal language, i.e., the transition from episodic to mimetic as well as the transition from mimetic to mythic culture, were driven by the heightened

---

[1] "Mithocondrial Eve" or "African Eve" is a name for the most-recent common ancestor of mankind, reconstructed on the mutation rate of the mitochondria that we inherit from the ovum, i.e. only from our mothers. According to these estimations this common ancestor lived in Africa, some 150-200 thousand years ago.

[2] Robin Dunbar, *Grooming, Gossip and the Evolution of Language*, Cambridge, MA: Harvard University Press, 1996.

[3] Steven Mithen, *The Prehistory of the Mind. The Cognitive Origins of Art, Religion and Science*, London: Thames and Hudson, 1996.

[4] Robert Worden, "The Evolution of Language from Social Intelligence", in James Hurford, Michael Studdert-Kennedy and Chris Knight (eds.), *Approaches to the Evolution of Language*, Cambridge: Cambridge University Press, 1999, pp. 148–166.

force of communication needs[5] that are, naturally, inseparable from social needs.

These theories are strongly supported by the investigations on the functions of present-day languages. Jean Aitchison drew up a list of the functions that human language fulfills only with difficulties, and of the ones language is suitable for. According to her categorization, language is moderately good for communicating small pieces of information but is fairly bad at explaining spatial information, and expressing sensations and emotions. Language is, however, an excellent tool for building and maintaining social relations, and for influencing others.[6] The former function can be recognized very often in talking without any "serious" content, in talking just for talking, and we know the latter function well from conversations in which we tell stories and opinions about others, or about ourselves. Language, deriving from these properties, plays an important role in gaining and maintaining power, especially because its abstract character provides an opportunity for cheating and lying as well.

Aitchison's suggestions are supported by the data gathered by Dunbar and his students[7] as well as by Emler's observations.[8] Experiences prove that the topic in two thirds of the conversations is the description of others' or our own behavior, and that we use language quite a lot to advertise ourselves in several ways.

The strong connection between our special sensitivity to social relations and language is proved by Cosmides' adapted version of the Wason Selection Test, in that it gives a clear evidence that humans solve the same type of logical problems much more efficiently if the problems are embedded into a social context than in an abstract logical frame,[9] although the problem is in both cases mediated by language.

To these notions we can add the less often mentioned results of sociolinguistic research. Based on the huge amount of sociolinguistic data it may be stated that whenever we speak, our language use inevitably signifies our group identity as well as our relation to the speech partner.

---

[5] Merlin Donald, *Origins of Modern Mind: Three Stages in the Evolution of Culture and Cognition*, Cambridge, MA: Harvard University Press, 1991.

[6] Jean Aitchison, *The Seeds of Speech*, Cambridge, MA.: Cambridge University Press, 1996.

[7] Robin Dunbar, *op. cit.*, pp. 120–121.

[8] Nicholas Emler, "Gossip, Reputation, and Social Adaptation", in Robert F. Goodman and Aaron Ben-Ze'ev (eds.), *Good Gossip*, Lawrence, KA: University of Kansas Press, 1994, pp. 117–138.

[9] Leda Cosmides and John Tooby, "Cognitive Adaptations for Social Exchange", in John Barkow, Leda Cosmides and John Tooby (eds.), *The Adapted Mind*, Oxford: Oxford University Press, 1993, pp. 162–228.

In other words, it always shows which group we belong to, and the position we have in the hierarchy of the group. As I have shown in another paper, this property of linguistic variability is adaptive, since it ensures intergroup isolation and intragroup stabilization at the same time. Both features are necessary to increase group cohesion, so ordered linguistic variability contributes remarkably to the development of group selection and, as a consequence, to the proliferation of human cultures.[10]

The use of a common language has been connected to group identity even to date. Not only in Europe and North America where language use has become a part of ethnic, national and social identity, but in non-industrial societies as well. In Papua New Guinea, for instance, there are neighbouring villages whose languages sound almost the same for the outsider, and the inhabitants of these settlements fully understand each other's dialects. However, since these people identify themselves with different tribes, they regard these idioms as different languages.[11] As several old and present-day examples show, people often see their own language as the only possible vehicle of meaningful communication while they look at the speakers of other languages as "barbarians" or "dumbs". In some cultures children are not held to be entirely human beings until they acquire language.[12]

There is another important property of linguistic variation that is relevant here. Variability is a prerequisite for language change. The permanent change of language is also an adaptive feature, for it makes life more difficult for free-riders who want to gain all the advantages of group life without paying the price for it. But to acquire and fluently speak a permanently changing language is a hard task without a continuous presence in the group.[13] It also means that the exclusion from the group of those who speak differently is probably as adaptive for the group as are other types of stigmatization, described by Kurzban and Leary.[14]

---

[10] Klára Sándor, "Language Change and Evolution: Linguistic Variation and Change as a Consequence of the Biological Embeddedness of Language", paper presented at the 29th *New Ways of Analyzing Variation* conference, East Lansing, MI, Oct. 7, 2000.

[11] Suzanne Romaine, *Language in Society*, Oxford: Oxford University Press, 1994, p. 9.

[12] Bambi Schieffelin, "Getting It Together: An Ethnographic Approach to the Study of the Development of Communicative Competence", in Elinor Ochs and Bambi Schieffelin (eds.), *Developmental Pragmatics*, New York: Academic Press, 1979.

[13] Klára Sándor, "Language Change and Evolution".

[14] Robert Kurzban and Mark Leary, "Stigmatization: The Functions of Social Exclusion", *Psychological Bulletin* 127/2, 2001, pp. 187–208.

The basic properties of human language, variability and change, do not simply offer an opportunity for stigmatizing people who speak differently from the way we do, but stigmatizing behavior actually seems to be quite useful for the group. Linguistic stigmatization may well have been born together with human language.[15] As the well-known Shibboleth story proves,[16] people have not only stigmatized each other on the basis of using a different language, but, for a long time, they have also been aware of the fact that language use is an appropriate tool for recognizing and, if needed, excluding others.

However, there is a very important feature of this period of tens of thousands of years of the history of linguistic stigmatization. In this first period the behaviour of the groups was reciprocal. Not only those who pronounced Shibboleth could kill the other group, it could have happened the other way round, too. Not only did the members of group A hold that people in group B are not entirely humans, 'cause they do not have "the" language, but likewise the members of group B thought the same of group A.

The Age of Disequilibrium:
The Development and Spread of Literacy

The second chapter of the history of linguistic stigmatization, I believe, started with the development of literacy. The appearance of literacy led to the birth of elite culture and this event overwrote the earlier relations of language and culture.

Before the development of phonetic scripts, to learn the art of writing and reading was a rather time-consuming activity. It was an exceptional capability, so it ensured high prestige to those who owned it. When writing became used for religious purposes as well, the sacralization of certain texts made highly respected also the written text itself. However,

---

[15] Klára Sándor, "Nyelvi megbélyegzés: a gének vagy a kultúra örökíti?" [Linguistic stigmatization: is it handed down by genes or by culture?], paper presented at the V. International Congress of the International Association of Hungarian Studies ("Language and Power"). Jyväskylä (Finland), August 9, 2001.

[16] "And the Gileadites took the passages of Jordan before the Ephraimites: and it was [so], that when those Ephraimites which were escaped said, Let me go over; that the men of Gilead said unto him, [Art] thou an Ephraimite? If he said, Nay; Then said they unto him, Say now Shibboleth: and he said Sibboleth: for he could not frame to pronounce [it] right. Then they took him, and slew him at the passages of Jordan: and there fell at that time of the Ephraimites forty and two thousand." (Judges, 12:5–6, King James Version Bible.)

before the development of phonetic scripts, the language used by literates for reading the texts was probably the same they normally spoke, just as Chinese signs are read in different Chinese dialects. Phonetic scripts determine much more strongly the phonetic interpretation of texts, and this creates the possibility for written and spoken language to diverge.

The process resulted in the appearance of a new phenomenon. To the earlier "speech" vs. "non-speech" or "language" vs. "non-language" opposition a new opposition was added: "correct language use" vs. "corrupted speech". Into this new opposition two components of the European-type cultures are encoded. One divides people who are natives of the same language into two groups, and labels one group as correct users of the language, while stigmatizes the other as incorrect language users. The other component opposes written text to speech. Resulting from the well embedded high prestige of writing, written text was interpreted as using good, and speech as damaged language. The impression that language can deteriorate was reinforced by the blooming of philology, and the development of text traditions. The fact that written texts are visible and touchable, as well as their durability suggested that the form of language used in written texts may well be one to be emulated. Also, the written form is the authentic, ideal form of language, while speech is only its paltry shadow.

This thought is still characteristic of cultures based on the Greek tradition. The idea of language correctness is widespread throughout the world, and the myth that writing is the real and pure form of language is shared by European and North American culture.[17] The Platonic interpretation of language pervades not only the folk linguistic ideas,[18] but two influential linguistic schools of the 20th century, structuralism[19] and generativism,[20] as well. The notion that speech is the main form of language and that speech markers are not unnecessary waste but essential in language has become the topic of linguistic research only recently, in sociolinguistics, and in discourse and conversation analysis.

The spread of printing strengthened the high prestige of written language, and increased the asymmetry of the linguistic situation. The

---

[17] Lars-Gunnar Andersson and Peter Trudgill, *Bad Language*, Penguin, 1990.

[18] Dennis R. Preston and Nancy A. Niedzielski, *Folk Linguistics*, Berlin and New York: Mouton de Gruyter, 2000, pp. 18–19.

[19] E.g. Ferdinand de Saussure, *Cours de linguistique générale*, 1916.

[20] E.g. Noam Chomsky, *Aspects of the Theory of Syntax*, Cambridge, MA: MIT Press, 1965.

codification of spelling was a practical need of the printing houses, however, because of the Platonic view of language, the rules of spelling became interpreted as the rules of grammar, and the rules of grammar in written styles were thought to be the rules of speech as well.

For instance, in the 17th century it was the general practice of the Hungarian printing houses that the typographers not only unified the spelling of the manuscripts but also rewrote the works they published, certainly in their own dialects, since each of them held his own vernacular the "correct" language.[21] The development of standard dialects in Europe followed the same ancient principle, that is, that "the language is what I speak".[22] Standard varieties evolved out of dialects of the social elite that had political, economic or cultural prestige, so that other groups would happily accommodate to its language use in order to show themselves to be members of this highly respected group. And, in addition, the social elite had the power to make its own dialect to be the dialect of literacy that, again, reinforced its authority.

The extreme prestige of both the written texts and of the standard varieties became widespread and stabilized with the extension of public education. Schooling actually trapped and traps pupils who wanted or want to rise socially: schools demand the use of the standard, and those whose vernacular is not this variety, that is, whose parents do not belong to the social elite, have disadvantages from the very first day they enter school. They need to learn not only what everyone has to learn, but also the language of instruction, and without a proficiency in the use of the standard they cannot be successful, independently of their knowledge of the subject.[23] Experiences show that the gap between the efficiency of standard and non-standard natives is generally increasing during education. It also means that in most European countries and in the United States, education is the most powerful institution to reproduce the linguistic aristocracy. Linguistic stigmatization in our days is so deeply embedded in our culture that – as James Milroy puts it – it is "the last bastion of overt social discrimination". Laymen, including teachers, usually interpret the use of non-standard dialects as an indexic sign of low

---

[21] Bárczi Géza, *A magyar nyelv életrajza* [Biography of the Hungarian language], Budapest: Gondolat, 1963, p. 210.

[22] James and Lesley Milroy, *Authority in Language*, London and New York: Routledge, 1991 (2nd rev. ed.).

[23] Peter Trudgill, *Accent, Dialect and the School*. London: Edward Arnold, 1975.

intelligence instead of looking at it as a symbolic sign of group identity.[24] Painful examples are well known from everyday practice, like for instance the case of African American kids who were labeled mentally deprived for their use of the African American Vernacular English.[25]

However paradoxical it may sound, language in the European-type cultures has got far from its original social functions as a consequence of the development of literacy and the growth of public education. Instead of corroborating group cohesion, the linguistic asymmetry we experience day by day disintegrates primary communities since the use of their own dialects is overtly stigmatized and thus it is associated with social shame. Linguistic aristocratism that forces the whole society to use one preferred language variety goes against our biologically encoded need of belonging to a primary, human-sized group. Thus not only does it reflect the situation which is characteristic for industrial societies, namely, that large societies are not the alliances of primary groups of people but a huge complex of alienated individuals,[26] but very effectively contributes to the maintenance of this unhappy state. This way of life is rather uncomfortable for human beings who, derived from their biology, would prefer living primarily in groups of about 150 people.[27]

The Surviving Forms of the Original Social Functions of Language: The Covert Prestige

Still, the original social functioning of language has survived. The power of standard varieties could never entirely supersede non-standard varieties. As is well documented in the sociolinguistic literature, people hold to their normal use of language, even if they judge their own dialectal forms incorrect under the pressure of the overt prestige of the standard.[28] The force that maintains non-standard varieties is called covert prestige, and works most obviously in small villages and in large

---

[24] Klára Sándor, "'A nyílt társadalmi diszkrimináció utolsó bástyája': az emberek nyelvhasználata" ['The last bastion of overt social discrimination': the language use of people], *Replika* 45–46 (Nov. 2001), pp. 241–259.

[25] For a summary of this myth (with a bibliography of the major works), see Walt Wolfram, "Black Children are Verbally Deprived", in Laurie Bauer and Peter Trudgill (eds.), *Language Myths*, Penguin, 1998, pp. 103–112.

[26] Vilmos Csányi, *Az emberi természet* [Human Nature], Budapest: Vince, 1999.

[27] Robin Dunbar, *op. cit.*

[28] Peter Trudgill, *Sociolinguistics*, Penguin, 1995 (3., rev. ed.); Lesley Milroy, *Language and Social Networks*, Oxford: Blackwell, 1980.

cities. In a small, isolated community the importance of local values outstrips the external values of society. On the other hand, it was in big towns that traditional bonds first broke up, but with the loss of these ties, the substitutes of the primary communities have emerged as well: teenage gangs, groups of people in slums and in working class districts, real or pseudo-communities of more or less elegant neighbourhoods and so on. The language use that is characteristic for a gang, that is their slang, is such an important identifier for the group members that it is actually obligatorily used.

In other cases the covert prestige of the vernacular is maintained together with the overt prestige of the standard. As we know from James and Lesley Milroy's research in Belfast, the stronger the social networks in a community, the more people in the community use their own non-standard dialect, while the socially and geographically mobile members move in the direction of the standard when they are outside the community.[29] However, as Lesley Milroy highlights, most people living in a modern urban environment do not have the opportunity to live in tight social networks.[30] This leads to a greater variability in their speech, and, very often, increases the feeling of linguistic insecurity. Industrial societies provide uncomfortable environments for human beings not only from a social, biological and psychological aspect but also from a linguistic point of view.

New Communication Technologies: Forward to the Past?

As we all hope, the new communication technologies of the mobile and networked information societies of the 21st century will be able to improve the unhappy world we lived in during the 20th century. Empirical data show that people use the internet not only for building new relations and maintaining loose friendships with those who live on the other side of the world. Actually, it is more common to maintain regular e-mail connections with people who live closer than with those who live far. Surveys carried out in Toronto, Los Angeles and Michigan prove that the internet strengthens the traditional community relations, and is not a subtractive but an additive form beside the former channels of information.[31] For people who living in urban societies missed the security

---

[29] Lesley Milroy, *Language and Social Networks*.
[30] *Ibid*.
[31] Barry Wellman, "Computer Networks As Social Networks", *Science* 293 (2001), pp. 2031–2034.

of close social networks, the internet offers a possibility to build up primary communities free from geographical bonds.

New technologies can change our linguistic world as well. The established status quo of standard and non-standard varieties will probably be unsettled. The balance between the uses of different varieties can be restored, non-standard varieties may regain much of their rights, and language may fulfill again all of its original social functions. This hypothesis is supported by two main factors.

One is that literacy that generated the asymmetry in the evaluation of linguistic norms seems to be losing much of its power. One reason of it is that the human energy, the time and the financial costs invested into writing, printing, multiplying and spreading texts are much lesser today than they were even ten years ago. Texts are easily reformatted and corrected by word processors and we do not need to wait months or years for an article to be published. If our partner misunderstands what we write in e-mail, we can almost immediately explain more clearly what was meant. Another reason is that although many texts which are mediated by the new communication technologies appear in a written form, they actually belong to the kingdom of speech and not to the kingdom of written texts. The texts of many e-mail and forum messages, and the texts of almost all chat and on-line messages contain spoken forms, expressed very often with an orthography that tries to imitate the phonetics of speech, adding also emphatic signs to it, in order to substitute for nonverbal communication. This means first that the number of the domains of language use associated with literacy is receding. And it also means that a new practice has developed which does not respect the process and product of writing, but instead handles it as a channel to communicate speech.

The other factor that contributes to the change of the communicational situation is that the reinforcement of old community ties as well as the development of new kinds of primary communities will probably strengthen group identity, and this process will most likely solidify also the language use that is characteristic of the group.

The strengthening of group identity is supported by several factors. One is the internal force that maintained the covert prestige and through it the overtly stigmatized language varieties. From a research conducted in Milton Keynes by Paul Kerswill, Jenny Chesire and Ann Williams, we have clear evidence that people in the 20th and 21st centuries, too, need and develop their own forms of language use that symbolizes their community, even if they live in loose social networks. Milton Keynes is an industrial town in England, near to London, founded quite recently, in 1967. The first inhabitants who settled there were people with varying dialectal backgrounds, and although their kids had the standard as a common dialect, since they used it at school, they have developed a new idiom which is now characteristic of the speech of youngsters in Milton Keynes.[32]

In urban environment, this encoded social need can be fulfilled with the help of modern technologies much more efficiently than earlier. The ability to keep up relations independently of time and space offers an opportunity for speaking about the really important things in life instantaneously and as much as we like: we can speak about the little events of everyday life, we can tell stories about others and ourselves that will not be relevant two hours later, we can express moods and we can get comfort. In other words, we can participate in each others' daily life, just as if we lived in small, coherent groups where the community members always see and hear each other, and they always know what is going on, who is friends with whom, who is happy or sad. According to a survey, human beings behave quite normally as regards the content of their mobile phone interactions: just as in face-to-face conversations, two thirds of the topics are "gossip".[33]

The form of mobile conversations is supposed to follow the content. It would be extremely difficult to communicate an informal content in a formal style, and when we talk with our group members, it would be strange to use a language variety other than the group's own dialect, even if we are surrounded by unknown people on a train, for instance. In situations like this, people normally hold it more important to show solidarity with their partners than to prove their proficiency in the overtly respected variety. The more we use our own dialect publicly, even if not to the public, the less social shame will be associated with it. The more we hear different dialects, the less strange they will sound, and, in the end, we may even be able to restrain our propensity for stigmatization.

Another force that strengthens non-standard varieties is a number of well-known phenomena of the 21st century. Globalization, computer networks, permanent availability, and mobile learning fortify the decentralizing tendencies, and support local or other, non-geographically organized communities that are smaller than a nation or a state. The

---

[32] Paul Kerswill and Ann Williams, "Creating a New Town Koine: Children and Language Change in Milton Keynes", *Language in Society* 21 (2000), pp. 1–26.

[33] Kate Fox, "Evolution, Alienation and Gossip: The Role of Mobile Telecommunications in the 21st Century", see http://www.sirc.org/publik/gossip.shtml.

new communicational situation may damage the prestige of the standard varieties that live in a symbiotic relationship with centralization, and will support, again, language varieties that symbolize group identities. Covert prestige may become overt again, and language use that first was attached to group, then to geographical identity, later on, in the industrial societies, signals social class, in the information society may well be associated with primary communities again.

The future that is not blurred anymore promises that one day language can be used fully, in all of its social functions, just as in the past that is not as obscure anymore. The dawn of the new age, I hope, will bring the fall of linguistic aristocratism.

Wolfgang Coy: Text and Voice –
The Changing Role of
Computing in Communication

> Some day – who knows? – there may come the poetry and grand opera of the telephone. Artists may come who will portray the marvel of the wires that quiver with electrified words, and the romance of the switchboards that tremble with the secrets of a great city. ...
> But these random guesses as to the future of the telephone may fall far short of what the reality will be. In these dazzling days it is idle to predict. The inventor has everywhere put the prophet out of business. Fact has outrun Fancy. When Morse, for instance, was tacking up his first little line of wire around the Speedwell Iron Works, who could have foreseen two hundred and fifty thousand miles of submarine cables, by which the very oceans are all aquiver with the news of the world? When Fulton's tiny tea-kettle of a boat steamed up the Hudson to Albany in two days, who could have foreseen the steel leviathans, one-sixth of a mile in length, that can in the same time cut the Atlantic Ocean in halves? And when Bell stood in a dingy workshop in Boston and heard the clang of a clock-spring come over an electric wire, who could have foreseen the massive structure of the Bell System, built up by half the telephones of the world, and by the investment of more actual capital than has gone to the making of any other industrial association? Who could have foreseen what the telephone bells have done to ring out the old ways and to ring in the new; to ring out delay, and isolation and to ring in the efficiency and the friendliness of a truly united people?
>
> Herbert N. Casson, *The History of the Telephone* [1]

The Computing Revolution

The short history of computing may be divided into three parts: the computing machinery as a number cruncher and computing *automaton*, the interactively usable computer workstation as a *tool* for the mind, and the ubiquitous digital *media* alias computer networks and large digital storages.[2]

Practical starting points of automatic computing were large amounts of repeated calculations. Konrad Zuse was impressed by the enormous number of simple calculations necessary for static computation in civil

---

[1] Herbert N. Casson, *The History of the Telephone*, Chicago: A.C. McClurg, 1910.

[2] Cf. Wolfgang Coy, "Automat–Werkzeug–Medium", *Informatik-Spektrum*, vol. 18, no. 1, 1995, pp. 31–38.

engineering. Though the basic calculations were rather simple they had to be repeated again and again with varying data in some rather schematic way. Describing himself as "lazy" Zuse considered a desk calculator with some control mechanism as a perfect solution of this problem.[3] From 1936 he constructed a series of "Ziffernrechenautomaten" that were able to repeat calculation and to decide automatically what branch of a calculation should be followed as a result of calculations already done. He even constructed infinite loops of calculations by means of a glued control tape – made of used 35mm-film punched with control code. At the same time, Alan M. Turing constructed a "paper machine" that was able to perform any conceivable computation that could be done by hand following strict rules of writing with a fixed number of symbols. Finally, it was the use of electronic circuitry used by Howard Aiken or Presper Eckert and John Mauchly that made fast computing practical. The developments of such electronic machines with the help of IBM and the U.S. government started the whole enterprise of commercial, military, and scientific computing machinery. John v. Neumann's basic "First Draft of a Report on the EDVAC" laid the foundation of a vivid growth of *computing automata*.[4]

In the early sixties semi-conductor technology made it possible to construct smaller and cheaper computing machinery. Digital Equipment Corporations PDP-1 and its successors up to the PDP-11 laid the foundation for a new class of computing devices. They were cautiously called *Peripheral Digital Processors*, not to be compared to the much more expensive IBM *computers*, but with their wide acceptance they ended in fact the absolute role of IBM. The next breakthrough came in 1972 with the invention of the first microprocessors (Intel 4004) and accompanying semiconductor memories like 1Kb-chips. This brought in intelligent workstations and personal computers that made the use of these machines an everyday experience. Of course, it was not primarily hardware that made computers a practical office aid, but the invention of clever software applications like word processors, simple data software and spreadsheets like VisiCalc. This combination of hardware and software defined

---

[3] Konrad Zuse, *Der Computer – mein Lebenswerk*, 2nd ed., Berlin: Springer, 1984.

[4] John von Neumann, "First Draft of a Report on the EDVAC", Moore School of Electrical Engineering, University of Pennsylvania, June 30, 1945. Reprinted in B. Randell (ed.), *The Origins of Digital Computers*, Berlin: Springer, 1973.

PCs as tools or "wheels for the mind", as Steve Jobs claimed for his Macintosh.

The digital Audio-CD, introduced by Philips and Sony in 1982, was the first cheap large digital storage (basically still fixed to the initially defined capacity of 650 MB). It opened the use of computers to their more general use as *Digital Media Machines*. Raster Displays, cheaper memories, faster processors, and the start of computer networking promised a transformation of computers to digital media that integrated existing media formats like audio recording, graphics, photos, or video in a single digital storage format and opened these multimedia machines to digital data communications over the already widespread telephone net.

Digital Essentials

Numbers, binary codes and binary numbers to be more precise, are the building stuff of these processes. Numbers unify storage and processing. They are forming a common digital data language. The common ground of binary coding defines a common digital storage for otherwise incommensurable media of numbers, text, images, and sound.

The development of digital storage demonstrates drastically the enormous potential of digital technology within the last decades. Exactly fifty years ago the first patent on data tapes was filed by IBM (U.S. Patent # 3,057,568 from Oct. 9, 1952). The twelve-inch diameter tape recorded and stored 1.4 Megabyte. Present-day tape cassettes approach Terabyte capacity. This million-fold expansion of removable storage spans 20 orders of binary magnitude, doubling tape capacity every 30 month. Disk capacity grew even more rapidly in the last 20 years, doubling every 18 month – a process even accelerating. Comparable growth rates are known for microchips, where Gordon Moore predicted already in 1965 a duplication of the number of switching components per chip within roughly every two years: "Certainly over the short term this rate can be expected to continue, if not to increase."[5] Nicknamed *Moore's Law*, it holds now for nearly 40 years with a steady duplication rate of 18 months and a common expectation of at least ten more years.

---

[5] Gordon E. Moore, "Cramming More Components onto Integrated Circuits", *Electronics*, April 19, 1965.

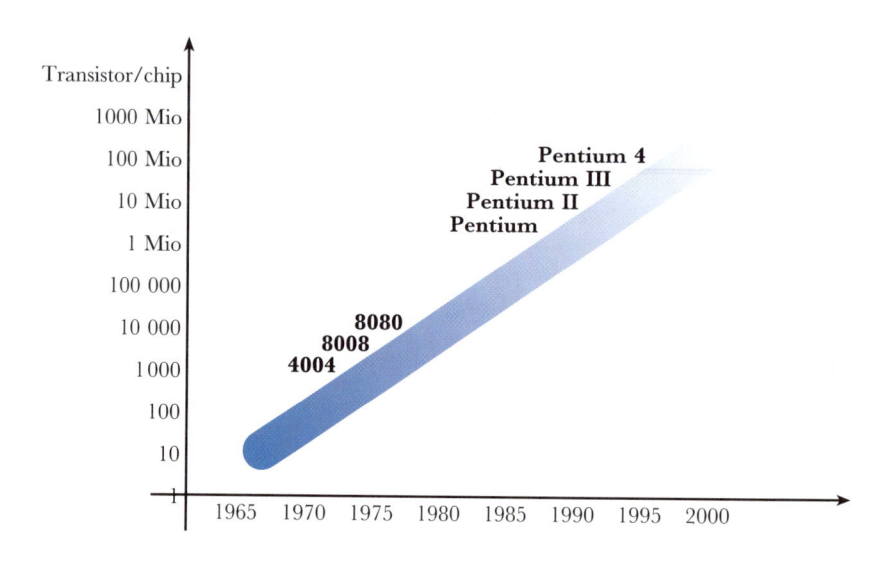

Intel processors under Moore's Law from 1965

While digital storage is the common denominator for all media formats ranging from text and numbers to images, videos, and sound – with olfactory, taste and tactual pressure data coming soon – the really new impact in digital media is programmed processing of data. Processors are usually thought as the core of computing because the complex transformations of data lead to new insights, and to automated applications.

The third element of digitalization stems from the technical convergence of computers and telephone networks. This is accomplished by digital coding of analogue signals. As a consequence the telephone net and its relatives were transformed by computers not only via the use of computer circuitry as switching elements (starting with AT&T's reed relay No.1 ESS digital exchange in the mid-sixties), but also by the unification of media data to uniform digital data. Networking changed the world of computing radically, but digitalization will change the world of networking even more radically.

Despite this shift towards digitized data and programmed procedures the unification of syntactic structures to digital data does not constitute a uniform semantic or pragmatic use of these data. Applications still remain in their originating field: images remains images, text remains text, recorded or transmitted voice remains voice and numbers remain numbers – though they all can now be stored, processed, and transmitted with the same machines, i.e. computers. New media forms may arise, but the old ones survive also in their digital form.

Embedded Systems: Vanishing but Ubiquitous Computing

Most things that look like a computer are computers, but the converse does not hold. Over 90% of all microprocessor chips are not even called processors; they are "microcontrollers". They form the technical basis of embedded digital systems, found in machines, cars, or any kind of sufficiently complex household appliance. These controllers are delivered as 8-bit or 16-bit machines, but there are also 32-bit processors like the Motorola MGT5100 (a disguised PowerPC 603). Even 64-bit machines are under consideration.

Microcontrollers have already begun their march into ubiquitous computing gadgetry. The once "General Purpose" computing machines turn into a gallery of nearly invisible but omni-present computing aids, enabling and enhancing other technical processes and machines. Though PCs are not directly an endangered species, they constitute only a fraction of the totally available computing power. Computing is vanishing into applications much like coding sophistications did before. And as nearly nobody thinks about the miracles of error-correcting codes that make DVDs possible and keep networks alive, computer programs meanwhile are the glue of actual and coming technologies. Computing became an everyday commodity like water supplies, electrical energy, or the global telephone network. The design and application of software has to be carried out, but it is hidden to most of its users – who will not even notice that they use it.

The microprocessor revolution that started in 1972 with the Intel 4004 has not yet reached its full potential, namely the ubiquitous spread of invisible computing and storage devices with specialized programs for any foreseeable service (as long as it can be paid for).

Internetworking

Communications networks have also experienced their digital revolution. Characteristics of this revolution are communication satellites, optical fiber cables, and the digitalization of data. Transmission as well as switching was enhanced by digital devices starting with Electronic Switching Systems – but it should be noted that switching was basically digital or numerical in character since the first automatic dialers.

Recall that most communication design was done with voice communication as the primary application in mind. This has changed rapidly in the last decade in favour of digital data, which means internet applications in an open, global network based on the worldwide telephone net. Actual communication networks reflect that trend. But even internet applications are not a single kind of communication. It all started with e-mail, a service that could easily be hidden in the overwhelming amount of phone talks. The situation changed nearly instantly with the advent of *Mosaic*, the first platform-independent graphical World Wide Web browser, soon replaced by Netscape's *Navigator*, and later on by Microsoft's *Internet Explorer*. The initially not so World Wide Web became the dominant form of data communication within a few years – surpassing all other internet traffic like mail, file transfer, or news. Digital Networks turned into broadcasters of Web content. Communication network design had to reflect that change. But within one decade the situation has changed again, and now peer-to-peer traffic, the individual exchange of media formats from programs, images, and audio tunes to movies defines the actual use of the internet. This is of course a direct result of multimedia PCs, but also of higher internet connection bandwidth via TV cable and better exploitation of the telephone net via DSL-technology.

Mobility: Wireless Networks and Mobile Data Communication

There is an inherent advantage of cabling over radio as a medium of distribution, because cable bandwidth may always be doubled by a second cable, while any frequency spectrum is limited by its physical nature. Nevertheless, the use of radio frequencies allows the freedom of mobility, and clever use of the working distance of radio transmissions and clever use of the actual accessible spectrum make wireless communication a viable option for intranets and internet.

Local frequency access was boosted by the development of two data protocols: The 2.4Ghz IEEE 802.11 family of protocols and the "Bluetooth" protocol. Both allow wireless local area nets (WLAN)), where IEEE 802.11 may be compared to Ethernet cable networks while Bluetooth may be compared to USB or IEEE 1394 Firewire serial access for printers, PDAs, and other peripheral devices.

Telephone providers try to open cell phones to the internet including its omnipresent multimedia content. These visions demand much more bandwidth than those actually available. This is accompanied by the profound technological change from line switching to data packet switching. With GPRS (*General Packet Radio Service*) and UMTS (*Universal Mobile Telecommunications System*) it is intended to transform cell phones to internet nodes. Such an effort was successful in Japan with NTT Docomo's iMode-technology. The hope to copy this experience in Europe assumes a comparable situation in the use of the internet. But this is rather questionable. The diffusion of private computer use and internet access is rather different in Europe, Japan, and the U.S. iMode phones substitute computers to some extent probably not because of a better usability but because of the lack of computer access. A similar process may be observed with specialized computer games hardware and it reminds of the rapid spread of hifi-equipment in Japan – said to be a substitute for family cars in the seventies. This does not mean that iMode, GPRS, MMS, or UMTS are bound for failure, but it also does not imply their overwhelming success outside the special conditions of Japan.

Thinking about the strong trend of digitalization, and the diversity of multimedia computer applications, it is much more probable that small computers, from Personal Digital Assistants (PDAs) to sub-notebooks, but also MP3-, TV-, or DVD portables may integrate phone functionality – as one of many functionalities. This will adopt the potentials of WLAN-connection, but may also include phone connectivity. A natural candidate for internet and phone connectivity is voice over IP, a technology already present, that has a strong potential to integrate phone functionality to computers – including mobile computers, whatever they may look like in the not-so-far future. Even though there is a strong indication of diversified computing devices instead of general-purpose PCs, they will hardly be shaped by the model of the mobile phone. It is much more likely that they will combine suitable functionalities to the successors of today's PDAs. This primarily depends on the achievable ease of use – apart from cost. As for the cost structure, it seems to be obvious that time-independent flat rates will be the adequate response to packet switching technologies, where restrictions on very large data volume may apply.

Speech versus Text in Communication Networks

Since modern society, science, and economy are so deeply indebted to the invention of the printing press, it seems to be only natural that the telegraphy revolution was a revolution of writing – from the Frères Chappes' optical telegraphs to Samuel Breese Morse's electrical telegraph which established the first global telecommunication infrastructure. Text as solid and reflected flow of thoughts, sustainable documents signifying revolutionary as well as imperial control. This empire of the written, optically and electrically codified words broke down within a few years with an invention that became the most important "Improvement in Telegraphy" – Alexander Graham Bell's patent # 174,465.[6]

Bell's beautiful invention of 1876 was shared by Edison's beautiful invention of voice recording and storage in 1877.[7] Suddenly the sound of human voices countered the written word in their importance. Both inventions were extremely successful. They did complement and replace relevant aspects of written language. As Bell wrote in 1876: "It is possible to connect every man's house, office or factory with a central station, so as to give him direct communication with his neighbors."[8] And as Thomas Alva Edison formulated it, well aware of the potential of his invention: "Speech, as it were, has become immortal." He also gave an illustrative interview to the *North American Review* in June 1878, where he announced as prime task of his invention: "Letter writing and all kinds of dictation without the aid of a stenographer." While Edison misinterpreted the power of his phonograph, it was Bell's invention that started a long crisis of the art of letter writing, just as newspaper reading and the associated ideas of an educated public opinion suffered from radio and TV broadcasts. Ever smaller and more personalized appliances like dictaphones, cassette recorders, video cameras, and mobile phones lead to media and communication environments where written language is pushed aside in favor of the immediate impression of voices and pictures.

Computers seemed to stop this process as they were controlled by written text and formulas, or better a combination of both called "programs". Programs as we know them are texts.

With the technical capacities of these machines their ability to use voice and other multimedia artifacts now becomes obvious. Digitized voice became a established member of the multimedia data family. Technical history generated a series of voice recording instruments with

---

[6] A. G. Bell, U.S. Patent # 174,465, granted March 7, 1876 (filed February 14): "Improvement in Telegraphy", covering "the method of, and apparatus for, transmitting vocal or other sounds telegraphically by causing electrical undulations, similar in form to the vibrations of the air accompanying the said vocal or other sounds".

[7] Th. A. Edison, U.S.Patent # 200,521, filed December 24, 1877, granted February 19, 1878: "Improvement in Phonograph or speaking machines", claiming: "The object of this invention is to record in permanent characters the human voice and other sounds, from which characters such sounds may be reproduced and rendered audible in future times."

[8] James Mackay, *Alexander Graham Bell: A Life*, New York: John Wiley & Sons, 1997.

moving parts describing the time flow. But Edison's wax cylinders, Erwin Berliner's records, Valdemar Poulsen's steel wires, Magnetophone's or Ampex' magnetic tapes, and Philips cassettes are to be replaced now by a simple device, the Digital Voice Recorder basically consisting of microphone and a memory chip. No more moving parts – only semiconductors and stored numbers. Time becomes a function of numbers, controlled by a quartz crystal.

Nevertheless the internet also demonstrated a revival of personal writing. E-mails as well as Internet Relay Chats or Internet Messengers demonstrate the power of written communication. This is technically influenced by the dominant type of computers – keyboards with monitors. E-mail has been complemented by another type of written electronic communication recently in the field of mobile telephony, where voice input and output is clearly easier than typing. "SMS-Texting" or more precisely *Short Message Services* (SMS) are meanwhile a cash cow for telephone providers – at least in Germany. Though SMS are only weak simulations of simple e-mail and not comparable to the versatility of enriched e-mail with all kinds of multimedia attachments, which in turn is not comparable to the richness of printed text or hypertext, they find their specific groups of users because of their usability that is improved in a single but very important point, namely "to be used nearly everywhere". The simple lesson is: *Usability is of prime importance* in technological innovation.

Digital Interfaces: Voice Input or Typing – or ... ?

A long time ago computers were controlled by punched cards or punched paper tape. The connection of teletypes as input and output devices transformed these number crunchers to "literary machines" (Ted Nelson[9]). Of course an even more direct input like a telephone seemed promising. But the use of voice as an input and output medium is not only an AI-dream. It has become a technical alternative to typed input and output since the mid-eighties, though there are still only few practical instances of voice-controlled computer applications. It is not surprising that phone applications are among them, but it is surprising that these capabilities did hardly find a way into the average computer environment. Even the actual use of IBM's well-advertised *ViaVoice* software is judged quite differently by average users.

---

[9] Theodore H. Nelson, *Literary Machines*, Sausolito, CA: Mindful Press, 1982.

In contrast to voice control, graphical interface elements (GUI) were enormously successful. Copying a file did no longer demand writing a command line like

cp x,y

or, more realistically,

cp x /usr/data/archive/y

with a hidden syntax to be learned by rote

cp [-R [-H | -L | -P]] [-f | -i] [-p] *source_file target_file*.

This was not supplemented by a spoken command but by simply selecting an icon, using a menu command and drawing that icon to another window. Doug Englebart's simple and elegant translation of the words to "select, point, move and click" was first ridiculed as WIMP: *windows, icons, mouse*, and *push-down menu*, but it started a complete interface revolution. The mouse-driven WIMP interface demonstrates that input and output was enhanced favourably by graphical elements and by gestures – not by writing nor by voice.

Certainly there are occasions for typing as well as there are conditions under which voice input and voice output are superior to text interfaces. This is obvious for some mobile applications – including the phone itself. But as long as writing remains a stable and valuable element of communication, it is hard to imagine that voice may take over as main interface. Nevertheless, it remains an open question how this aging text interface may develop under the conditions of multimedia with growing processing power and growing storage capacities. Not only speech, but also graphics, moving pictures, sounds, deictic elements, or tactile feedback are competitive elements in this rally for better user interfaces and usability.[10]

---

[10] On the role of images cf. Kristóf Nyíri, "The Picture Theory of Reason", in Berit Brogaard and Barry Smith (eds.), *Rationality and Irrationality*, Vienna: öbv-hpt, 2001 (http://www.fil.hu/uniworld/nyiri/krb2000/tlk.htm).

Voice, Text, and Culture

Alexander Graham Bell tried to improve the telegraph – a writing machine. As he soon found out, he had invented the base technology for a voice machine. But his team also invented a beautiful piece of human–machine interface, soon copied throughout the world. Instantaneously talking to someone else over a decent distance was a thrilling experience. It was also a first step towards a kind of *secondary orality*. The separation of microphone and loudspeaker, long-distance capabilities and automatic dialing greatly enhanced the ease of use for the telephone.

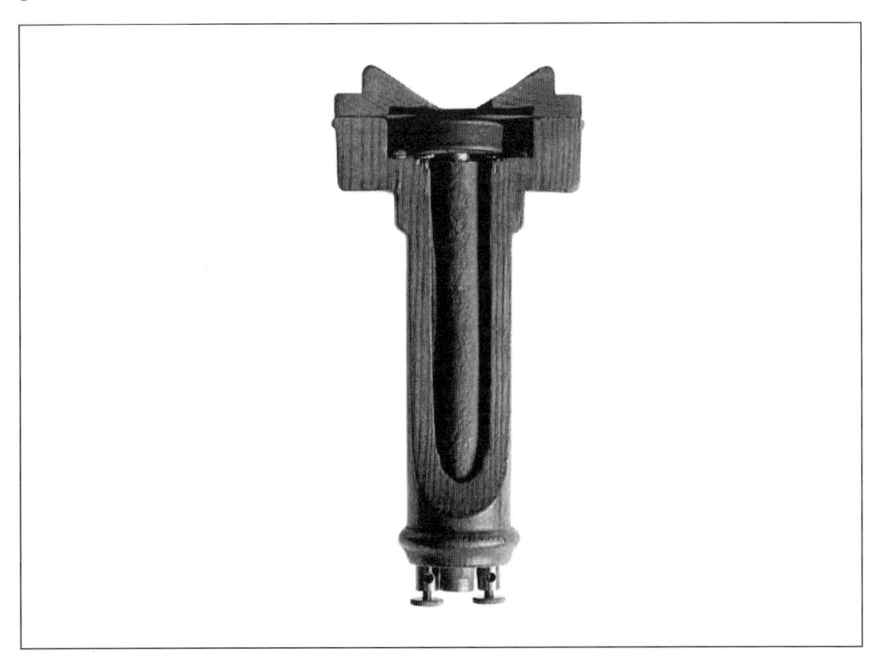

Bell's integrated microphone and loudspeaker – a simple, easy to understand interface

The second step towards secondary orality followed with the introduction of radio. Though this invention was initially open in its use, it was focused under military and political pressure to a broadcast form – also adapted by TV. A comparison of two-way radio versus telephone proves the enormous importance of simple interfaces and sound network infrastructures.

The third step towards secondary orality consists in the blending of the mobile radio and telephone. The rapid spread of mobiles includes the spread of phone access to hitherto inaccessible areas and groups. Mobiles open up rural areas, are a support to homeless people, also to playing children, or the physically challenged. The use of speech technology as computer input and output may constitute a fourth step towards secondary orality, including the use of voice technology as input or output for embedded systems.

The term *secondary orality* refers to the fact that many of theses applications are oral by their nature but demand a certain ability of expression and training to use. This is obvious for speech input systems like IBM's *ViaVoice* that demand a certain articulation and training, but it holds also for the use of answering machines that demand a certain attitude of use to be learned. It was also obvious for earlier voice technologies – from Edison's *Dictaphone* wax recorders to actual Digital Voice Recorders.

Secondary orality counters the long-term growth of *literacy* as the basic communication structure of our society – from the Greek alphabet and its forerunners to Gutenberg's invention and the resulting processes of general alphabetization and education. Literacy stabilized the educational processes from learning by reading to learning by writing. Learning by reading was a long cultural process that included important steps like silent reading without moving the lips, over copying notes in lectures, to readers of newspapers as an informed public sphere. Learning by writing includes the formulation of stepwise argumentation, the maintenance of cultural memories, and the development of scientific styles of thinking and argumentation.

It is obvious that literary technologies were under severe pressure from media development in the last 100 years. Telephone, radio and TV supported the spoken word up to the point that newspapers and letter writing were really pushed back in the last 30–50 years.

Present-day developments in communication technology support something like a *secondary literacy* that may be called *"Realtime-Writing"*. It started with usable and affordable fax machines in the mid-eighties, where real-time access to distant offices became practical, comparable to a phone call, but with the qualities of a written letter. E-mail was the next step. E-mail combines some of the advantages of telephone, fax, and letter writing, while it may be enhanced by voice mail and multimedia attachments. E-mail may be very fast, even reaching the status of a mutual conversation (converging to Internet Relay Chats or Instant Messaging), but it has also the solid qualities of letters or fax, delivering written text or copied (scanned) documents. Attached documents like images, drawings, sound, or movies make e-mail a powerful medium of communication. Even SMS-texting is a simplistic mobile form of real-time-writing.

Computing power allows the replacement of the written word by speech to some extent: Voices as input signals as well as output streams. It is difficult to predict the exact nature of that extent. Both forms, text as well as speech show inherent qualities.

• Spoken words may be easily uttered and are easily understood. We assume voice to be volatile, but this holds no longer in times of abundant digital storage.[11] Spoken word is the first choice in everyday situations.

• Text on the other hand is only slowly generated, but it allows for reflection in thought, and it has a documentary character usually not attributed to speech – except in the well-planned form of lectures or public addresses.[12]

Looking deeper we may note that the written word is the foundation of our culture, science, and technology. Text has much stricter rules of argumentation than oral communication. Stringent logic and complex proofs are the results of alphabetization. Text grossly extends the chains of argumentation by storing intermediate results – as texts, books, or lines of research and education. Text is also well-structured – e.g. by chapters, paragraphs, indices, and tables of contents. All these elements are not yet developed for stored speech and it seems to be a long way until stored voices, images, or videos will be organized as usefully as texts are in books, journals, and libraries – if ever.

It is hardly imaginable that the concise documentary and argumentative power of the written text may be replaced by speech in a foreseeable future.

---

[11] It is being contemplated to build digital storage devices like wrist watches that store every spoken word of its bearer. Of course cell phones are a logical (and probably unavoidable) first step for such gadgets.

[12] The importance of ancient rhetoric is a simple consequence of the technical lack to reproduce and distribute speeches in sufficient numbers

Péter György: Virtual Distance

> Distance has died many deaths. It met its end when the Internet reduced space to a Send command. Before that, the jetliner transformed global travel into a day trip; before that, the car, the phone, the railroad, and the telegraph all destroyed our sense of distance and replaced it with another.
>
> Jeff Howe[1]

The origin of the contemporary idea of "globalization" lies in the eighteenth century experience of the "planetary consciousness" of natural historians and travellers. "The systematising of nature ... is a European project of a new kind, a new form of what one might call planetary consciousness among Europeans... Unlike navigational mapping, however, natural history conceived of the world as a chaos out of which the scientist *produced* an order" – writes Mary Louise Pratt in her book on travel writing and transculturation.[2]

The travellers' experiences required a framework of scientific interpretation in order for the travellers to be able to narrate (write and draw) what they had come across in the uncharted fields of continents only just discovered. They travelled to faraway places, across the oceans, where they collected instances of the various species indigenous to those new, unfamiliar countries. The classification system of natural history helped them to distinguish the essential from the trivial, to create order. The victory over distance was an essential part of this planetary consciousness: the explorers and travellers succeeded in connecting and interpreting vastly disparate cultural and natural phenomena within the single framework of natural history. Unlike *Wunderkammers* and curiosity cabinets, modern consciousness relied on invisible laws, on the paradigm of typology, and had an understanding of development, of the rules governing change in time and space. Linnaeus's system offered a

---

[1] Jeff Howe, "The Next Wave", *Wired*, January 2002.

[2] Mary Louise Pratt, *Imperial Eyes, Travel Writing and Transculturation*, London and New York: Routledge, 1992, pp. 29 f.

standardisation of the natural world in the period of early capitalism; the systematisation of nature preceded the Industrial Revolution. The Victorian Mind,[3] Darwinism, and ideas about the hierarchy of life forms substituted the paradigm of evolution for typology. Planetary consciousness became increasingly important and widespread.

The 18th century, the classical age of colonialism controlled, divided, and ruled the planet — not too successfully from the European point of view as evidenced by the First World War. However, the real question is not which European country controlled the world; the essence lay in the philosophy and the writing practice employed by this control, which lead to the development and the heyday of Orientals.[4] *The West and the rest* was the common ground of colonialism. Those who belonged to the white race dominated the "rest". The so-called racial maps, eugenics, and the ladder of civilisation, were gatekeeper concepts in the intellectual navigation system. The classification system was globalised: the European scientific and technological superiority was the one globally accepted social practice, the only way in which things were understood. Primitivism was the permanent enemy.[5] Every culturally distant society, class, or community, was easily designated "primitive". Distance remained crucial during the Victorian decades: a small minority of travellers informed the whole community, most of which almost never left their region or village.

In the 20th century, the question of distance — which is connected to Geert Hofstede's category and metaphor of "power-distance" — has changed dramatically: the planet has become smaller and smaller every decade. As it is primarily the various forms of telecommunication and the invention of broadcasting that are responsible for this change, its main exponent is the emergence of the "small planet" feeling, and not the growing number of travellers.

The telegraph was the first step in the progression towards simultaneity, which is (hitherto) the most important and characteristic element in the created social space of modern societies. The telegraph was the most successful unifying influence of colonialist culture. Asa Briggs and Peter Burke quote a 19th-century Australian opinion: "To us, old colonists, who have left Britain long ago, there is something very delight-

---

[3] George W. Stocking, Jr., *Victorian Anthropology*, New York: The Free Press, 1987.

[4] Edward W. Said, *Orientalism*, Pantheon Books, 1978.

[5] Marianna Torgovnick, *Gone Primitive. Savage Intellects, Modern Lives*, University of Chicago Press, 1990. – Susan Hiller (ed.), *The Myth of Primitivism. Perspectives on Art*, London and New York: Routledge, 1991.

ful in the actual contemplation of this, the most perfect of modern inventions... let us set about electric telegraphy at once."[6]

However, the telegraph, and a few decades later the telephone, which opened up the promised land of simultaneity, were and are limited to one-to-one communication. (Although in Budapest a first attempt at broadcasting was made by Tivadar Puskás, who invented a telephone news broadcasting service). The telephone is the technology of freedom, as Ithiel de Sola Pool teaches,[7] and was the first step in the process of the privatization of social space. In the early days of the telegraph and the telephone, when access to these rare instruments was limited, the public aspects of these new technologies were the most important: they had a unifying influence. Now that these technologies are living their heyday and telephones are omnipresent, they facilitate the creation of individual relations in private, intimate space.

In the history of media and space, of the struggle to overcome distance, the second turning point was the invention of radio and later television.[8] Broadcasting, this new system of dissemination, created a new type of social space, termed "media space" by Monroe Price.[9] Media space is censored and stringently controlled, unified and simultaneous. Within a few decades media space dramatically changed the concepts of foreign policy, of the validity of nation states, of the meaning of political communities, of the cultural hierarchy, and of canons in the market of loyalties. In media space, distance became a technological and political issue. Technologically, it is simply the calculation of the energy needed to overcome a given distance. There is, of course, a price to be paid: transmission over long distances is not cheap, and can be politically difficult. The messages and radio programs that were transmitted beyond enemy lines became part of the art of warfare.[10] Media space was always watched over by the gatekeepers of this period, politicians. Censorship was different in democratic societies and in the one-party-system Comecon countries, but technologically there was no difference in the implemen-

---

[6] Asa Briggs and Peter Burke, *The Social History of Media*, London: Polity Press, 2002, p. 141.

[7] Ithiel de Sola Pool, *Technologies of Freedom*, Cambridge, MA: Harvard University Press, 1983.

[8] Brian Winston, *Media Technology and Society. A History: From Telegraph to the Internet*, London and New York: Routledge, 1999.

[9] Monroe E. Price, *Media and Sovereignty: The Global Information Revolution and Its Challenge to State Power*, Cambridge, MA: MIT Press, 2002.

[10] Monroe Price, *Television, Public Sphere and National Identity*, Oxford and London: Oxford University Press, 1997.

tation of control. Media space did not only influence the political circus, it probably also reshaped the nature of political debate, and the technology of war. In the second World War, radio propaganda was an essential element of warfare; during the Gulf War, the media became the playground of the war. CNN did not just cover the war, it partially created it.

The third turning point is the current digital revolution: the phenomena of convergence, of the multimedia and internet revolution, and last but not least of the recent fusion of the various mobile and wired/wireless interactive communication tools and structures. This revolution, this new paradigm has now also created a new kind of social space: cyberspace or virtual space.[11] Cyberspace is a domain shared by the public and the private sector, it is the expression and the manifestation of virtual identity, of virtual neighbourhood, and of virtual distance. In cyberspace traditional concepts, such as distance, and the distinction between private and public, collapse and disappear. There are competing communities, there is a lively market for loyalties, and there is cultural alignment, but all this without control or censorship, without gatekeepers such as ruling classes, politicians, or nation states. Since cyberspace is now irreversibly part of discourse on politics, media, communication, and cultural development, one is often confronted with both over- and underestimation of the importance of this brave new world (e.g. a world of universal freedom versus a global Big Brother, the digital divide versus a world without boundaries, etc.).

One crucial aspect of this virtual space – the locus of planetary consciousness – is that it lacks the compulsory categorisation systems and the classificatory forms and norms of the 18th century. In this new world order, or playground, in this world of virtual distance, there is a fundamentally new possibility to change the traditional institutions of cultural domination and the rules of social perception.

There are a number of global institutions and organisations in the off-line world that have their roots in physical geography, and that represent a technology of power and control that is based on a traditional notion of distance. The following example clearly illustrates the difference between the worlds of media space and of virtual distance. The WIPO, the World Intellectual Property Organization succeeded in making the parliaments of almost all countries in the world ratify legislation that represents the European approach to and notion of intellec-

---

[11] Kevin Kelly, "From Places to Spaces", in *New Rules for the New Economy*, http://www.kk.org/newrules/newrules-7.html.

tual property. All developed countries have to accept that intellectual property and trade marks are not just big business, but also expressions of a political philosophy that values authenticity and individuality – the most sought-after values in our cultural and political hierarchy – over anything else. (Genius theory would be unthinkable without the cult of authenticity and individuality.) Yet we all know what has happened on the internet: the domination of intellectual property in the forms developed during the centuries of the printing press and broadcasting has rapidly come to an end. This is not only because of MP3 and the permanent worldwide exchange of various digital databases and collections, in a cyberspace where distance does not play a role anymore, where geographical control is just a narration in the garden of cultural memory, or perhaps a website that commemorates this historical fantasy. The new developments often simply reject or disregard copyright.

The real revolution lies in the fact that there now is a world of cooperation, a virtual neighbourhood in cyberspace, where everybody can meet everybody, and the only remaining question is what system of navigation to use. There is a huge difference between the age of the great explorers and their discoveries and the current age of planetary consciousness. In the past, the system of geographical map making, the art of navigation, and natural history created a system of control.

However, in the case of the internet this is all different: navigation systems and uncharted cyberspace exist side by side. There are a number of recent phenomena that deserve a brief analysis:

1. Virtual archives and the open source code movement are among the most important benefits of virtual distance: anybody can offer their cultural products, and collect what they need. Virtual and personal archives are the best examples of mobile interactive communication institutions: virtual archives are always under construction, there never is a final version. Interactive archives rewrite the traditional boundaries between written and oral culture. What is an e-mail archive? Who is the collector? What does the collector collect: the chain of messages? As the internet archive by Brewster Kahle (www.archive.org) illustrates, it is also unclear what exactly an internet archive is. Does it still make sense to distinguish copies from originals in the case of digital databases? How should media archaeology deal with digital copies? Brewster Kahle has been influenced by the Alexandria Library, the Museion. But where is Alexandria in cyberspace? On my screen? On whose screen?

2. Personalized collaborative filtering technology and the new boundary between private and individual. This is crucial: individualised cyberspace means a fragmented and permanently temporary system of

information.[12] In this context: what is a weblog site, this *virtual institution?* A blog (Weblog) is an online forum usually with one main author/contributor who frequently posts his or her thoughts. What is a weblog-site: an individual archive or a temporary document of personal communication?[13]

3. The transpublication system, an idea proposed by Ted Nelson, the founding father of Xanadu, and the inventor of hypertext. Transpublication is the copyright system of the Net: it recognises the fundamental role that collaboration plays in every intellectual product. The work of art, the artifact does not exist in a final version anymore, only in a process of permanent communication. This permanent activity is documented in archives. There is the idea and practice of an interoperable e-print archive, of self archiving – invented, among others, by Stevan Harnad. The idea of self archiving is connected to the Open Archive Initiative Protocol[14] and the Budapest Open Access Initiative.

4. The renaissance of the curiosity cabinet as a valid type of collection: the recognition and reinterpretation of outsider artists and collectors, and marginalized culture. The end of the traditional cultural hierarchy.[15] The internet is the best example of a post meta-narration, post master-narration world.

---

[12] Kevin Kelly, *Out of Control*, http://www.kk.org/outofcontrol. The question is connected to the problem of emergence, cf. Steven Johnson, *Emergence: The Connected Lives of Ants, Brains, Cities, and Software*, New York: Scribner, 2001. – "Emergence is what happens when the whole is smarter than the sum of its parts. It's what happens when you have a system of relatively simple-minded component parts – often there are thousands or millions of them – and they interact in relatively simple ways. And yet somehow out of all this interaction some higher level structure or intelligence appears, usually without any master planner calling the shots. These kinds of systems tend to evolve from the ground up." ("Steven Johnson on 'Emergence'", http://www.oreillynet.com/pub/a/network/2002/02/22/johnson.html.)

[13] "Like any ecosystem, the Blogosphere demonstrates all the classic ecological patterns: predators and prey, evolution and emergence, natural selection and adaptation. I've often thought that anthropologists were best equipped to deconstruct the emerging blogging sub-culture, but now I'm convinced I got it wrong: the greater mysteries of the Blogosphere will be unlocked instead by evolutionary biologists." (John Hiler, "Blogosphere: The Emerging Media Ecosystem", http://www.microcontentnews.com/articles/blogosphere.htm.)

[14] Cf. http://www.openarchives.org/documents.

[15] Eric S. Raymond, "The Cathedral and the Bazaar", http://www.firstmonday.dk/issues/issue3_3/raymond/#d1.

5. The collapse of global ideology-based institutions, such as the WIPO and the UNO, and the rise of institutions that radically criticize globalization. The rebirth of multiculturalism, avant-garde, and counter cultures.

Summary

The world of virtual distance is a world of new freedoms and rights, of new technologies of cultural identity, of new principles of authenticity, of communicative, dialogue-based personalities and communities. New creativity, new art forms, new coalitions, new hierarchy against meta-structures and globalization.

The emerging world of virtual distance is a world of new artistic activity and new types of movements against globalization. There are new technology-based *widerstandformen:* SMS, mobile phone calls, e-mails, internet: a digital continuum of new technologies of political freedom and community creation. *The world of Emergence, instead of the tradition of the transparent Archive.*

Herbert Hrachovec: Mediated Presence

This presentation will offer 9 propositions, divided into 2 parts. The initial 5 theses are dealing with concepts, while the remaining set of claims will address more tangible problems in media studies.

1. The hype surrounding tele-presence deserves to be taken seriously.

Quite a number of scholars frown upon recent excitement about an alleged new dimension of experience, called cyberspace. In view of the slogans widely circulated they seem to have a good point. There is an irritating resemblance between advertisements for stylish digital gadgets and pronouncements coming from certain quarters of post-modern media theory. Captions like "Telepresence: A Technology Transcending Time and Space" or "Telepresence: live, interactive, look where you want video on the Internet" evoke flights of metaphysical phantasy together with more robust reflexes, familiar from e-commerce. Yet, as William J. Mitchell has noted with respect to the term cyberspace: "It's a figure of speech that has emerged to cover a gap in our language."[1] Responding to this need, here is a well-considered definition:

> Telepresence is the art of enabling social proximity despite geographical or temporal distances through the integration of computers, audio-visual, and tele-communicative technologies.[2]

Such clear and useful explanations do not make the headlines, though. It seems that "the gap in our language" which accounts for the

---

[1] William J. Mitchell, "Replacing Place", in Peter Lunenfeld (ed.), *The Digital Dialectic: New Essays on New Media*, Cambridge MA: MIT Press, 2001, p. 113.

[2] Gerald M. Karam, "Telepresence – Current and Future Technologies for Collabaration. (Did the Interstate System Kill Route 66?)", in *Ontario Telepresence Project. Final Report.* Information Technology Research Center, Telecommunication Research Institute of Ontario, 1995. Available at http://www.dgp.toronto.edu/tp/tphp.html. (Accessed: 2002/05/15.)

excitement in popular discourse, does not call for a simple patch. Tele-presence is touching on magic and mystery; one cannot easily resolve this semantic surplus within a sober analytical account.

Perhaps this is not even a good way to proceed. The lack of technical expertise in common talk about digital technologies is a genuine symptom of its tenuous hold on the underlying issues. It does not help to kill the messenger. Consider the following phrases picked from a paragraph written by the German philosopher and journalist Florian Rötzer: "the disappearance of distance and duration ... space traffic cancels out all boundaries between cultures ... a pluralization and rela-tivization of reality."[3] These are pathetic words but everyone will recognize the problem. Spatial distance and temporal duration seem indeed to have vanished in the age of global, inter-active telecommunication. It might be objected that networked computers have obviously neither abolished space nor time. True enough, but this objection marks a fallback position without facing the challenge.

2. We cannot afford current, easy explanations of tele-presence.

"Transcending time and space" or "the abolition of distance and duration" are indications of a genuine disturbance, yet those locutions have to be handled with care. There are no laws against poetic exaggerations in the public relations industry and it might seem unobjectionable to use speculative license to capture the exhilaration and awe that comes with borderless information interchange. But such constructions, offered as explanations, turn into thought hazards. Take, for example, distance. Tele-presence is supposed to eliminate distance. But if you really push the loss of distance you end up with mysticism. Understanding technology turns into zen-like utterances.

One way to see the problem is to observe that we cannot make sense of the puzzlement we are faced with without a working distinction between proximity and distance. Paul Virilio complains that:

> closer to what is far away than to what is just beside us, we are becoming progressively detached from ourselves.[4]

There is no way to comprehend the complaint but to master the

---

[3] Florian Rötzer, "Virtual Worlds: Fascination and Reactions", in Simon Penny (ed.), *Critical Issues in Electronic Media*, New York: SUNY Press, 1995, p. 126.

[4] Quoted in Barry Brown, Nicola Green and Richard Harper (eds.), *Wireless World: Social and Interactional Aspects of the Mobile Age*, London: Springer, 2002, p. 26.

ordinary use of closeness. It has to be presupposed and supplemented with the additional twist suggested by the author. Imagine someone lacking any understanding of closeness: she will not profit by being told that newly available techniques are bringing distant events close to her. We need a concurrent mastery of *tele-distance* to be able to distinguish between the physical environment and those peculiar impressions we want to classify as close by, yet coming from afar. And we have to keep this separate from the close distance a phenomenologist might want to describe, e.g. the tension arising between persons keeping away from each other in an elevator.

The reason for the confusion often encountered in promotional talk about tele-presence is quite simple. Certain concepts such as "left and right" or "true and false" work in pairs, hence the occasional temptation to overstress one component. A notorious example is Baudrillard's "universal simulation". Such conceptual extravaganzas almost inevitably lead into dead ends. As soon as it is recognized that deception only makes sense vis a vis knowledge the pendulum swings back: If there is no knowledge, there is no deception either. The dialectics between proximity and distance is a case in point. If we take "the abolition of distance and duration" as anything but shop talk from media journalists we embark upon a journey that can only end in philosophical embarrassment.

3. Our web of belief is under stress. Tele-presence calls for a re-examination of some basic concepts in epistemology.

A contradiction seems to have emerged. How can one state that hype has to be taken seriously and yet insist that this leads into a dead end? One way out is to accept the surface paradox of ubiquitous presence as a first impression and look elsewhere for a more promising approach to the problem thus emerging. A good way to start is the time-honored epistemological scenario developed in parallel with modern science. According to this paradigm human perception is regarded as an essential ingredient in the acquisition of knowledge. Humans are sentient organisms, interacting with their environment in space and time, according to their capacities of apperception. It is trivially true that sensual input into the nervous system has to be triggered by stimulation arising within the vicinity of the receiving entity. Anti-metaphysical empirical philosophy, in due course, established sensory affection as a prerequisite of the epistemological process.

Causal chains are, however, not restricted to the neighbourhood. A person can be affected by nuclear radiation or by the depletion of the earth's ozone shield. The scope of technologically mediated impingement upon the human subject has been spectacularly enlarged in the preceeding century, just think of electricity, wireless communication and computer networks. Our familiar epistemological scenario has been developed to model the cognitive process accompanying the lighting of a candle, but it is seriously overtaxed in dealing with a light switch. Yet, interestingly, the advent of electricity has not forced any revisions upon epistemology. The probable reason for this is that causal connections are really not the important part of the story. Space can be bridged by extremely fast physical processes, but this is not in itself a challenge to the established concept of knowledge, since it is carefully separated from causal machinery.

The characteristic ingredient in any epistemological account is the use of signs. Semiotic dimensions are orthogonal to causal dependencies. Perceiving a word or a picture is not just a case of submitting to a physical input. The recognition of an actress in a newspaper, to pick an example, is peculiarly exempt from her physical whereabouts. The workings of human cognition have usually been discussed within certain semiotic frameworks, the most prominent tools of mediation being concepts or sentences. Such bearers of information content seem to occupy a realm very different from electrical currents running though a wire. Still, in a way that's ancient history. One important presumption underlying the classical setup has become obsolete.

Old signs were pretty static: spoken words, texts, pictures. Their presence to the senses was an all or nothing affair. A meaningful utterance has to be heard by someone, sharing the speaker's location. A given text had to be perceived within a narrowly defined environment. There simply *was* no option of a text being presented via causal mechanisms from the opposite end of the world in real time. Signs, even though they mediate possibly distant content have to be embedded in the range of sensual perception. A dramatic change has, however, occurred on the level of technological mediation: contemporary machinery allows us to significantly enhance the causal underpinnings of sign systems. It has become impossible to base knowledge claims exclusively on neighbourhood perception. A live report on TV does not fit into the pattern of the testimony of the senses. When a reporter addresses her audience via a screen we assume a causal chain leading far beyond the living room and giving credibility to her sentences. Classical epistemology distinguishes between sensual affections and conceptual activity. It does not provide a place for cognitive content transmitted by instant tele-mediation.

4. Presence refers both to a mode of time and to a spatial quality. This link-up is under serious stress and should be used with care.

Language provides a nice illustration of the preceeding claims about the tele-epistemological innocence of classical philosophy. It offers the same expression, namely "presence", to designate a given moment and attendance *at* a given moment. "To be present" easily extends into "at the present time". The reason is quite clear. Given the typical scenario of knowledge acquisition prior to the advent of telecommunication, sensual perception of spatial objects – exempting objects seen through a telescope – coincided with their actual presence. Signs have, of course, always been able to bridge large distances. But they were simply not hooked into an extended causal framework of technologies transmitting information from a given place to distant places with practically no delay.

The outcome is well known: telephone, radio, TV and the internet offer a kind of semiotic globalization, i.e. they provide regimes of symbols that are no longer governed by the constraints common to ordinary speech, writing and print. Make no mistake: *qua* signs the color dots on the monitor are not at all "immediate". Their pervasive presence is not a means to overcome the distance between signifier and signified. Still, we can hardly escape the strong impression of something one might call "representational immediacy" which is a tentative description of a specific techno-semiotic arrangement, namely the instant availability of a set of symbols around the globe at any given time. Just think of the huge TV-screens installed in some soccer stadiums. They depict the game, as seen in million homes, to the crowd attending the actual event. To talk about the disappearance of distance and duration *does* seem to make sense in such circumstances.

It is, nevertheless, a misguided move as can be shown by the following argument. Spatial categories, it is true, fail us in a certain, significant sense, as the crowd's enthusiasm is fed by pictures manipulated in a remote recording studio. This does not, however, imply the breakdown of duration, quite the contrary. The whole point of the exercise is to let spectators across the continent participate in a given moment. Presence in the temporal sense remains very much in force.[5] It is impossible to have tele-presence without a common spatial and temporal grid, but both differ in a significant way. The entire planet can be regarded at one moment in time – it cannot similarly be positioned at one single spatial

---

[5] One might attempt to additionally jump out of the time frame, but this is not the topic of my talk.

coordinate. All of mankind may for certain purposes be treated as being co-present in a temporal sense, but it cannot be physically joined together in Budapest. We have to come to terms with a pervasive break of symmetry as the spatial meaning of presence is split off from its temporal meaning. In tele-presence people are sharing a particular moment, but they do *not* share a common place in a comparable meaning of the term. An internet chat proceeds in real time, yet the chatroom is a software construct. The category of "being present" in a chat divides into "sharing the actual moment" and "inhabiting a virtual environment".

5. Life originates in the Here and Now. When its symmetry is broken, the likely result is information overload.

Think of a person arriving at a cinema, wanting to spot a friend among the mass of people queuing for a movie ticket. She calls him on his mobile phone. Both want to attend the same film at a particular time, but are they present at the same place? In a trivial sense they certainly are, yet in the light of media theory things are more complex and more interesting. The friend's location, if he answers the call, is not just a slice in the common three-dimensional coordinate system; his presence is mediated via an elaborate mechanism of wireless signals, possibly by extra-terrestrial radio devices. While their common time frame is unaffected – both wait for the film to start at 7 p.m. – the space they occupy is an intricate hybrid phenomenon. Take another example. A person stands in front of a camera and looks into a monitor which shows her picture as it is simultaneously transmitted on TV. Permit me to skip the detailed analysis of this kind of proximities and tele-distance and suffice it to say that it would be hopeless to base it on traditional spatial presences.

"Mediated presence" suggests the following picture: something is close at hand, even though we employ tele-transmission to bridge a real life distance. This might be good enough to describe a two way intercom, but it is insufficient to deal with more advanced forms of tele-presence. Mediation, in those cases, covers the planetary space in a single move. With only minimum exaggeration one can talk of a tele-communicative continuum which covers all relevant agents simultaneously, even though they remain seperated by vast distances. Presence is *temporal* actuality and the challenge is to master this presence against the backdrop of multiple information channels constituting a second nature environment, namely *virtual* space.[6]

---

[6] To discuss virtuality is beyond the scope of this paper.

6. Symbolic systems depend on material signifiers. Ubiquitous digital telecommunication disturbs many of their familiar patterns.

It is mainly under the impression of electronic data exchange that scholars have become aware of the close fit between traditional means of communications (like speech, writing and print) and their informational content. A well-established mature technology like the printing press can, with the benefit of hindsight, be seen as a stabilizing factor in the social production, propagation and administration of knowledge. This does not only hold for Gutenberg-type interchange, but extends to more recent forms like photo, telephone or radio. In every case a technical medium was domesticated into a set of devices and conventions that imposed its restrictions onto the possible *Gestalt* of its symbolic outcome. There are genres of phone conversation or radio programs just like the well-known literary genres.

This situation is currently changing. The category of so-called "secondary orality" which was introduced to designate the post-Gutenberg option of spontaneous communication directly transmitted in broadcasting and computer networks is inadequate to capture what is happening in the field of electronic media. Photos and films, to pick just one example, are still widely seen in historical terms, as outcomes of a certain photo-chemical process. But it is obvious that this story has been increasingly undermined by digital procedures. As pictures and sounds can be freely generated and transformed by multi-media software their surface appearance and their concomitant social role become mere epiphenomena of an underlying electronic design that does not distinguish between text, picture and sound.

We *do* still, to be sure, distinguish a monitor from a speaker and a printer. The sensory modalities served by those respective machines are unlikely to disappear. But, like in the case of tele-presence, electronic information processing blurs previously natural distinctions. Prior to maximum-resolution graphical software the optico-chemical mechanism of photography certified the authenticity of the picture, prior to the advances of psycho-acoustical modeling a high fidelity recording was the most authoritative source of audio rendition. Such analog media-techniques loose their traditional capacity to shape content.

7. *Several defining distinctions between established types of communication are no longer well-founded.*

An engineer will strive to optimize signal transmission, but his expertise is embedded in institutional practice. We were socialized into a culture that made a difference between telephone, radio and computer networks, but it is impossible to guess the future course of wireless transmission. Take the development of digital audio web-casting. It takes only a moderate amount of expertise to make a computer into a private radio station. You can play music from the CD-drive or pipe a live event through the sound-card. It will instantly be received on a global scale. The consequences are widely unforeseen. Imagine several million radio stations, each running on a standard PC. This is, of course, not going to happen, since it would spell the abolition of the social pattern ordinarily associated with radio stations. As long as the term makes sense there have to be comparatively few of them, governed by government regulations and largely intended to make money. Such institutional constraints simply don't fit web-casting which will, in all likelihood, thoroughly change the established patterns of public as well as commercial broadcasts.

Technology change is closely linked to politics in this area.[7] The electro-magnetic spectrum used to be subdivided into frequency bands for radio transmission. Since those resources were limited it was deemed necessary for governmental agencies to supervise the allocation of segments of the spectrum. This is, of course, just a fancy way to express the common wisdom that radio stations have to be fitted into the available bandwidth. It's clearly the opposite of the internet protocols and – as it turns out – it is in fact an incorrect assumption. Conventional radio technologies were "shouting" across the whole range of their alloted bandwidth, i.e. they used strong signals to overcome noise and disruptions. There are more economical ways of safely propagating radio signals. Equipped with computer chips receivers can pick out and process information in more sophisticated ways. "Spread spectrum" methods allow a practically limitless number of transmissions over the whole range of the spectrum. Digital supplement radio does not, at least as far as interference-free transmission is concerned, require government regulation. And it is fit for the handling of IP/TCP which adds another

---

[7] Lawrence Lessig has written an elucidating analysis of this. Much of what follows is inspired by his book *The Future of Ideas: The Fate of the Commons in a Connected World*, New York: Random House, 2001.

twist to this already somewhat confusing account of transgressive technological developments.

A radio set connected over the internet protocols is a two-way device and can, given a suitable digital connection, receive and send data. One use for such machines is environmental information gathering in regions difficult to access, i.e. monitoring certain parameters in tropical rainforests. Comparatively cheap radios or web-cams that can be manipulated via an IP-address are just precursors of things to come.[8] Now, for a final point, consider that the next generation mobile phones, implementing the UMTS standard, employ precisely spread spectrum technology to boost performance and increase available connections. Our habitual attitudes towards information genres are becoming increasingly detached from their *de facto* implementation as the convergence of technologies drain the meaning out of familiar distinctions like one-to-one, one-to-many and many-to-many communication.

8. To cope with mediated presence a new kind of geography will have to be developed.

In former times typical representations were closely dependent on place and change of place. A painting by Rembrandt has to be moved to an exhibition outside Amsterdam, and – even discounting the aura – its photographic similes occupy definite locations. The tense present of telecommunication imposes different rules on verbal and pictorial content. Even though a politician's speech might still be delivered to a local audience, there is all the difference between this occasion and its being reported on television. TV politics is clearly the dominant force in contemporary democracies. It offers a symbolic system built upon the simultaneity of audio-visual information. The title of Austrian TV's main news show actually sums it up pretty well: "Zeit im Bild", roughly "Depicted Time".

These are relatively modest implications of tele-presence; challenges we have had half a century to face. But, as a glance at recent technical advances shows, the comparatively familiar informational set-up of the 20th century is in turmoil. Jacking a microphone into my sound-card and assuming a certain set of software tools I can talk to any person on the internet for very little money for an unlimited amount of time. How

---

[8] For more detail see *The Cook Report: Broadband Spread Spectrum Wireless Extends Internet Reach of ISPs & Field Research Scientists.* Available at http://wireless.oldcolo.com/biology/progress2000/cookjul.pdf. (Accessed: 2002/05/17.)

should this option be called? It's neither radio, nor telephone in any established sense, just as web-cams are neither films nor TV. The situation is similar to 19th century architecture which superimposed its ancient canon of forms upon the new building materials. Mediated presence is full of surprises and possible embarrassments.

But isn't this just – modern – life? One plausible reason for the Enron debacle is that fund managers of the cheated trusts were not up to the highly sophisticated instruments of accounting and credit developed in the preceding decade. Viewed against widespread economic dissatisfaction and geo-political upheaval I seem to have dealt with extremely benign confusions. The preceeding remarks have, admittedly, to be put into perspective. Their purpose has not been to proclaim yet another new age, but rather to draw attention to two structural features of information society: (1) a certain detachment of space from time and (2) a profound rearrangement of the very framework of the tele-communication industry. If this is the diagnosis, stripped from sensationalism, what does remain of the more alluring side of cyber-philosophy?

9. *History is impossible without bodies, which are impossible without distance.*

The hype surrounding tele-presence deserves to be taken seriously. But how to avoid profound hype? Here are some tentative observations on a high level of abstraction, combining both descriptive content and metaphysical impact. The nuclear bomb was the first device which made people aware of the fact that a single, local action could have instant global repercussions up to the destruction of the planet. On a more peaceful note the moon landing was a historical moment, demonstrating how, at a certain date, the entire globe could be considered one united location. The quality of temporal presence can thus be projected onto the spatial framework. Nuclear energy and broadcasting are comparatively unsophisticated examples to make this point. Mediated presence has become much denser. In 2001 private mobile phones rather than the military power of the United States provided immediate responses to an ongoing terrorist attack. Such incidences seem to suggest that we will have simultaneity plus ubiquity in the not too distant future, i.e. tele-presence in the strong sense.

This prognosis rests upon a conceptual confusion. Symbol systems are capable of literally *presenting* states of affairs across big distances and they can, nowadays, be linked to their sources with the speed of light. This makes for causal simultaneity which may even go both ways, including feedback to the originating source. And causally triggered events can, in the limiting case, engulf the entire space-time. But here is the catch as far as tele-*communication* is concerned: symbols are different from causes. To put it in more cautious analytic terms: we are dealing with two autonomous levels of description, difficult to reconcile. Global warming is a causal process affecting the entire planet, but it does not carry any particular information. Pristine electro-magnetic waves are, likewise, ubiquitous and uninformative. The fact that engineers have managed to encode content into such natural phenomena should not lead us to confuse causal connections with symbolic features. Even if the symbolic medium is, in a way, omnipresent, this does not mean that we are in the presence of the things symbolized. To use a symbolism amounts to recognize a categorical distinction between the material of the signifier and its designation. This holds for pointing to an adjacent tree as well as for recognizing the face of a singer on TV. The speed of light and feedback mechanisms simply do not enter into this equation.

The conclusion is not that one should be insensitive towards the implications of instant global signification technology. It's just a reminder that symbols differ from simple objects. Human evolution is built upon this mild case of schizophrenia which makes us able to present an object that is physically absent. Tele-presence seems to hold the promise of this gap to be eventually closed. But think again. What would be achieved if signs were to be fused with designations within a single cosmic instant?

Cosmological theory tells us that the history of the universe can only be reconstructed from radiation caught by our observation instruments in earth-time. To arrive at an astronomical understanding such signals have to be mapped back onto space-time, reintroducing distance, absence and process. Now imagine the planet viewed in God-like immediacy from a far away galaxy. All significant spatial relationships would be merged into a tiny spot of light. An intelligent being out there would have to unravel the mystery, re-introducing a pattern of spatial coordinates and symbolic communications bridging its extension to understand the human condition. The thought experiment can have a sobering effect. If you are tempted to regard tele-presence as an overcoming of distance and duration, think of yourself as looked upon from a distant galaxy. You are an unremarkable blob, waiting to be reverse engineered into a story within time and space.

Valéria Csépe: Children in the Mobile
Information Society:
Cognitive Costs and Benefits

The nature of literacy and learning is rapidly changing as new technologies for information and communication such as cellular phones appear, providing us with new challenges and new opportunities as we consider how best to be prepared for changes to the human cognitive structure. By their very nature, humans love to communicate, love to express themselves, as is well shown by the intensive use of cellular phones. In the world of five senses, people freely experiment with language, voice modulation, gestures, and facial expressions – all as ways to communicate nuances in meaning. Cellular phones used for talking or for different types of messages (SMS, MMS, e-mails) still do not provide many of these options.

The human capabilities of using the recent generation of cellular phones and catching up with recent technical changes has set many limitations especially when flexibility and ease of use of manipulating a new or slightly different device are taken into consideration. However, when immersed in a medium that places some restrictions in the path of their communication needs, humans get downright clever and creative in overcoming those barriers. The very few studies run by psychologists, mostly using questionnaires, have mainly focused on the general habits of cellular phone users. In a previous study[1] we used the cellular phone as a device for getting online information on text composing, combined with questionnaires in order to elicit information on cognitive changes assumed to occur in recognizing space and time due to the intensive use of mobile devices. As it was shown by an additional result of the study, the younger the subjects were the more flexible and faster they manipulated the test device. A detailed inspection of the teenagers' perform-

---

[1] Valéria Csépe, "Kognitív fejlődés és mobil információs társadalom" [Cognitive Development and the Mobile Information Society], in Kristóf Nyíri (ed.), *Mobil információs társadalom: Tanulmányok* [The Mobile Information Society: Essays], Budapest: MTA Filozófiai Kutatóintézete, 2001.

ance gave us the idea that some particular features of the memory system may be responsible for the better performance in device manipulation of the young subjects as compared to that of adults.

The Memory System and Its Development

Already Proust has well understood the evocative power of memory. In his famous novel[2] he describes visiting his mother, who serves him tea and pastries. As he dips the little pastries known as petites madeleines into his tea, all of a sudden he is overcome by vivid memories and unexpected emotions. As Proust writes: "I sensed that it was connected with the taste of the tea and the cake, but that it infinitely transcended those savours." As a consequence of these intensive emotions, the source of the memory reveals itself to him, past experiences related to his aunt, Leonie. What is the most interesting in Proust's writing about the process of remembrance is the distinctive components of a particular memory type called explicit memory. It is easy to recognize for a psychologist how different is the access in Proust's description to the item and to the source memory.

Sigmund Freud, Proust's contemporary and the father of psychoanalysis has stressed the importance of specific childhood events and memories. He was deeply convinced that the repression of memories plays a particular role in the development of various types of psychopathology. Freud also presaged another type of memory now known as implicit memory. In contrast to explicit memories, like Proust's remembrance of specific madeleines past, procedures for how to relate to others are encoded in the same way that other skills such as learning to ride a bike are acquired. Procedural memory encodes *how to do something*, whereas explicit memory is memory for specific events or facts.

There are several important implications of understanding forms and roles of the procedural memory.

First, events encoded in procedural terms may operate outside conscious awareness in a passive fashion. Our ways of doing things are frequently opaque. We are not very good at telling someone how to ride a bicycle. The main reason of this is that we have learned to do it through practice, and any person who wants to acquire this knowledge has to learn it through practice, too.

---

[2] *Remembrance of Things Past* (Á la recherche du temps perdu).

Second, neuroscientists now know that implicit memories are encoded directly in the cerebral cortex through slow, incremental changes in the connectional strength of cortical neurons. Learning a procedure takes time because changes in the neuronal connection occur slowly. There are not too many people who learn to ride a bike or a horse in just one try. Why do these changes require so much repetition? One of the possible reasons is that the processes having an objective of creating an average prototype need a particular time range for building up a representation.

Third, there is a striking difference between the brain structures underlying explicit and implicit memory processes. While the cerebellum is responsible for implicit memories, the hippocampus is one of the most important brain areas responsible for storing experiences and facts. The hippocampal memory traces are often laid down in one trial, then transferred to the cortex for long-term storage.

While the procedural memory is prominent and robust in young children, the explicit memory may undergo a longer maturation and does not begin until the age of 2.5 or 3. The longer maturation of the explicit memory may be influenced by the fact that certain parts of the hippocampus have not developed in young children, so that procedural memory is all they have. The difference between the development courses of the two types of memory may be linked to the often-experienced phenomenon that children under 14 manipulate high-tech devices with particular ease and become skilled users in a relatively short time. When designing our experiments the main assumption has been that the superior skills that teenagers exhibit for manipulating mobile phones are a positive indication that their procedural memory has developed sufficiently for tool acquisition.

Cognitive Architecture and Memory

As part of the cognitive structure, learning and memory are especially important factors of the information processing. The classical approach to memory processes deals with three very important memory functions such as encoding, storing and structuring, as well as retrieval.

There are several studies investigating developmental processes expressed in quantitative and qualitative changes. It is especially important to understand these changes if we want to reconcile them with the relative stability of the cognitive architecture. The cognitive architecture consists of all the basic structures and features of information processing. The specific stages of this processing rely on a relative constancy even during development. This constancy means that mostly effectiveness and capacity are changing during development, while the architecture does not.

When any performance relying on procedural learning of children and adults is compared the question arises if two types of acquisition, one typical for adults and another one for children should be assumed which is related to a particular type of use? However, it is also possible that not only the acquisition is different but the type and effectiveness of tool manipulation as well. The fact that 10–12 year old schoolchildren use mobile phones with an amazing skill leads to the assumption that learning and memory functions developed early accelerate their performance when using complex tools. Of course there are many possible factors attached to the phenomenon that cellular phones are "overrun" by youngsters. We often see how easily young teenagers (10–12 years of age) use cellular phones.

Our recent study aimed to shed light on the main factors tool acquisition might rely on. Moreover, we searched for some possible evidence corroborating the impression that children perform better than adults, when the use of a new high-tech device is acquired. If we adhere to one of the main assumptions of cognitive psychology, namely the constancy of the cognitive architecture, we have to take into account that some underlying cognitive functions should act as main factors contributing to the fast and easy acquisition of using mobile phones.

Implicit Learning and Tool Acquisition

One of our main hyotheses is that the level of development of procedural memory in children is one of the reasons they are adept in using mobile phones. There are indicators that point to this. First, procedural memory relies on fast and automatic processes, therefore explicit access (declarative function) is denied, and we see that when observing children using technical devices. Secondly, children almost exclusively start using technical devices through manipulation instead of using instructions. Thirdly, procedural memory is the most developed memory type up to the teenage years. Fourthly, manipulative tasks that lack explicit instructions are "easier" for children than for adults. In these tasks the solution is mainly, sometimes even exclusively, based on combining experience and non-declarative results.

There are several experimental methods for studying the role of procedural memory, though the most common is following it with measuring the results of implicit learning. Explicit and implicit memory are the end results of information processing. In contrast, when focusing on implicit and explicit learning, it is the acquisition process itself, including encoding and storing as well as structuring, that we want to understand. During implicit learning the role of executive and strategic functions is less important, while explicit learning is an active process requiring attention, hypothesis formation and explicit rule extraction. Perceptual skills as well as motor skills are acquired by implicit strategies and the same is valid for rule extractions, or probability learning. The end result of implicit learning is an implicit knowledge often studied in typical paradigms such as artificial grammar, effect of redundancy on serial responses (sequence learning) as well as control of complex systems. In our empirical study two main factors of implicit learning were investigated, the implicit rule extraction and the flexibility of the rule application. The first is a latent or unconscious sequence learning of probabilities measurable in reaction time; the second is reversal-shift learning.

Rule Acquisition and Application

Our experimental hypothesis was that in implicit learning tasks such as sequence learning children would perform better than adults. Our question was whether the rules extracted in the implicit task lead to a better performance in children than in adults, and if so whether a conscious access to the rule is equally denied. We also assumed that the inferior performance of adults is related to that difference in performance shown in categorization and classification tasks based on individual examples instead of rules. Therefore explicit rules used mainly by adults would interfere with item recognition.

The implicit learning paradigm used in the experiments was a computer-generated version of the paradigm used by Lewicki and his colleagues.[3] The subjects' task in this paradigm is to respond to stimuli

---

[3] P. Lewicki, T. Hill, and E. Bizot, "Acquisition of Procedural Knowledge about a Pattern of Stimuli that Cannot Be Articulated", *Cognitive Psychology* 20 (1988), pp. 24–37.

in each of four locations in a 2x2 matrix. Stimuli occur in each location with equal frequency, but every seventh item is predictable on the basis of the pattern of the preceding stimuli. Subjects demonstrate implicit learning by responding faster to the crucial "7th stimulus" while they are unable to report the predictive relationship.

In our computerized task the subjects' task was to detect a target stimulus of a particular shape by pressing a button. Our hypothesis was that if the implicit rule, that is the predictability of the seventh stimulus' location was learned, the reaction time for the target occurring as seventh was shorter than in other positions. Moreover we expected a measurable difference in the performance of the children and adults investigated.

The participants were 9 and 12 year old boys (10–10 subjects), half of them already mobile users. Their data was compared to the data of adults with higher education (10 male subjects). The analysis of the reaction times (RI) revealed a significant difference between adults and children. A significant difference was found between the RIs given to the target in predictable and unpredictable position in the children group only. The largest difference in the RI for "the seventh" was found between the 12 year old mobile users and the adults. No adequate report on the assumed rule was available in either group. That does not mean that neither the children nor the adults had a conscious access to the implicit knowledge, although the RI difference found in children's RI to the predictable and unpredictable could be explained only by that they relied on the implicit rule when performing. This combination of the task and feedback without having an access to the rule extracted indicates implicit learning and well functioning procedural memory. As we know from the literature on implicit learning it is not necessary to assume that subjects are developing elaborate rules, on the contrary searching for rules may interfere with the task performance which tends to be far from perfect.

Moreover, it seems that the subjects' performance, especially that of the children shown in our modified Lewicki paradigm, proves that implicit behavior is rule-based and may be one of the implicit strategies used in acquiring mobile phone operations.

The Flexibility of Rule Application

Over the last decade, research on implicit learning produced a lot of interesting questions and generated more research than any other aspect of human memory and learning. Although cognitive psychology cannot provide a consistent model of the whole memory system, it is rather probable that the implicit memory does not constitute a single system. It seems to be more correct to assume the contribution of different learning mechanisms that have in common that they are incapable of generating recollective memory.

As we saw above, one of the magic tasks of implicit learning is the rule extraction, probability or sequence learning. However, it is advisable to take into account other, less often investigated factors, such as the flexibility of rules acquired through implicit learning. The assumed flexibility may provide the necessary basis for transfer, often needed when devices used in the past undergo changes due to a recent technological development. Flexibility and transfer is badly needed when we switch to a new mobile telephone having different searching tools, or a differently organized menu system. How to measure this flexibility or transfer? In order to judge the differences expected between children and adults a new task was introduced.

In the second series of our experiment a newly developed learning task was used. The task was similar to some computer games where a particular combination of features leads to a rewarded performance. In the first session the subjects' task was to generate an example by focusing on a particular attribute of the sequenced stimuli, for example color or size. In the second and third session the task could be performed successfully if a combination rule was generated. In the "reversal" task the example generation had to focus on the stimulus attribute not used in the preceding task and a feedback. In the "extra-dimensional" task the example generation had to rely on combining the task, the feedback and a possibly relevant fact. Subjects participating in the first experiment were performing the task in a different experimental session. The number of trials needed to learn the tasks was measured.

Performance of the adults and children did not differ significantly in the "reversal" task, while a striking difference was found in the "extra-dimensional" task. Children of 9 and 12 years of age showed a significantly better performance (Figure 1) than the adults. When the children group was split into two subgroups, fast and slow learners, the comparison revealed a further difference. Fast learners were superior to all the groups investigated in both tasks and were better in an additional task transferring their skills from a known device to a new one. The mobile phone user children were especially well performing in the transfer task as compared to their age-matched controls as well as to adults.

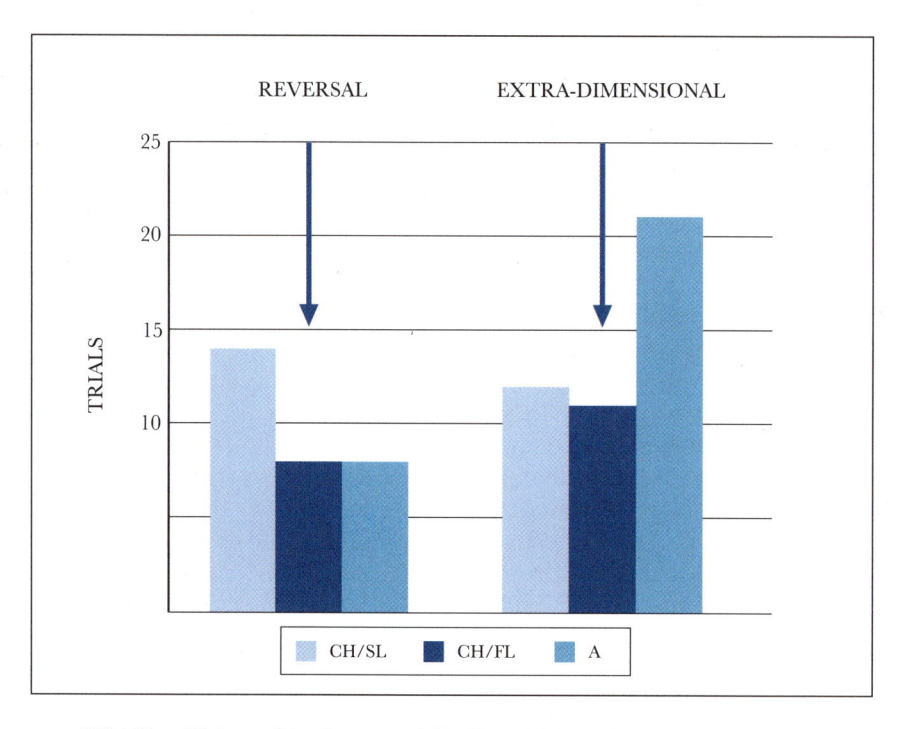

CH/ SL: children, slow learners, CH/ FL: children, fast learners, A: adults
See description in the text

The Role of Implicit Strategies

According to our recent results children rely much more on implicit learning strategies than adults. However, this well developed and often used learning type plays a crucial role in easy acquisition of technical devices, and the mobile phone is one of those. As it is proven by our empirical data this implicit rule extraction is very effective. This type of learning, which is incapable of generating recollective memory, provides a sufficient condition for using cellular phones and video games without user instructions. It is possible that one of the crucial factors that teenagers are able to use mobile phones so easily and happily is the fact that this subsystem of the cognitive architecture is developed well enough and provides a good basis for acquiring the use of different high-tech devices. This is the possible reason for the fact that children learn to use various tools through consecutive trials instead of relying on explicit verbal instructions.

We may also assume that the implicit and explicit strategies have a different weight in acquisition during development, and the explicit strategies, due probably to school experiences, training and maturation overcome the more natural implicit ones. We do assume that the differences found are not related to any inferiority of adult implicit learning; rather, adults cannot avoid using explicit strategies in tasks that would lend themselves more to intuition and procedural learning. It is rather probable that children who are not very good at focusing on particular properties combine task and feedback without using any other possible relevant facts even in explicit learning situations.

As we see everywhere the new devices are intensively used by children, and not only because these tools are good, nice or trendy. They use them because the skills necessary can be acquired more easily due to the fact that some cognitive functions have matured early enough. The cellular phone is one of those devices that can be learned by implicit strategies in relatively few trials. Why are our children called the "mobile phone generation"? Why did we not speak, earlier, about Morse or typewriter generations? Children in the past could not use devices which required developed cognitive functions necessary for learning to use those devices.

The cognitive benefit of an easy acquisition is that the use gets easily automatic and the content of communication may be in the focus. Whether our children rely on this benefit, we do not exactly know. It is not known either if there are cognitive costs as well. Do we need to assume that an overuse of the different devices leads to a delayed development of the explicit strategies? That is hard to believe. However, further studies are needed to shed light on these questions.

Csaba Pléh: # Communication Patterns and Cognitive Architectures

The Concept of Architecture

One of the leading ideas in present-day cognitive science is the recognition that human cognition is characterized by special structural constraints that are referred to as mental architectures. These are assumed to be constraints on the one hand, structural aspects of information coding on the other. The notion of architecture covers issues like:

- the knowledge types used (propositions, images, skills)
- their temporal parameters
- and internal organization

In a sketchy way one is entitled to talk about biological, more fundamental architectures on the one hand, and newer ones on the other. Their coexistence in the mind is responsible for the realization of the entire human architecture. Some proposed features of these two types are outlined in Table 1.

Primitive architecture	Culture, modern architecture
Evolved	Unbound
Fixed	Flexible
Fast (ms, s)	Slow (minutes, hours, years)
Formed over millions of years	Centuries, decades

Table 1
Primitive and newer mental architectures

These structural determinants are characterized both on the individual level and on the level of human groups by characteristic formation and processing times. A short summary of these is given in Table 2, in accordance with a classic view.[1] The table indicates that there are very fast procedures to deal with information that took millions of years to evolve, which are formed relatively early at the individual level, while the more newly formed procedures take a longer time to unfold in the individual as secondary networks.

Domain	Function time	Evolution time	Individual formation time
Biological, neuronal nets	10^{-2}–10^{-4} sec	Millions of years	Years
Cognitive acts, actions	10^{-1}–10 sec	Centuries	Hours, years

Table 2
The temporal scale of human actions according to Newell

Present-day information technology raises the question as to whether the new tools that simplify our life, and at the same time make our life more vulnerable, e.g. as regards our time structuring, do not lead to the formation of new secondary architectures by changing our way of thinking.

Many classical philosophical and psychological arguments are raised in this context, and we are basically faced with questions having a distinctly enlightened flavour. A traditional issue along Humboldtian lines has been whether language is primarily an internal, intimate reality, or a medium of communication. This traditional issue of internal or external determination is rephrased as the issue of the primacy of new communication devices in determining thought. Do new communication tools and their respective protocols change human mental life? In fact we have to realize that with regard to relationships of communication media and architectures two visions are currently entertained. These are set out in Table 3 as the opposition between the external and internal determination of thought.

---

[1] Allen Newell, *Unified Theories of Cognition*, Cambridge, MA: Harvard University Press, 1989.

Inward	Outward
Socialization	Innate Structure
Interiorization	Expression of thought
Relativism	Universalism
Tools are decisive	Tools are but instruments

Table 3
Two visions of mental determination and communication

The first extreme position is the strictly modular view as proposed by Fodor. It holds that all mental architectures and even contents are innately specified.[2] According to the extreme cultural relativist view, on the other hand, all architectural aspects are rewritten by external cultural influences. Most present-day methods look for a compromise regarding the variability and changeability of architectures. It is assumed that some relatively stable processing modes do exist, but that some parts of the entire architecture are under the influence of cultural domains. There are strong biological architectures, and culture has had an impact only on the higher output levels of these computations and cannot rewrite everything.

Modifications of Architectures: The Proposals of Merlin Donald

One of the most comprehensive proposals encompassing biologically given architectures and at the same time emphasizing the formative influence of culture has been made by Merlin Donald.[3] The uniqueness of

---

[2] Jerry A. Fodor, *The Modularity of Mind*, Cambridge, MA: MIT Press, 1983. For a more subtle present version see Fodor, *The Mind Doesn't Work that Way*, Cambridge, MA: MIT Press, 2000.

[3] The original proposal was outlined in Merlin Donald, *Origins of the Modern Mind*, Cambridge, MA: Harvard University Press, 1991. The new version of the exposition gives a detailed consideration regarding the newest developments in neuroscience and the evolution of the mind (Merlin Donald, *A Mind So Rare: The Evolution of Human Consciousness*, New York and London: W. W. Norton & Co., 2001). Donald provides us with his own interpretation of how his theory relates to the issue of historical plasticity: "The Mind Considered from a Historical Perspective", in David M. Johnson and Christina E. Erneling (eds.), *The Future of the Cognitive Revolution*, New York: Oxford University Press, 1997, pp. 355–365.

the approach lies in the fact that Donald assumes correspondences between communication and representation, external and internal worlds. Neuropsychological organization, the world of communication, and economy in memory all have a place in his interpretation of architectures. Table 4 gives a summary of his views extending towards present-day knowledge vehicles.

Culture	Species, age	Memory organization	Transmission
Episodic	Apes, 5 millon years	Episodic events	None
Mimetic	Homo erectus, 1,5 million years	Body representation Social enactment	Enactment, imitation
Mythical	Homo sapiens sapiens, 100 000–50 000 years	Linguistic semantics	Myths, narrative knowledge and transmission
Modern	Modern humans 10 000 years	External storage Hierarchical store	Fixed knowledge External authority
Gutenberg	Printing	Mass meme diffusion	Textual authority
Networks	20 years	Distributed in networks	Personal and impersonal

Table 4
The conception of Donald on changes in systems of representations and cultures

The general conception of Donald commences far from the considerations of present-day communications patterns. He starts by outlining a sequence of representational systems in anthropogenesis. Essentially, the three representational systems comprise different organizational compositions and knowledge transmission characteristics, namely mimetic culture, mythical culture, and theoretical culture. The primate mind is characterized by a fourth, more primitive episodic culture. In episodic culture knowledge is always personal and contextualized. The real human change appeared with the advent of a social semantics, with the appearance of shared knowledge, and thus an overcoming of the solipsistic mind. Mimetic culture was the first social system of knowledge, well before natural language started to evolve about 1.5 million years ago. It established a world of intentional representations demonstrated by the body. These representations, entailing an open generative system, with communicative intentions of a referential nature, use internally reproduced representations. The domain of this culture is visual and motoric, involving hand gestures, the use of body posture and facial expressions. Its neurologiocal precondition is a relatively precise representation of the own body and the outputs of the episodic system.

With regard to cognitive architecture, mimetic culture implies a more precise control over our own body, executive functions being able to "turn inward" as well. "Attention had to be redirected inward, away from the external world, and toward their own actions."[4] This meant that the perceptual world and the mind of primates was replaced in early hominids by action-oriented representations making action the object of tradition.

From then on, concepts become shared, distributed. Social play, organized teaching systems of transmission are born, as well as coordination through communication and joint representations, as in social hunting.

Mimetic culture at the same time was very conservative and slowly changing. The reason for this was that mimetic culture always required an episodic anchoring, its contents being provided by contextually bound episodic knowledge.

In the route towards natural language some additional neurological changes were required making possible sound-based communication. These changes are summarized in Table 5.

Cognitive function	Its role in language
Working memory	Lexical learning, sentence parsing
Divided attention	Lexical learning, contextual interpretation
Cortical plasticity	Lifelong learning
Increased long term storage	Word storage
Growth of semantic brain parts	Richer contextual meaning

Table 5
Cognitive / neurological preconditions of natural language according to Donald

---

[4] Merlin Donald, *A Mind So Rare*, p. 270.

A sound-based language also implies a culture characterized by faster social changes. Donald refers to this as *mythical culture*, due to the prevalence of narrative language used in the early stages. The dominant new organization of knowledge is through action and protagonist oriented narratives. Integrative myths of a group are an outgrowth of narrative patterns. Narratives are essential for change as well. "On a cultural level, language is not about inventing words. Languages are invented on the level of narrative, by collectivities of conscious intellects."[5]

The third turn was established by a formation of theoretical culture that involved the discovery of external storage mechanisms. Writing embodied this external storage space. In episodic, mimetic and mythical cultures knowledge was represented in the brain of an individual, according to the social nature of the language being distributed, and its respective origins in language-based (mythical) culture. Following the advent of writing these became independent social systems, with the establishment of a division of labour occurring between our own working memory system and the external supporting memories. External memory can exist in many physical forms, it is unbound, stable, and in principle always accessible. This *in principle* is of course questioned by the long stories of sacred knowledge, censorship and the like, and in a way the modern network-based knowledge carriers are in fact proposing that network-based knowledge provides for real constant accessibility. But compared to our individual brains, books are certainly a more accessible system. Writing creates a system that with the new organization of knowledge leads to new epistemologies and visions of knowledge in general.[6] From there on can we talk about a symbolic theoretical culture that has become the main governing principle of formal education with the image of a noetic system that has an independent existence. According to Donald, due to writing our mental apparatus is relieved from overload: on any given occasion it only has to contain some arrows pointing to relevant external memories, and sometimes the written "frame" as an external aid carries allusions to internally stored locations.

Representational changes are the moments that allow us to better understand the relationship between brain reorganization and hominid evolution. According to this vision – not unlike the one proposed by

---

[5] *Ibid.*, p. 292.
[6] Cf. Kristóf Nyíri, *Tradition and Individuality*, Dordrecht: Kluwer, 1992.

Luria and Vygotsky in the thirties[7] – higher cortical functions are subjected to cultural organization. "We are a culturally bound species and live in a symbiosis with our collective creation. We seek culture, as birds seek the air. In return, culture shapes our minds, as a sculptor shapes clay."[8] This creates a peculiar bridge between biology and culture.

According to Donald, the four cultures do not replace each other but create inclusive relations. It is this inclusiveness that leads to a new kind of consciousness, self organization and creativity in communicative and representational systems. Creativity, as it was emphasized by many, is the ability to overhear between otherwise separated systems. In the framework put forward by Donald this appears as the option provided by mentally coexisting cultures.[9]

As Donald puts it, the peculiarly human development leads to the birth of *hybrid minds* who live in *cognitive communities*. "The evolutionary origins of language are tied to the early emergence of knowledge networks, feeling networks, and memory networks, all of which form the cognitive heart of culture. Language was undoubtedly produced by Darwinian selection, but evolved indirectly, under conditions that favored those hominids who could make their shared cognitive networks more and more precise. ... [the] emergence of language could not have initially been and end in itself... The first priority was not to speak, use words or develop grammar. It was to bind as a group, to learn to share attention and set up the social pattern that would sustain such sharing and bonding in the species."[10] "The great divide in human evolution was not language, but the formation of cognitive communities in the first

---

[7] For an available English summary see A. R. Luria and L. S. Vygotsky, *Ape, Primitive Man, and the Child: Essays in the History of Behavior*, New York: Harvester, 1992.

[8] Merlin Donald, *A Mind So Rare*, p. 300.

[9] Traditional examples of creativity as crosstalk between otherwise separated domains is provided for the case of scientific discovery by Frederic Bartlett in his book analysing great structural discoveries by people like Helmholtz (*Thinking: An Experimental and Social Study*, London: Allen Unwin, 1958). Similar visions were entertained regarding all aspects of creativity by Arhur Koestler in his book *The Act of Creation* (London: Hutchinson, 1964). This logic is extended now to the issue of antropogenesis by other people beside Donald. Steven Mithen for example claims that the human mind is characterized by a crosstalk between very general types of originally isolated, modular intelligences, such as social, technical, naturalistic, and communicative intelligences (*The Prehistory of the Mind*, London: Thames and Hudson, 1996).

[10] Merlin Donald, *A Mind So Rare*, p. 253.

place. Symbolic cognition could not spontaneously self-generate until those communities were a reality. This reverses the standard order of succession, placing cultural evolution first, and language second."[11]

Architectural Changes and Contemporary Information Society

The permissive visions provided by Donald are designed to find some compromise between the external and internal attitudes, allow for a new look at contemporary information society and at the issue of possible architectural changes related to this. Table 6 presents some descriptive contrasts regarding these systems by contrasting formal knowledge systems.

Traditional	Network based
Decades of learning	Less years in school
Slow access	Faster access
Knowledge as property	Distributed knowledge
Certainty an elaborated property	Certainty being formed now

Table 6
Traditional and new information and knowledge transmission

Rather than surveying all the possibilities of new communications I would like to highlight some essential issues that go beyond the enthusiasms created by the new tools, and which are of fundamental significance to a cognitive psychologist. In a way, this should be interpreted as a continuation of the issues raised by Donald in modern society.

External–internal relationships. The traditional two visions, the inward and outward visions on the relationships between culture and the mind summarized in Table 3 also emerge in the middle of electronic communicative changes as aspects of users and creators. With regard to *users*, e-communication shows the success of centripetal thought: we are using new messages and change our thoughts accordingly. Communication di-

---

[11] *Ibid.*, p. 254.

rects human thought, and its changing patterns do alter our thought. Under the impact of new communicative surfaces we do become, as emphasized by many, less linear, more image-oriented, and recognize the laws of imaged-based thinking.[12]

The situation seems to be different, however, when considering the creators of new communicative forms. In *creators* the emphasis is on creating new representations, and not on their communication. This is true both for minor details of technology and in the creation of fundamentally new systems (user surfaces). It is exactly this starting point in the thought processes that allows communicative innovation on the part of the users. This very asymmetry does indeed exist not only on the level of noisy phrasings by sociologists and cultural critics (meaning that the new media carry hidden contents and make us slaves of certain ways of life), but it shows up in the quieter level of cognitive architectures as well. Communication does shape thinking in most of us, but rapid technological change makes even clearer the presence of an inverse process: we can as well shape our systems of representation.

Initiation and passivity. All of this directly touches upon the issue of our activity in the world of new media. Certainly, as users we are passive compared to the R & D people: our frames are received as givens. However, this is the case even with natural language! Thus, the division is not as new as first thought. At the same time, we are initiators in many respects: network search itself, for example, is a rather active and initiative process contrasted with waiting to be served in traditional libraries. Even within the same domain, that of the screen, one can identify an entire scale of activities.

Researchers, just to take a well researched minority in the world of electronic correspondence that seems to be passive since it easily connects us to our childish dependency circles, find a channel that is free both financially and personally, compared to traditional correspondence. Electronic correspondence as a next step facilitates the creation of new scientific communities where language becomes an important virtual "niche creator". This virtual horse riding, however, raises the spectre of phantasy-dominated architecture, the danger of never growing up and creating a world of electronic Don Quixotes.

---

[12] Kristóf Nyíri, "The Picture Theory of Reason", talk given at the 23rd International Wittgenstein Symposium, Kirchberg am Wechsel, August 13–19, 2000. In Berit Brogaard and Barry Smith (eds.), *Rationality and Irrationality*, Vienna: öbv-hpt, 2001.

Some Empirical Data on the Use of New Electronic Media

Our pilot investigation on the use of electronic media indicates however, that instrumental and dependency-related uses are distinct clusters. Analyzing the communicative habits of a frequent internet user group, factor analysis reveals the profile presented in Table 7.[13]

Browsing – information seek	Mail – communication	Entertain – dependency
Browsing in general 0,85	E-mail – known person 0,91	Chat 0,81
Browsing information 0,81	E-mail 0,88	E-mail – unknown person 0,76
Browsing entertainment 0,71		

Table 7
Internet use functions

The different factors presumably imply different motivational needs. One of the main functions seems to be browsing which is independent of the other uses. This function is characterized by the search for information as contrasted to entertainment. The second function is e-mail that mostly implies communication with known partners. The third function implies uses that mainly characterize internet-dependent people, including chat and correspondence with unknown partners. It is noteworthy that the factors do not group possible uses simply according to technical options, but according to motivational factors. Mail for example is divided into two factors depending on whether it is with known persons or with "strangers", since these two uses imply different needs.

Abstract world and real people: Don Quixote in the world of today. With regard

---

[13] Data is from the study by: Attila Krajcsi, Kristóf Kovács, and Csaba Pléh, "Internethasználók kommunikatív szokásai", in Kristóf Nyíri (ed.), *A 21. századi kommunikáció új útjai: Tanulmányok* [New Perspectives on 21st-Century Communications: Essays], Budapest: MTA Filozófiai Kutatóintézete, 2001, pp. 93–110. In English by the same authors: "Habits of Communication of Internet Users", *Periodica Polytechnica*, in press.

to the new communicative media it is emphasized that these tools focus on virtuality, promising freedom. The virtual world creates inner and outer roads of unknown dimensions, it thus carries a vision of freedom. One travels to places and libraries where ordinarily one would not only lack the means, but also the time to do so.

This freedom is the positive side: it appears from e-commerce to travel sites in many respects, including the world of research as well. But as the fears concerning multimedia consuming children have already indicated, there is an other side as well: the threat of losing control of reality.[14] This is the problem of Don Quixote, since the noble Spaniard was suffering from being a victim of virtuality at the dawn of the printed word. We are familiar with this problem from our adolescent times: after a few years of escape into the bookish world we started to wish to escape to our real world, to make real trips and to turn to real persons, like real girls.

Thus, the worry is not new. What is new, however, is that in this transformed world the ratio of secondary information, or virtualities, is rising. We observe life paths where virtuality becomes reality. The new world of communication certainly does change our way of life, thereby rearranging the relative weight of our motives. Some of us become dependent on our tools, and at the same time the new Don Quixotes try to get away towards objects, towards nature and real life. Time has a central role in this process.

Emotional time: The issue of time management. The logo of the world of new media is constant availability. It is a commonplace sociological truism that the new media do lead in certain strata of society towards mixing of work and private life, and to new types of interaction-based alienations. Due to our participation in the system we ought to have open channels all the time, but we sometimes feel the need to switch off entirely. But then we would become nonentities even in our own eyes. The psychological issue that touches architectures and mentalities seems to be simple: in order to regain our personality we may again regulate our own communicative patterns, and reconsider what time we spend on

---

[14] Other, more sociological and legal aspects of these fears are surveyed by László Z. Karvalics. See his "The Security Aspect of Information Society as a Global Biocultural System", in print.

what. A simple aspect of this is how much time do we spend on *finding and obtaining* the constantly refreshed pieces of knowledge, and how much time is spent on *using this valuable information*. There is no easy solution, but there certainly is an intellectual task and a social problem, that touches on the ecology of mental resources.

Figure 1 shows the communicative time dynamics of a select group taken from our empirical study.

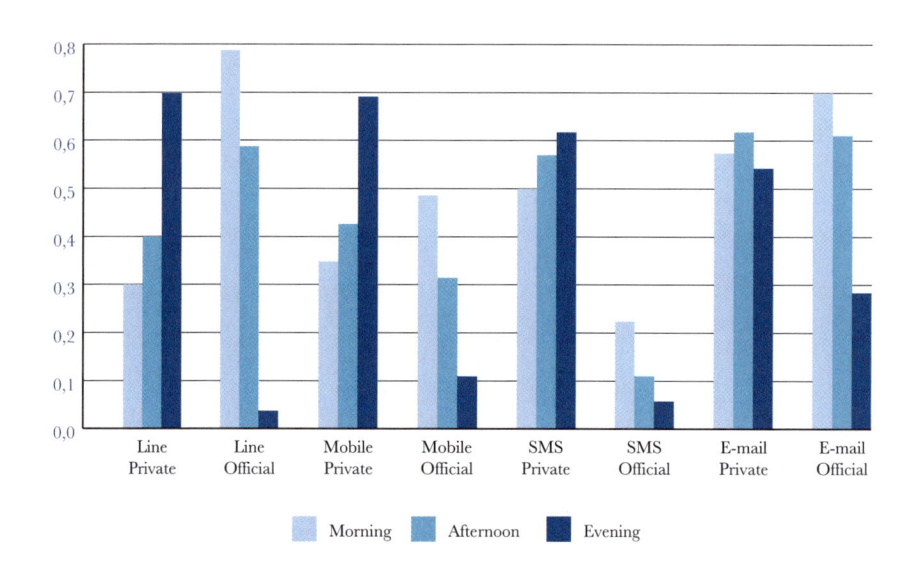

Figure 1
Communicative media use according to daily schedules of regular internet users

It seems to be that mornings are for business, and evenings for private matters. That should not surprise anyone. However, with SMS and e-mail, we have two not easily controllable uses, enabling us to attend to our private matters at any time of the day.

Relations between knowledge and skill. The new media force us to reconsider the role of explicit knowledge in the formation of the human mind. What amount of knowledge has to be packed into the user perceived as a moving encyclopedia? The weight of skills increases relative to the weight of knowledge when not only "sacred books" are the social storehouses of knowledge. Learning obsolete knowledge becomes questionable. However, if skills are elevated to the High Table then what do these skills operate on? These are issues of a psychological and educational nature,[15] and have been with us for at least a century in the debate between conservative and progressive curricula. The issue of new media reactivates the debates since new communications are a skill-based entry to stored knowledge according to some, and according to others they turn us away from the accepted canons.

Teaching methods. Lifelong learning is not merely a social issue related to the workplace market. Humans are unique in the animal kingdom by being instructional creatures. The traditional organizing frame is vertical transmission of knowledge whithin a relatively stable environment. This went together with skill formation and even explicit knowledge transmission as part of our bookish culture, being limited to certain early ages, unaffected by a growing life expectancy. With the rapidly changing environment, with growing life expectancy and new communicative patterns not only does lifelong education appear, but the importance of horizontal transmission also increases. This implies learning and teaching to be more fun, but also to involve new tensions. Society in fact is not prepared to deal with this issue, but some retraining and supervising fractions of it (such as psychotherapy, language teaching, and the like) have accumulated knowledge in this area. We should learn from them how to deal with the need to learn.

New media and old ethological constraints. Beside the entirely internalist and entirely externalist views of the mind, there are some trends that emphasize that even the most modern technologies in a way become accepted and widespread because they somehow become harmonized with the ethological constraints of the mind. Theoreticians in this group believe in the stability of biological systems that can only be slightly modified by new technologies. Evolution built in some quite stable needs and possibilities into human beings that cannot be changed by cultural influence. The nightmare of Orwell cannot be realized, because human beings are unable to suffer loneliness or restriction of information for longer periods of time. Along these lines, Dunbar describes several examples of chatrooms that fit into long-established motivational and cognitive systems. In our research we intended to provide some empirical evidence for this otherwise strongly theoretical debate through a survey on the communication habits of internet users. But this is also true

---

[15] For some recent discussion of the explicit–implicit, knowledge–skill dimension in present-day cognitive reserach see Z. Dienes and J. Perner, "A Theory of Explicit and Implicit Knowledge", *Behavioral and Brain Sciences* 22 (1999), pp. 735–808.

for sociological theories that show how the wired net can be interpreted as a sociological network.[16]

Theories of secondary orality[17] and the re-personalization of technological communication patterns imply that the new media use old available tools of network formation building with traditional tools an inner world that becomes very much new due to cognitive ecology. The task of a scientist here is to analyze the universal aspects of this process. In order to do this there is a need for more cross-talk between disciplines, and communicative tolerance, with regard to exactly what these new tools were meant for.

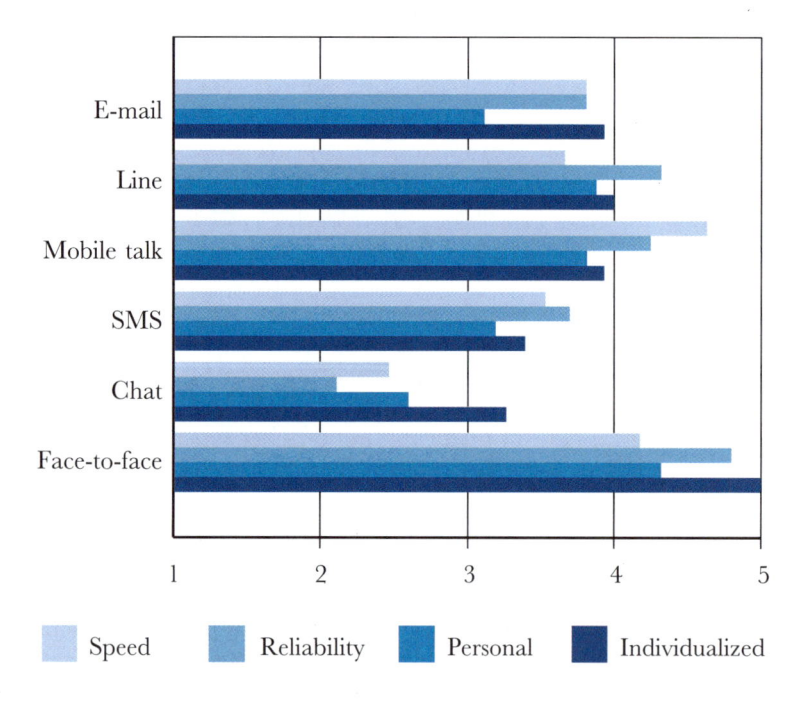

Figure 2
Relative ranking of different communication channels on different scales

---

[16] On the first issue see R. I. M. Dunbar, *Grooming, Gossip and the Evolution of Language*, Cambridge, MA: Harvard University Press, 1996, and also his paper in the present volume; on the second Barry Wellman, "Computer Networks As Social Networks", *Science* 293 (2001), pp. 2031–2034.

[17] See Nyíri, *Tradition and Individuality*.

As everyday users we are already aware of the variability of our tools. Figure 2 shows that with regard to speed, personal touch, and trustworthiness we are by far not naive users of those tools.

There is of course still a long way to go until we become as flexible and versatile in our science dealing with communicative media, as we are in our subjective judgment, and in our mental architectures.

Barbara Tversky: Some Ways Graphics Communicate[1]

Graphics count among the oldest and newest forms of communication. Maps, for example, have been drawn in the sand or incised in stone or imprinted in clay for millennia. Maps now appear on mobile phones or are downloaded from websites or are updated in car navigation systems. Ancient maps and modern ones, maps produced by professionals and those created by novices, by children and by adults, share many features. They schematize the information, eliminating some of it and simplifying other.[2] Long distances with little of importance are shortened, curves are eliminated, and turns are simplified to 90 degrees. Maps also display information not present in the terrain, names of landmarks, icons for churches or markets, and boundaries. Maps may present perspectives not possible in the world, showing overviews of networks of roads and frontal views of salient landmarks. These distortions and embellishments of actual space seem to facilitate the uses for which maps were intended. An aerial photograph doesn't generally make a good map.

Space of Graphics

Using Diagrammatic Space to Represent Real Space. Maps use space to represent space, as do architectural sketches, engineering designs, and instructions to operate devices. Such diagrams are ancient, and have appeared in many cultures. Other graphics use space to represent concepts and relations that are metaphorically spatial, for example, organization charts, flow diagrams, and economic graphs. Graphics using space

---

[1] Some of the research reported here was supported by Office of Naval Research, Grants Number NOOO14-PP-1-O649 and N000140110717 to Stanford University.

[2] B. Tversky, "Some Ways that Maps and Graphs Communicate", in C. Freksa, W. Brauer, C. Habel, and K. F. Wender (eds.), *Spatial Cognition II: Integrating Abstract Theories, Empirical Studies, Formal Methods, and Practical Applications*, New York: Springer, 2000, pp. 72–79.

143

to display metaphorically spatial concepts and relations began to appear in the late 18th century.[3] Interestingly, the early uses of such graphs are still the most common of graphs, plotting change over time.[4]

Using Diagrammatic Space to Represent Metaphoric Space. Using space to represent space has cognitive immediacy, is readily comprehended. Yes, there is the issue of scale; except for Borges' mythical case,[5] maps are smaller than the spaces they represent. But understanding reduction of scale seems almost effortless. Children and adults spontaneously gesture when describing space, even large spaces not currently viewed.[6] They also spontaneously build models of space using props or on paper. For both gestures and models, the representing space is typically smaller than the represented space. Spatial language, terms like "near", "above", and "along", is claimed to be scale-independent. Using space to represent metaphorically spatial concepts is apparently not as immediate as using space to represent space. Graphics using space metaphorically are a recent, Western invention, undoubtedly reflecting their relative lack of transparency. This is in spite of the fact that languages all over the world use space metaphorically. Talented students are said to be at the top of heap or the head of the class, people are said to fall ill or into depressions, fields are described as wide open for those who wish to take the road less trodden. Gestures, too, reflect these spatial metaphors, high five, thumbs up or down. Up, on the whole (unemployment and inflation excepted), is good, more, powerful, strong, healthy.

Children Use Diagrammatic Space to Represent Metaphorically Spatial Concepts. Despite their late appearance, there is evidence that graphics that use space metaphorically do so in cognitively natural ways.[7] We asked children and adults in three language cultures to put stickers on paper to

---

[3] J. R. Beniger and D. L. Robyn, "Quantitative Graphics in Statistics", *The American Statistician* 32 (1978), pp. 1–11. – E. R. Tufte, *The Visual Display of Quantitative Information*, Cheshire, CT: Graphics Press, 1983.

[4] W. S. Cleveland and R. McGill, "Graphical Perception and Graphical Methods for Analyzing Scientific Data", *Science* 229 (1985), pp. 828–833.

[5] J. L. Borges, *On the Exactitude of Science. Collected Fictions.* Translated by Andrew Hurley. New York: Penguin, p. 325.

[6] J. Iverson and S. Goldin-Meadow, "What's Communication Got to Do with It? Gesture in Children Blind from Birth", *Developmental Psychology* 33 (1997), pp. 453–467.

[7] B. Tversky, "Cognitive Origins of Graphic Conventions", in F. T. Marchese (ed.)., *Understanding Images*, New York: Springer-Verlag, 1995, pp. 29–53. – B. Tversky, "Spatial Schemas in Depictions", in M. Gattis (ed.), *Spatial Schemas and Abstract Thought*, Cambridge, MA: MIT Press, 2001, pp. 79–111.

represent three entities that varied in space, time, quantity, or preference."[8] Children were asked, for example, to place stickers on paper to reflect the time they ate breakfast, the time they ate morning snack, and the time they ate dinner, or to reflect a TV show they disliked, one they liked a little, and one they liked a lot. Only a few of the preschool children failed to put the stickers on a line, as if they were representing three different and unrelated entities, categorical relations. Most of the children put the stickers on a line, that is, they represented these concepts at the level of ordinal information. Only the older children and the adults used space to represent nonspatial concepts at the interval level of information. Their placement of stickers reflected the order among the elements, but also the interval between the elements, so that the stickers for breakfast and morning snack were closer than the stickers between morning snack and dinner. The directions of increase conformed to the linguistic and gestural metaphors, that is, increases were portrayed as upwards or leftwards or rightwards, but downwards increases were avoided. Interestingly, the direction of the written language did not affect the direction of increases, except in the case of temporal relations. For temporal relations, increases tended to go rightwards for writers of English and leftwards for writers of Arabic, with Hebrew writers in between. In Arabic, both letters and numbers go leftwards, at least in early years of education, but in Hebrew, letters go leftwards but numbers go rightwards. In addition, Hebrew-speakers are more likely to be exposed to European languages.

Proximity in Diagrammatic Space Signifies Proximity in Metaphoric Space. The basic spatial metaphor underlying graphics is one of proximity. The closer things are in real or conceptual space, the closer they are represented in diagrammatic space. Proximity may preserve relational information at several levels of information. Categorical uses include putting things into piles or groups by type, as in sorting nails and screws or knives and forks, or people by country or occupation. Ordinal uses include putting things in orders that correspond to other orders, for example, listing children by age or groceries by the order of encounter in the supermarket. Networks reflecting various hierarchies, such as taxonomies or organizational charts, are common uses of partial orders, a combination of categorical and ordinal uses of space. Interval uses include graphs of statistical data. For these, both the order of elements and the distance

---

[8] B. Tversky, S. Kugelmass, and A. Winter, "Cross-Cultural and Developmental Trends in Graphic Productions", *Cognitive Psychology* 23 (1991), pp. 515–557.

between elements are meaningful. Where there is a natural zero, space is used on a ratio scale in which case, ratios between elements are meaningful.

Graphical space may mix metaphors. A poignant graphic by Minard depicts Napoleon's failed campaign on Russia. The graphic is on a schematic map that highlights the major battles and geographic features from the French border to Moscow. Space is also used to indicate the changing size of Napoleon's army, a thick band leaving France, a trickle returning. At the bottom of the diagram, space is used to convey the diminishing temperatures of the winter. Distance, quantity, time, and temperature all use space to tell a sad story graphically.

Elements of Graphics

Icons and Figures of Depiction. Graphics use elements as well as space to convey meaning. The simplest and most direct kind of element is an icon, where the element bears resemblance to the thing it represents. These are as old as ideographic languages, where schematic animals and edibles represented their real-world counterparts, and as new as the latest computer or Olympics icons. But many useful concepts cannot be readily depicted. Figures of depiction have been spontaneously adopted, again since ancient times. Synechdoche, where a part represents a whole, is common, as in the horns or head of a sheep to stand for sheep. Similarly, metonomy, where an entity associated with a concept stands for the concept, as in a crown for a king or scales for justice or scissors for delete. The same devices, of course, appear in figures of speech. Icons that are related to the things they represent by figures of depiction also appeared in ancient scripts and appear in contemporary machinery. The advantage of icons and figures of depiction is that their meanings are readily understood and remembered.

Morphograms. There is another kind of element that is prevalent across a wide range of graphics and that is readily understood in context. Lines, crosses, arrows, and blobs are simple, schematic geometric figures that are an integral component of many kinds of graphics, maps, graphs, and mechanical diagrams for examples. Their meanings are related to the their geometric or Gestalt properties. Lines, for example, connect, they serve as paths from one point to another, suggesting a relationship between the points. Crosses are intersections of lines. And arrows are asymmetric lines, suggesting an asymmetric relationship. Blobs are two-dimensional, suggesting an area. Their amorphous shape suggests that shape is irrelevant. Like words in language, morphograms can be combined in various ways to create varying meanings. Like words in language, there are constraints on how they can be combined. It is time to illustrate these claims with research.

Bars and Lines in Graphs. Line and bar graphs appear widely, not only in scientific journals, but also in daily newspapers, often interchangeably, seemingly dependent on the creativity of the graphic artist. An examination of their geometric and Gestalt properties, however, suggests that they may be interpreted quite differently. As noted, lines connect, indicating a relationship. Bars, by contrast, contain and separate. Bars are boxes or frames. A line between X and Y suggests that there is a relationship between X and Y, that X and Y vary on the same dimension. A bar for X and a bar for Y suggests that all the X's share some property and all the Y's share a different property.

To ascertain whether people interpret lines and bars differently, Zacks and I[9] asked people to interpret an unlabeled line graph or an unlabeled bar graph. In accordance with the current analysis, people overwhelmingly interpreted lines as trends and bars as discrete relations. So for line graphs, people said, there's an increase from A to B or a trend from A to B. For bar graphs, people said, the B's are higher than the A's or there are more B's than A's. The next step was to provide content to the graphs, either continuous content, so compatible with lines or trends, or discrete content, so compatible with bars. In both cases the graphs depicted height; for the continuous case, of 10 and 12 year olds, and for the discrete case, of women and men. As before, participants were asked to interpret the graphs. And, as before, the form of the graphic affected the interpretations. There were more trend interpretations of line graphs and more discrete interpretations of bar graphs, in many cases, conflicting with the nature of the underlying variable. There was an effect of the underlying variable, continuous or discrete, but the effect of the graphic format was greater. Some participants even said, as people get more male, they get taller.

The third step was to provide continuous or discrete interpretations, and ask participants to construct graphs depicting them. The same variables were used, height of 10 and 12 year olds or height of men and women, described either as a trend, height is greater for 12 year olds (men) than for 10 year olds (women), or as a discrete comparison, 12 year olds (men) are taller than 10 year olds (women). The type of description

---

[9] J. Zacks and B. Tversky, "Bars and Lines: A Study of Graphic Communication", *Memory and Cognition* 27 (1999), pp. 1073–1079.

affected the type of depiction: more participants drew lines for trend descriptions and bars for discrete comparisons, again overriding the underlying nature of the variables in many cases. The correspondence between the language of the interpretations and the "language" of the graphics is striking.

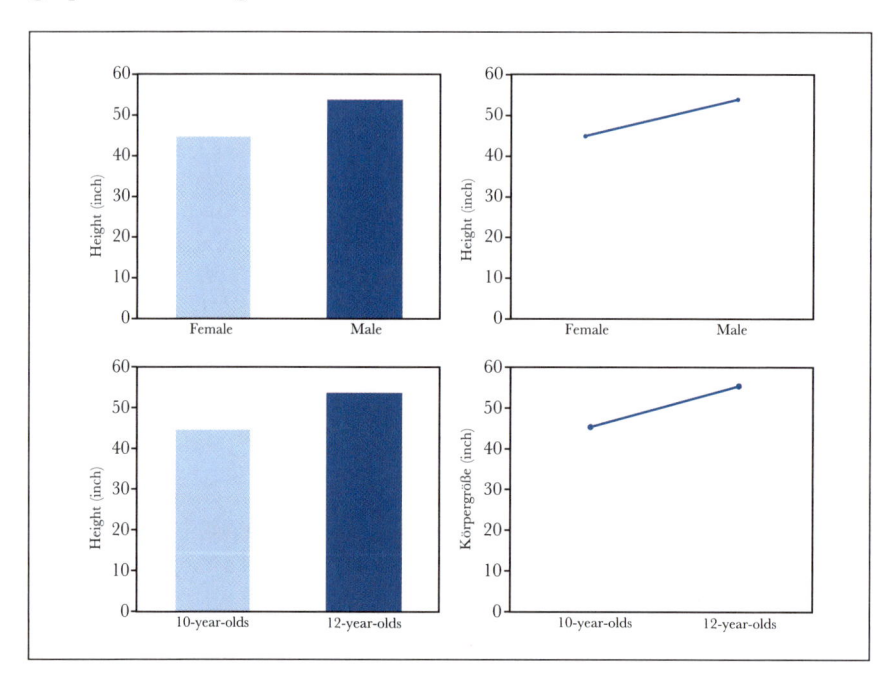

Figure 1. Examples of bar and line graphs[10]

Lines, Curves, Crosses, and Blobs in Route Maps. The correspondence between the language of description and the language of graphics is no less striking in route directions. Lee and I[11] caught hungry students outside a dormitory and asked them if they knew the way to a local fast food

---

[10] J. Zacks and B. Tversky, *op. cit.*

[11] B. Tversky and P. U. Lee, "How Space Structures Language", in C. Freksa, C. Habel, and K. F. Wender (eds.), *Spatial Cognition: An Interdisciplinary Approach to Representation and Processing of Spatial Knowledge*, Berlin: Springer, 1998, pp. 157–175. – B. Tversky and P. U. Lee, "Pictorial and Verbal Tools for Conveying Routes", in C. Freksa and D. M. Mark (eds.), *Spatial Information Theory: Cognitive and Computational Foundations of Geographic Information Science*, Berlin: Springer, 1999, pp. 51–64.

restaurant. If they did, we handed them a piece of paper, and asked them to either sketch a map or write instructions to location. Both map sketches and verbal directions varied widely, in length, detail, and elegance. Despite this variability, they both had the same underlying structure.

> From Roble parking lot
> R onto Santa Theresa
> L onto Lagunita (the first stop sign)
> L onto Mayfield
> L onto Campus drive East
> R onto Bowdoin
> L onto Stanford Ave.
> R onto El Camino
> Go down few miles. It's on the right.
> Go down street toward main campus (where most of the buildings are as opposed to where the fields are) make a right on the first real street (not an entrance to a dorm or anything else). Then make a left on the 2nd street you come to. There should be some buildings on your right (Flo Mo) and parking lot on your left. The street will make a sharp right. Stay on it. That puts you on Mayfield road. The first intersection after the turn will be at Campus drive. Turn left and stay on campus drive until you come to Galvez Street. Turn Right. Go down until you get to El Camino. Turn right (south) and Taco Bell is a few miles down on the right.
>
> Go out St. Theresa
> Turn Rt.
> Follow Campus Dr. way around to Galvez
> Turn left on Galvez.
> Turn right on El camino.
> Go till you see Taco Bell on your Right

Table 1. Examples of Route Directions[12]

---

[12] B. Tversky and P. U. Lee, "How Space Structures Language".

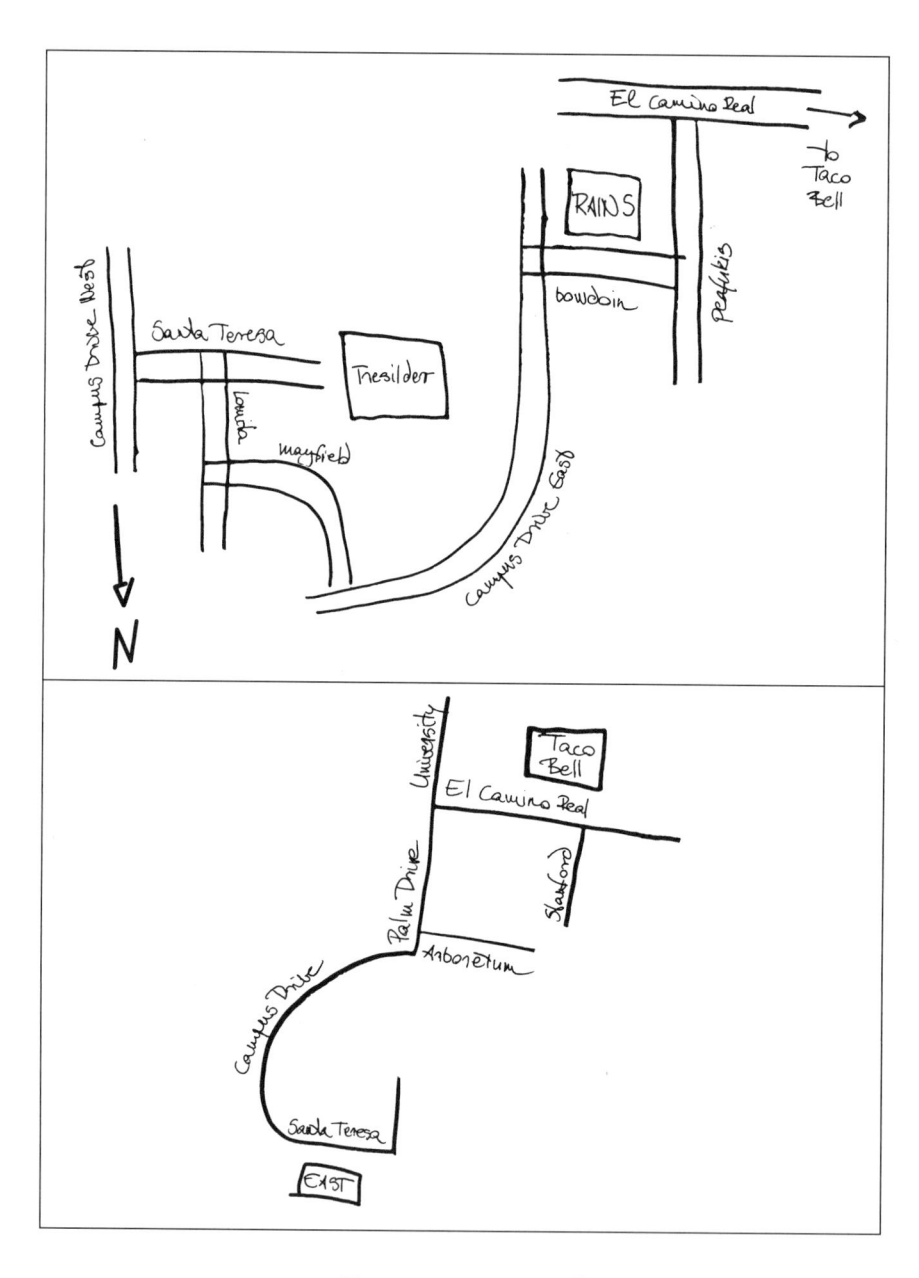

Figure 2. Sketch maps.[13]

---

[13] *Ibid.*

The structure of the route directions and maps was analyzed using a scheme developed by Denis.[14] He found that route directions could be decomposed into a series of segments. Each segment in turn had four elements: a start point, an orientation, a progression, and an end point, as in "exit the Central Square station, turn left, go down Mass Avenue until you come to Café Centro". Not only could the route directions be decomposed into a series of those four segments, but also the route maps. Interestingly, there was more missing information in the directions than in the maps. The directions frequently omitted the progression and either the start or end point, as in "left on Mass Ave., left on Magazine, right on William". Both missing start or end points and progression can be easily inferred from context. Sketch maps rarely omitted information as the graphic medium forces completion.

Not only could the sketches and descriptions be decomposed into the same four types of elements, but also there was remarkable correspondence between the linguistic and graphic components. Start and end points were represented by landmarks. In the case of descriptions, these were names, usually of streets or buildings. In the case of sketches, landmarks were blobs and streets were lines, often labeled. Orientations in descriptions were accomplished primarily by "turn", "make a", and "take a". In depictions, turns were indicated by +'s or T's or L's depending on the nature of the intersection. In both descriptions and depictions, the exact angle of orientation was not indicated. This is more surprising for sketch maps, as they could be analog, could represent the exact angle of the intersection. The same phenomenon occurs in representing progression. Descriptions tended to use "go down" or "follow around", where "go down" corresponded to a straight path and "follow around" corresponded to a curved path. Maps also made primarily a dichotomous distinction between straight and curved paths, again, in spite of their potential to reflect the actual spatial relations. Distance was not represented analogically in sketch maps either. Long straight distances were shortened, and short distances that had tricky turns were enlarged. This corresponded to differences in relative length in descriptions. The correspondence between descriptive and depictive elements suggests that they both derive from a common underlying conceptual structure.

In all, both route directions and route maps consisted of a small number of elements, used in combinations. This led us to think that we could provide people with verbal or graphic tool kits that would suffice

---

[14] M. Denis, "The Description of Routes: A Cognitive Approach to the Production of Spatial Discourse", *Cahiers de Psychologie Cognitive* 16 (1997), pp. 409–458.

to create routes. We gave verbal or visual versions of tool kits representing the four types of segments to new groups of participants. We asked them to use the tool kits to create a large number of route directions or maps. We told the participants that the tool kits would probably not be sufficient for their purposes, and they should feel free to add to the tool kit when needed. Despite this suggestions, few participants added few elements to either tool kit. A few participants added freeway ramps, for example. These graphic devices commonly produced by people have been incorporated into an algorithm for generating route maps, which have met with great enthusiasm on the part of users.[15]

The sketch maps, then, not only schematize, but also distort the actual information. Does it matter? Probably not. Sketch maps are ancient. They have undergone countless spontaneous user tests. Sketch maps are typically used in an environment. The environment disambiguates and corrects the schematized information. If a turn on a map is 90 degrees, but the intersection is 60, the navigator has little choice but to turn 60 degrees. After all, route directions also suffice to bring travelers to their destinations, and they, too, underspecify and schematize the information. Both have pragmatics associated with them as well as syntax and semantics. The pragmatics includes the implicit knowledge that turns and distances are approximate. These pragmatics of route directions and depictions are understood by their creators and users alike.

Arrows in Mechanical Diagrams. Another graphic device used by about half the participants was arrows, indicating direction. As noted, arrows are like lines; they indicate a relationship. But arrows are asymmetric, so they indicate an asymmetric relation. The very form of arrows has natural equivalents, not just in the arrows used in hunting, but also the arrows created by fluids descending pliable matter. Arrows serve a multitude of functions in diagrams, expressing asymmetric relations. Arrows were redundant in route maps as the maps only showed the roads relevant to the route, and the start and end points were known. In route maps, they indicate spatial order and direction. In maps and in mechanical diagrams, arrows can be used to label parts; they link a name with a part, or point to a part. In mechanical diagrams, arrows can indicate temporal order and direction; they can also indicate directions of motion, and manner of motion. Just as spatial proximity can represent

---

[15] M. Agrawala and C. Stolte, "Rendering Effective Route Maps: Improving Usability through Generalization", *Proceedings of SIGGRAPH '01* (2001), pp. 241–250.

proximity on abstract dimensions, so arrows can indicate order and direction of abstract dimensions, notably, causality.

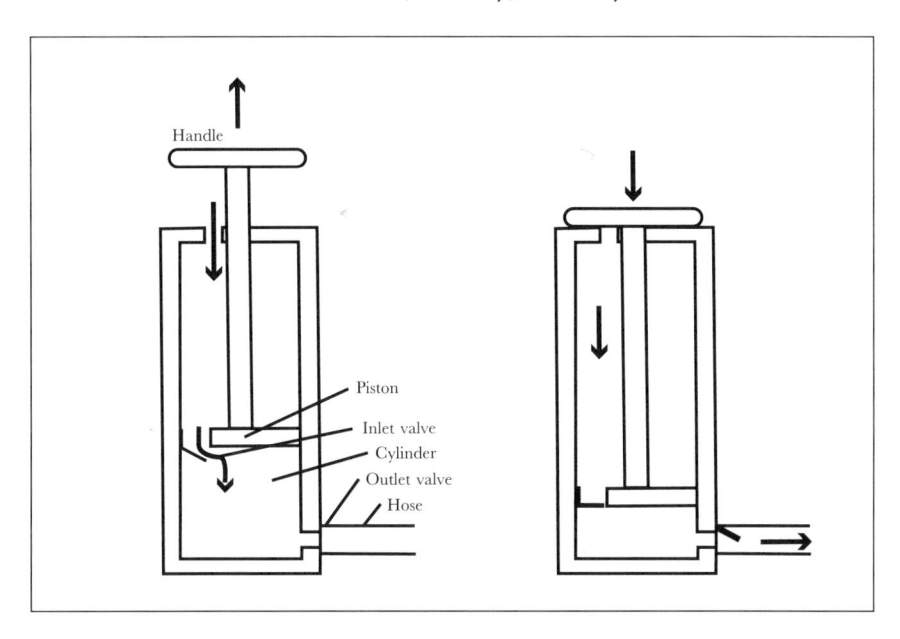

Figure 3. Bicycle pump with arrows.[16]

To understand the role of arrows in mechanical diagrams, Heiser and I[17] asked participants to write descriptions of diagrams. Each participant described a single diagram, either of a bicycle pump or a car brake or a pulley system, either with arrows indicating the operation of the device or without. When participants saw diagrams without arrows, they wrote primarily structural descriptions, providing details of the spatial relations among the parts of the system. When participants saw diagrams with arrows, they wrote causal, functional descriptions. The

---

[16] J. Heiser and B. Tversky, "Descriptions and Depictions of Complex Systems: Structural and Functional Perspectives". Manuscript submitted for publication. Figure adapted from J. B. Morrison, *Does Animation Facilitate Learning? An Evaluation of the Congruence and Equivalence Hypotheses*, dissertation, Stanford University, 2000, there adapted from R. E. Mayer and J. K. Gallini, "When Is an Illustration Worth Ten Thousand Words?", *Journal of Educational Psychology* 82 (1990), pp. 715–726.

[17] J. Heiser and B. Tversky, "Descriptions and Depictions of Complex Systems".

arrows provided the temporal order of the operation of the device. The inference from temporal to causal was apparently immediate. As in the previous examples, routes and graphs, we ran the mirror-image experiment, asking participants to produce diagrams from descriptions of the devices. As expected, more participants produced diagrams without arrows for structural descriptions and more participants produced diagrams with arrows for functional descriptions. Arrows, then, allow mental animation of systems; they promote understanding of a system's dynamics and function. Actual animations are computationally expensive and not easily transported. What's more, animated and static graphics have been compared in a multitude of contexts, concrete and abstract. When the content of animated and static graphics is equated, and when interactivity is equated, there is no evidence to support the superiority of animations.[18]

Morphograms, such as lines, arrows, crosses, and blobs, appear in a wide range of diagrams. They have interpretations that are readily understood in context from their geometric or Gestalt properties. They can be combined in a multitude of rule-bound ways to create different graphical ideas. Thus, they have many properties in common with semantic elements, words, in spoken or written language. Morphograms parallel language also in meaning; the meanings of words like relation, intersection, and field, spatial concepts all, not only correspond to lines, crosses, and blobs, but are rich in possible meanings, which contexts specify.

The "Language" and Functions of Graphic Communication

Graphics use space and elements in space to represent concepts that are inherently spatial and concepts that are metaphorically spatial. The elements, whether icons or figures of depiction or morphograms, bear many relations to semantic elements of spoken and written language, morphemes. They can be combined to create many complex meanings. How they are combined and spatially arrayed is systematic, not random. The conventions of combination and array bear resemblance to syntax. There is a pragmatics to graphics as well. For example, in sketch maps, graphic space is not meant to be interpreted metrically, in contrast to completed architectural drawings and topographic maps, where graphic space is meant to be interpreted metrically.

---

[18] B. Tversky, J. B. Morrison, and M. Betrancourt, "Animation: Can It Facilitate?", *International Journal of Human Computer Systems* 57 (2002).

Graphics serve a multitude of functions. They record information, preserving it over time. They are a cognitive tool, taking over from working memory some of its functions, notably, storage and computation. They can be inspected and reinspected, leading to new inferences and insights. They are public, allowing a community to think about a set of issues collectively and revise conceptions collectively. The use of space in graphics facilitates comprehension and capitalizes on human efficacy to make spatial inferences.

Kristóf Nyíri: Pictorial Meaning
and Mobile Communication

"Words make division, pictures make connection."
Otto Neurath, *International Picture Language* (1936)

A picture, as the saying goes, is worth a thousand words. Words are of course often spoken hurriedly when voiced through the mobile phone, and they have to be used sparsely when composing an SMS message. The assumption that in mobile communication pictures could be usefully employed should then not come as a surprise. But why, exactly, would a picture be worth a thousand words? Sometimes, indeed, the opposite seems to be the case. Words are needed to index, explain, and disambiguate pictures, as well as to express abstract concepts, logical relations, and linguistic modalities.

In this paper I will, first, present arguments for the view that images, not words, are the primordial stuff of thought. This view, never doubted in everyday thinking, was practically forced underground by the psychology and philosophy of the first half of the twentieth century, but it is a view to which science is returning. Once more the hypothesis sounds convincing that in the course of human phylogeny and ontogeny it was *the language of gestures*, and not verbal language, which introduced conceptual order into the episodic imagery of pre-linguistic thought; verbal language, pervaded by metaphor, builds on the meanings and semantic relationships created by the language of gestures. But if the dimension of verbal language is not so much the foundation of thought, as rather, merely, a more abstract framework of the same, then words supplemented by pictures, indeed sometimes pictures by themselves, could be better suited as vehicles for *communicating* thought, than words alone.

Secondly I will argue that although pictorial communication is seldom entirely successful if not accompanied by words, and any visual language needs the background of convention, pictures can indeed function as *natural symbols* due to their resemblance to the objects and facts represented. Thirdly I will stress that, precisely because they resemble what they represent, pictures are eminently suited for conveying visual information. However, the employment of pictures for the communication of knowledge was impeded, throughout the millenia of alphabetic literacy, by the limited means for the creation and duplication of graphics. This has changed dramatically with the new capabilities we enjoy thanks to computers. As I will attempt to show fourthly, even the dream of *iconic languages*, it appears, can now be realized. And with the advent of multimedia messaging, I will then point out, devices capable of creating and communicating pictures will become ubiquitous. By way of conclusion I will suggest that with visual elements re-entering the process of communication, and with communication remaining continuous even over great physical distances, personal relationships can retain or regain an intimacy that has been largely lost in the world of modern communications, an intimacy recalling the condition of close communities.

Thinking in Images

The story commences with Plato and Aristotle. Important new beginnings occurred with the so-called "imagery debate" in the late 1960s and early 1970s. I will mention some of them further below, but let me here start by referring to the book *Descartes' Error* by a leading neurophysiologist, Antonio Damasio, published in 1994.[1] It is in the form of images, Damasio holds, that the factual knowledge required for reasoning and decision-making is present to our minds. Images are not stored as facsimile pictures of things, or events, or words, or sentences. We are all aware, writes Damasio, that in recalling a face, or an event, we generate not an exact reproduction but rather some sort of re-interpretation, a new version of the original which will in addition evolve over time. On the other hand however we all equally have the sensation that we can indeed conjure up, in our mind's eye, approximations of images we previously experienced. Images form the main content of our thoughts. Of course "hidden behind those images, never or rarely knowable by us", there are numerous processes that guide the generation and deployment of images. "Those processes ... are *essential* for our thinking but are not a *content* of our thoughts."[2]

---

[1] Damasio, *Descartes' Error: Emotion, Reason, and the Human Brain*, New York: Putnam, 1994.

[2] See *Descartes' Error*, pp. 96–108. – Images, mental pictures, are subjectively experienced, are however not accessible to the external observer. Neurophysiological research today is in the process of discovering certain correspondences between visually experienced impressions on the one hand and topologically organized neural patterns on the other. (Stephen Kosslyn, the main protagonist on the "pictorial" side of the imagery debate,

Recall that throughout the twentieth century the view that visual images play a substantial role in rational thought, and that pictures are important carriers of information, was a minority position in philosophy. The position was defended by Russell, who in 1919 wrote: "If you try to persuade an ordinary uneducated person that she cannot call up a visual picture of a friend sitting in a chair, but can only use words describing what such an occurrence would be like, she will conclude that you are mad." To which he added: "The 'meaning' of images is the simplest kind of meaning, because images resemble what they mean, whereas words, as a rule, do not."[3] Russell's views were taken up by H. H. Price – Professor of Logic in the University of Oxford – in his *Thinking and Experience* (1953). Price insists that some of us do indeed use images in our thinking. Images, says Price, have a superiority over words, in that "they come *nearer* than words do to being instances of the concepts brought to mind by means of them". The mental picture of a dog is more dog-like than the word "dog". Mental pictures are *quasi-*

---

could refer to an interesting example as early as 1994, in his *Image and Brain*, Cambridge, MA: The MIT Press; a recent publication on the topic is the paper by James V. Haxby et al., in *Science*, Sept. 28, 2001, where one reads: "the pattern of response in ventral temporal cortex carries information about the type of object being viewed".) However, it is obvious that the ontology of cortical patterns is very different from that of conscious images. The issues here opening up lead into the depths of the philosophy of science, and of course cannot be pursued in this essay. I must restrict myself to a reference to one of the first contributions to the imagery debate, Allan Paivio's *Imagery and Verbal Processes* (New York: Holt, Rinehart and Winston, 1971). Paivio represents an entirely clear methodological position. "Mental images", writes Paivio, belong to the order of "postulated processes", they are "theoretical constructs", "inferential concepts", i.e. entities or processes themselves not observable, but having observable aspects and implications. Introspective experiencing of visual images on the one hand, and the objective recording of neural phenomena on the other, are empirical observations of a very different sort, but they refer to one and the same theoretical construct of a "mental image". Paivio contrasts his own methodology with "the classical approach to imagery" in which "the term image was used to refer to consciously-experienced mental processes". (*Imagery and Verbal Processes*, pp. 6–11.) This contrast became blurred again in the later discussions.

[3] "I see no reason whatever", concludes Russell, "to reject the conclusion originally suggested by Galton's investigations, namely, that the habit of abstract pursuits makes learned men much inferior to the average in the power of visualizing, and much more exclusively occupied with words in their 'thinking'." (Bertrand Russell, "On Propositions: What They Are and How They Mean" [1919]. *Aristotelian Society Supplementary Volume* 2, pp. 1–43. I am here quoting from J. G. Slater [ed.], *The Collected Papers of Bertrand Russell*, vol. 8: *The Philosophy of Logical Atomism and Other Essays, 1914–19*, London: George Allen & Unwin, 1986, pp. 284 f. and 292.)

instantiative particulars, "whereas words ... are completely non-instantiative particulars. Thus when we think in images, thinking in absence comes much nearer to perceiving in presence than verbal thinking can." However, Price also insists that although mental images are quasi-instantiative particulars, they are not the only ones. "Models, diagrams, pictures drawn publicly in the light of day with nothing 'mental' about them, ... public cinematographic reproductions ... all these entities and occurrences have the same quasi-instantiative function as images have." Now the quasi-instantiative function of both mental images and physical replicas clearly relies on *resemblance*. Price does not believe that the notion of resemblance is unproblematic. However, he points out that where the single picture fails to convey an unambiguous meaning, a series or a *temporal sequence* of pictures might well succeed to do so. Let me add, also, that Price has provided some profound analyses on the issue of mental images as carriers of *concepts*. He emphasized that precisely because mental images are often fleeting, blurred, sketchy, can they represent *generic meanings*.[4]

"We have the misfortune", wrote Price, "to live in the most word-ridden civilization in history, where thousands and tens of thousands spend their entire working lives in nothing but the manipulation of words. The whole of our higher education is directed to the encouragement of verbal thinking and the discouragement of image thinking. Let us hope that our successors will be wiser, and will encourage both." Price here also made the telling remark: "some people are almost incapable of drawing".[5]

A philosopher who was certainly capable of drawing was Ludwig Wittgenstein. His full work has become available only recently, with the publication of a CD-ROM edition.[6] The *printed* corpus, as published during the decades after Wittgenstein's death in 1951, only partially conveys the richness, complexities, continuities of, and changes in, his ideas on pictorial representation. And it fails to convey the significance of the later Wittgenstein's method of explaining philosophical points with the help of drawings and diagrams – his *Nachlaß* contains some 1300 of them. Wittgenstein's later philosophy was for many years regarded as the decisive formulation of the doctrine of imageless thinking. But if his complete corpus is taken into consideration, a very differ-

---

[4] H. H. Price, *Thinking and Experience*, London: Hutchinson's Universal Library, 1953, pp. 235, 254 ff., 272, 275, 284 f., 292.

[5] *Ibid.*, pp. 252 and 258.

[6] *Wittgenstein's Nachlass: The Bergen Electronic Edition*, Oxford University Press, 2000.

ent Wittgensteinian position emerges. According to this position verbal languages on the one hand, and the language of pictures on the other, function jointly, acting on each other; pictures, like words, are instruments embedded in our life. However, while words are predominantly conventional, pictures are in essential respects natural carriers of concrete meanings.

It is only against the background of such a reinterpretation of Wittgenstein's later philosophy that his formerly published passages receive their proper place value. Thus, for example, this remark in the so-called *Philosophical Grammar*: "How curious: we should like to explain the understanding of a gesture as a translation into words, and the understanding of words as a translation into gestures. – And indeed we really do explain words by a gesture, and a gesture by words."[7] The language of gestures – a pre-verbal, visual language – appears to possess a certain autonomy. Let me quote two other striking passages from the same volume. The first: "Thinking is quite comparable to the drawing of pictures." The second: "for the picture to tell me something it isn't essential that words should occur to me while I look at it; because the picture should be the more direct language."[8] In the *Blue Book* Wittgenstein calls attention to the possibility of "a picture which we don't interpret in order to understand it, but which we understand without interpreting it". There are, he writes, "pictures of which we should say that we interpret them, that is, translate them into a different kind of picture, in order to understand them; and pictures of which we should say that we understand them immediately, without any further interpretation". Later in this rather exceptional passage Wittgenstein acknowledges that there occur mental images making up as it were a *pictorial language*.[9]

---

[7] Ludwig Wittgenstein, *Philosophical Grammar*, English translation by Anthony Kenny, Berkeley: University of California Press, 1974, p. 42.

[8] *Ibid.*, pp. 163 f. Kenny has: "the picture was supposed to be the more direct language". In the German original: "Denn das Bild sollte doch die direktere Sprache sein."

[9] As he puts it: "in some cases saying, hearing, or reading a sentence brings images before our mind's eye, images which more or less strictly correspond to the sentence, and which are therefore, in a sense, translations of this sentence into a pictorial language". Ludwig Wittgenstein, *Preliminary Studies for the "Philosophical Investigations". Generally Known as the Blue and Brown Books*. Oxford: Basil Blackwell, 1958, repr. 1964, p. 36. For a more detailed analysis of Wittgenstein's views on pictorial representation see my "Pictures as Instruments in the Philosophy of Wittgenstein", in Rudolf Haller and Klaus Puhl (eds.), *Wittgenstein and the Future of Philosophy: A Reassessment after 50 Years*, Wien: öbv&hpt, 2002, pp. 328–336.

A fundamental work arguing for the pictorial nature of thought was Rudolf Arnheim's 1969 book *Visual Thinking*, a book that found little recognition at the time it was published. "I shall suggest", Arnheim here writes by way of introduction, "that only because perception gathers types of things, that is, concepts, can perceptual material be used for thought; and inversely, that unless the stuff of the senses remains present the mind has nothing to think with." Perception, as Arnheim, referring to the discoveries of Gestalt psychology, puts it, is a grasping of general structural features. And similarly, also thinking that deals with the generic, the abstract, operates on pictorial structures. "How can conceptual thinking", ask Arnheim, "rely on imagery, if the individuality of images interferes with the generality of thought?" In attempting to answer this question Arnheim cites some psychological experiments conducted early in the twentieth century and concludes that the *indistinctness* and *incompleteness* of mental images is "not simply a matter of fragmentation or insufficient apprehension but a positive quality", facilitating abstraction. (Curiously, Arnheim does not mention Price.) And just as mental images, physical pictures, too, are suitable vehicles of abstract reasoning. In this connection, Arnheim calls attention to the potentials of diagrammatic and schematic drawings. And he stresses that the difference between "mimetic and non-mimetic shapes" is only one of degree: this manifests itself, for example, in the case of *descriptive gestures*, "those forerunners of line drawing". As he puts it:

> the perceptual qualities of shape and motion are present in the very acts of thinking depicted by the gestures and are in fact the medium in which the thinking itself takes place. These perceptual qualities are not necessarily visual or only visual. In gestures, the kinesthetic experiences of pushing, pulling, advancing, obstructing, are likely to play an important part.

From our present point of view the most important passages of *Visual Thinking* are to be found in chapter 13: "Words in Their Place". Looking back at the overall argument of the book Arnheim here begins by stating: "concepts are perceptual images and ... thought operations are the handling of those images". This is not to deny, he goes on to say,

> that language helps thinking. What needs to be questioned is whether it performs this service substantially by means of properties inherent in the verbal medium itself or whether it functions indirectly, namely, by point-

ing to the referents of words and propositions, that is, to facts given in an entirely different medium. Also, we need to know whether language is indispensable to thought. – The answer to the latter question is "no". Animals, and particularly primates, give clear proof of productive thinking. ... However, animal thinking may be inferior to that of humans in one important respect. It may be limited to coping with directly given situations.[10]

Arnheim's book had an influence on Merlin Donald's work *Origins of the Modern Mind*, published 1991. (Another important influence on Donald I should here mention came from Dunbar's earlier writings.) In his paper in the present volume Csaba Pléh provides a detailed account of Donald's theory. What I myself at this point would like to stress is that according to Donald the rudimentary capacity of thinking *directly* with images, without verbal mediation, seems to belong to our biological makeup. The theory distinguishes three evolutionary transitions in the development of humankind. The first transition, from apes to *Homo erectus*, was characterized by "the emergence of the most basic level of human representation, the ability to mime, or re-enact, events". To Donald's hypothesis of a *mimetic culture* we will return shortly. The second transition, from *Homo erectus* to *Homo sapiens*, completed the biological evolution of modern humans. "The key event during this transition", writes Donald, "was the emergence of the human speech system, including a completely new cognitive capacity for constructing and decoding narrative." The third transition was "recent and largely nonbiological, but in purely cognitive terms it nevertheless led to a new stage of evolution, marked by the emergence of visual symbolism and external memory as major factors in cognitive architecture." To the third transition Donald allots "three broadly different modes of visual symbolic

---

[10] Arnheim, *Visual Thinking*, Berkeley: University of California Press, 1969, pp. 1., 105 ff., 116 ff. and 227 f. – Arnheim's argument is taken up in the fascinating paper by Robert Scott Root-Bernstein, "Visual Thinking: The Art of Imagining Reality", *Transactions of the American Philosophical Society*, 75 (1985). "A purely linguistic approach to thought", writes Root-Bernstein, "seems to me to be misguided. Neither our experience of nature nor our ability to think about it are limited to, or are even mainly confined to verbal forms. Thoughts may, in fact, be translated into language only for communicating. But pictures, music, and other nonverbal forms of thought also communicate and can me manipulated logically" (*Transactions*, p. 62).

invention", which he designates as "pictorial, ideographic, and phonological". Of these, the pictorial mode emerged first; and the point Donald makes is that this signaled the beginnings of "a new cognitive structure", already enabling some primitive forms of "analytic thought", i.e. "formal arguments, systematic taxonomies, induction, deduction".[11]

Donald's hypothesis of a mimetic culture serves to explain prelinguistic intelligence. Mimesis is distinct from imitation, since it adds a representational dimension to the latter; it is "the re-enacting and re-presenting" of an event or relationship; it is symbolic. Gestures, facial expressions, postural attitudes, tones of voice all belong to the instruments of mimetic representation. Donald points out that this level of representation even today plays a central role in human society. He refers to cross-cultural similarities in the domain of non-verbal expressions, as investigated by Eibl-Eibesfeldt or Ekman, and emphasizes that

> the mimetic layer of representation survives under the surface, in forms that remain universal ... because mimesis forms the core of an ancient root-culture that is distinctly human. No matter how evolved our oral-linguistic culture, and no matter how sophisticated the rich varieties of symbolic material surrounding us, mimetic scenarios still form the expressive heart of human social interchange.[12]

Verbal language builds on the foundations of nonverbal communication, and is then again supplemented by new dimensions of the same. Nonverbal communication as it were regulates verbal exchange on a meta-communicative level. Not backed by direct face-to-face communication, writing, in particular alphabetic writing – actually the main foundation of Western rationality[13] – is from the outset a constricted channel

---

[11] Merlin Donald, *Origins of the Modern Mind: Three Stages in the Evolution of Culture and Cognition*, Cambridge, MA: Harvard University Press, 1991, pp. 16 f., 278, 284, 273.

[12] *Ibid.*, pp. 168 ff. and 188 ff. – Fundamental on the interpretation of pictures as archaic carriers of knowledge is John E. Pfeiffer, *The Creative Explosion: An Inquiry into the Origins of Art and Religion*, Ithaca, NY: Cornell University Press, 1982.

[13] Pioneering on the topic of literacy and rationality is the work of the Hungarian historian István Hajnal. On Hajnal see my essay "From Palágyi to Wittgenstein: Austro-Hungarian Philosophies of Language and Communication", in Nyíri and P. Fleissner (eds.), *Philosophy of Culture and the Politics of Electronic Networking*, vol.1: *Austria and Hungary: Historical Roots and Present Developments*, Innsbruck and Wien: Studien Verlag / Budapest: Áron Kiadó, 1999, pp. 1–11, as well as my volume *Tradition and Individuality: Essays*, Dordrecht: Kluwer, 1992.

of communication. But written language, too, relies on the support of nonverbal elements: word spacing, punctuation, layout, paragraphs, underlining, etc. Gutenberg Man learned to make do with such auxiliary means in the course of his solitary reading and writing. However, in the case of digital communications, the attempt at *interactivity* once more collides with the limits of the medium of writing: the poverty at nonverbal possibilities again and again leads to failures in communication.

In the jumbled literature on nonverbal communication the early publications by the neurologist Macdonald Critchley[14] still represent a singularly clear, and also philosophically perceptive,[15] approach. One of the most convincing arguments given by Critchley for the primordial nature of nonverbal language relates to communication among deaf-mutes. As is well-known, deaf-mutes use contrived sign-languages. However, as Critchley points out,

> all deaf-mutes possess another and lesser-known system of communication. This is a kind of pantomimic shorthand, whereby a single gesture signifies – not a letter – but a word, a phrase, or even a sentence. This "natural sign-language" of the deaf and dumb as it is generally called, is largely unfamiliar to outsiders and indeed many are unaware of its very existence. ... Even very young deaf-mutes communicate freely with each other and the presence of this natural sign-language at an age prior to their receiving systematic instruction points to an "instinctive" or at least a primitive type of symbolization.[16]

---

[14] Notably his *The Language of Gesture* (London: Arnold, 1939) and his collection *Aphasiology and Other Aspects of Language* (London: Edward Arnold, 1970), in the latter especially the paper "Kinesics; Gestural and Mimic Language: An Aspect of Non-Verbal Communication", based in part on the 1939 book.

[15] Cf. e.g. his remarks related to Plato and Locke (*Aphasiology...*, pp. 100 f.), Suzanne Langer (*ibid.*, p. 139) and H. H. Price (*ibid.*, p. 161).

[16] Critchley, "Kinesics...", pp. 305 f. – Among the classics of the topic are also David Efron, *Gesture and Environment*, New York: King's Crown, 1941 (new ed. 1972: *Gesture, Race and Culture*, The Hague: Mouton), Paul Ekman and W. V. Friesen, "The Repertoire of Nonverbal Behavior: Categories, Origins, Usage, and Coding", *Semiotica* 1 (1969), pp. 49–98, as well as Jurgen Ruesch and Weldon Kees, *Nonverbal Communication: Notes on the Visual Perception of Human Relations*, Berkeley: University of California Press, 1956 (new ed. 1972). Mark L. Knapp (*Nonverbal Communication in Human Interaction*, New York: Holt, Rinehart and Winston, 1972) adopts the conceptual framework of Ekman and Friesen, which in its turn is markedly influenced by Efrons's work. Critchley, too, finds Efron interesting (cf. "Kinesics...", pp. 311 f.), but describes the latter's formulations – rightly, I am afraid – as "rather involved".

The natural gesture language of the deaf and dumb.
Sign on the left indicates "heaven", on the right "over there".

(After Critchley)

Many elements of nonverbal communication are culturally specific. Critchley presents, e.g., a series of Italian gestures, each having a well-defined, conventional, meaning. However, there also exists, no doubt, a universal dimension of gestures and facial expressions.

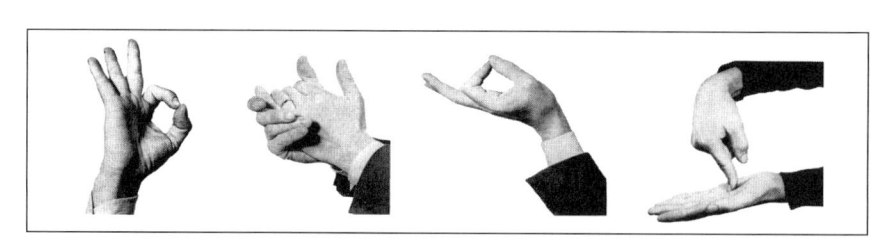

| Approval | Contentment | Excellent! | I insist |

Italian gestures

(After Critchley)

Of those in recent years arguing for a priority of the language of gestures, William C. Stokoe is perhaps the best-known representative. In his last book *Language in Hand*, which was published in 2001, he summarizes his earlier arguments. A fascinating thesis of Stokoe is this: that not only the *semantics*, but also the *syntax* of verbal languages, in particular the subject–predicate structure, is prefigured in gestures.

Motionless handshapes function as names, they represent "people and animals and things"; *moving* handshapes function as verbs, representing "actions and changes". Together, they amount to *sentences*.[17] – The hypothesis of a transformation leading from the language of gestures to verbal languages is augmented by the theory of George Lakoff and Mark Johnson.[18] Lakoff and Johnson on the one hand argue that our language and *thinking* are deeply and thoroughly metaphorical;[19] and, on the other, that the source of those metaphors is the human body itself – its parts, postures, and movements.[20]

Convention and Resemblance

According to the famous trichotomy of Peirce, a sign may be classified as an *icon*, an *index*, or a *symbol*.[21] Icons *resemble* what they denote; indices stand in a *causal relationship* to what they indicate; symbols refer

---

[17] William C. Stokoe, *Language in Hand: Why Sign Came Before Speech*, Washington, D.C.: Gallaudet University Press, 2001, pp. xiii and 12 f. – The thesis is of course not without antecedents. Stokoe himself e.g. refers repeatedly to the paper by Ted Supalla and Elissa Newport, "How Many Seats in a Chair? The Derivation of Nouns and Verbs in American Sign Language", published in Patricia Siple (ed.), *Understanding Language through Sign Language Research*, New York: Academic Press, 1978.

[18] George Lakoff and Mark Johnson, *Metaphors We Live By*, Chicago: University of Chicago Press, 1980.

[19] Thus e.g. in the above half-sentence "on the one hand", "point out", "thinking" (which stems, etymologically, from "appearing"), "deeply", and "thoroughly" are metaphors, "language" (from *lingua* = "tongue") a metonymy. – The idea that originally all word meanings are "non-literal" (*uneigentlich*), was propounded by Herder and Nietzsche already, cf. my paper "The Picture Theory of Reason", in Berit Brogaard and Barry Smith (eds.), *Rationality and Irrationality*, Wien: öbv-hpt, 2001, p. 243.

[20] The approach by Lakoff and Johnson is not mentioned in Stokoe's *Language in Hand*, but referred to in the volume William Stokoe, David Armstrong, and Sherman Wilcox, *Gesture and the Nature of Language*: "Our mental life is run by metaphor, and, some would argue, so is the structure of our languages, as metaphorical representations of our own bodies and their interactions with the environment. We have argued that syntax is metaphorically *embodied* in the direct actions, that is gestures, of our hands and other parts of our bodies." (Cambridge: Cambridge University Press, 1995, p. 235.)

[21] Cf. Charles Sanders Peirce, *Collected Papers*, vols. I—II, ed. by Charles Hartshorne and Paul Weiss (1931), Cambridge, MA: Harvard University Press, 1960, vol. I, p. 295 and vol. II, p. 143.

to what they mean on the basis of *conventions*. In his book *Seeing Is Believing* A. A. Berger explains this classification using pictures:

Simple drawing of a man *A house on fire.* *A cross*
"Where there's smoke, there's fire."

(After A. A. Berger)

Of course all three pictures here are iconic, since each of them resembles what it depicts; beyond that, the picture of the man is an icon in the sense that we directly see what it portrays; the second picture is of an indexical character, in that we *know from experience* that the smoke coming through the window is likely to be caused by some fire; and the third picture is a symbol for those who have *learnt* to associate the cross with Christ's crucifixion. At the same time the cross also has a metonymical function, standing for Christianity.[22] Quoting Lakoff and Johnson, Berger refers to the pervasive role metaphors play in language, and emphasizes that *visual language*, too, is largely metaphorical.[23] He mentions the snake as a metaphor of deception for those familiar with the Old Testament tradition.[24]

Striving to enrich mobile communication by a visual language involves a twofold task. First, a unified system of appropriate conventions has to be introduced – I will come back to this problem further below.

---

[22] Arthur Asa Berger, *Seeing Is Believing: An Introduction to Visual Communication*, Mountain View, CA: Mayfield, 1989, 2nd rev. ed. 1998, pp. 32–35.

[23] *Ibid.*, pp. 39–43.

[24] Cf. Gen 3:13.

Secondly, the potential of pictorial likeness as a natural dimension for conveying meaning should be exploited. Note however that the border between resemblance and conventionality is not a sharp one. Stokoe again and again stresses that gestures, originally, are based on resemblance, i.e. they are *natural* signs, but become, gradually, conventional ones.[25] And conventional signs can come to be treated as natural ones. Wittgenstein has some interesting remarks on this. It would be possible, he noted for example, "that we had first to learn with some pains to understand a method of depiction, in order to be able later on to use it as a natural picture".[26] Two years later he wrote: "Just think of the words exchanged by lovers! They are 'loaded' with feeling. And surely you can't just agree to substitute for them any other sounds you please, as you can with technical terms. Isn't this because they are *gestures*? And a gesture doesn't have to be innate; it is instilled, but, after all, *assimilated*."[27] In 1938 he wrote – and drew – in connection with a familiar pictorial convention (MS 159):

The symbol of the spoken word: characters in a loop which emerges from the mouth of the speaker.

This picture strikes us as quite natural, although we have never seen anything like it.

---

[25] Stokoe, *Language in Hand*, pp. 23 f., 69 and 74 f. On p. 69 Stokoe refers to Thomas A. Sebeok's *Signs: An Introduction to Semiotics* (Toronto: University of Toronto Press, 1994), and writes: "Conventional linkage connects a symbolic sign to a meaning through a convention – users and interpreters agree; but a sign may become conventional through use, even though it is an icon or an index (similar to, or naturally shaped by, its meaning)."

[26] Ludwig Wittgenstein, *Remarks on the Philosophy of Psychology*, transl. by G. E. M. Anscombe, Oxford: Basil Blackwell, 1980, vol. I, § 1018. The passage comes from MS 135 (1947), cf. *Wittgenstein's Nachlass: The Bergen Electronic Edition*.

[27] Cf. Ludwig Wittgenstein, *Last Writings on the Philosophy of Psychology*, vol. I, ed. by G. H. von Wright and Heikki Nyman, transl. by C. G. Luckhardt and Maximilian A. E. Aue, Oxford: Basil Blackwell, 1982, § 712, cf. e.g. MS 138, entry of January 17, 1949. The following telling remark by Wittgenstein dates from the same day: "There really

Indeed it is not just the speech bubble as such that we have come to experience as a natural sign, but also its particular varieties. As William Horton indicates, convention and intuition both play a role in the family of speech balloon symbols. He presents speech balloons of various shapes –

– and prompts us to consider what meaning they convey. "What kind of message", he asks, "would you expect each of these speech balloons to deliver?"[28] And indeed the various forms do suggest to us different moods, sentiments, meanings – even though we might have never encountered them before, have never learnt any conventions relating to them. Speech bubbles have been with us for centuries; they have evolved from ancient and medieval *speech bands*.

In the so-called Part II of the *Philosophical Investigations* Wittgenstein makes it quite clear that for him there are some kinds of pictures which convey unambiguous meanings even though we have never been taught how to interpret them. He introduces the example of a "picture-face",

and remarks: "In some respects I stand towards it as I do towards a human face. I can study its expression, can react to it as to the expres-

---

are those cases where the meaning of what one wants to say is much clearer in one's mind than one could express it in words. (This happens to me quite often.) It is as if one distinctly remembered a dream, but was not able to tell it well."

[28] William Horton, *The Icon Book: Visual Symbols for Computer Systems and Documentation*, New York: John Wiley & Sons, 1994, p. 69. On the emergence and the varieties of the speech bubble as a comics and cartoon convention, cf. also Carl G. Liungman, *Dictionary of Symbols*, New York: Norton & Co., 1991, pp. 358 f., original Swedish edition 1974,

sion of the human face. A child can talk to picture-men or picture-animals, can treat them as it treats dolls."[29]

There are pictures we do not interpret at all, but react to, as Wittgenstein puts it, in an *immediate way*. Whether we do so react, can be influenced by "custom and upbringing"[30], such influence however is sometimes very slight. Wittgenstein's view was corroborated by John Kennedy's findings in his 1974 book *A Psychology of Picture Perception*.[31] Understanding photographs or line drawings generally does not presuppose any previous training in pictorial conventions. At the same time Kennedy points out that static pictures are not always unequivocal. He refers to a certain crowd scene about which it has been noted that some African people tend to interpret it as showing people fighting, whereas other African people may see the same scene as part of a dance. "Frozen pictures tend to be ambiguous, of course", Kennedy writes, "and the viewer's culture can be expected to predispose him toward one imaginative story rather than another."[32] Writing at the time he did, it is perhaps understandable that the idea of *animations* as a means of disambiguation does not occur to Kennedy;[33] both Price and Wittgenstein however did hit on that idea when confronted by the problem of ambiguous pictorial meaning.

Knowledge and Visual Communication

In his paper "Visualization and Cognition" Bruno Latour points to "writing and imaging craftmanship"[34] as the ultimate ground of modern

and Robert E. Horn, *Visual Language: Global Communication for the 21st Century*, Bainbridge Island, WA: MacroVU, 1998, pp. 141f.

[29] Ludwig Wittgenstein, *Philosophical Investigations*, transl. by G. E. M. Anscombe, Oxford: Blackwell, 1953, p. 194.

[30] *Ibid.*, p. 201.

[31] John M. Kennedy, *A Psychology of Picture Perception: Images and Information*, San Francisco: Jossey-Bass, 1974, see esp. pp. 47–84.

[32] *Ibid.*, pp. 69 f.

[33] Colin Ware's *Information Visualization* (San Francisco: Morgan Kaufmann, 2000) came to my attention as the present volume went to print. Ware acknowledges his indebtedness to Kennedy, and in a sense continues where Kennedy left off. While providing a magisterial summary of the natural sign versus conventional sign theme ("sensory" versus "arbitrary" representations, in his terminology), Ware also focusses on the cognitive powers of animation. I will come back to the subject further below in notes 43 and 50.

[34] Bruno Latour, "Visualization and Cognition: Thinking with Eyes and Hands", *Knowledge and Society: Studies in the Sociology of Culture Past and Present*, vol. 6, Greenwich, CT: JAI Press, 1986, p. 3.

science. Through the technologies of writing and pictorial representation the objects of cognition become *mobile*, and at the same time *immutable*; they can be collected, presented, and combined with one another in the power centres of knowledge.[35] Latour does not mention István Hajnal, although the work of the latter is, partly at least, accessible also to non-Hungarians;[36] but otherwise he provides a comprehensive survey of the recent literature on the topic. He refers in particular to Jack Goody's *The Domestication of the Savage Mind*,[37] a book analyzing the role of alphabetic literacy in the emergence of systematic, logical thinking, and to Elizabeth Eisenstein's major work *The Printing Press as an Agent of Change*, describing the close connection between the spread of printed books and the beginnings of modern science.[38] A work Latour is particularly indebted to is the brilliant book by William Ivins, *Prints and Visual Communication*, published in 1953. The observation with which Ivins begins is that "the backward countries of the world are and have been those that have not learned to take full advantage of the possibilities of pictorial state-

---

[35] *Ibid.*, p. 7. – "Economics, politics, sociology, hard sciences", Latour writes, "do not come into contact through the grandiose entrance of 'interdisciplinarity' but through the back door of the *file*. ... domains which are far apart become literally inches apart" (*ibid.*, p. 28). Latour refers to the "new branches of science and technology that can accelerate the mobility of traces, perfect their immutability, enhance readability, insure their compatibility, quicken their display: satellites, networks of espionage, computers" (*ibid.*, p. 30).

[36] I have in mind especially his "Le rôle social de l'écriture et l'évolution européenne", *Revue de l'Institut de Sociologie Solvay*, Bruxelles, 1934.

[37] Cambridge: Cambridge University Press, 1977.

[38] "More abundantly stocked bookshelves", wrote Eisenstein, "obviously increased opportunities to consult and compare different texts. Merely by making more scrambled data available, by increasing the output of Aristotelian, Alexandrian and Arabic texts, printers encouraged efforts to unscramble these data. Some medieval coastal maps had long been more accurate than many ancient ones, but few eyes had seen either. Much as maps from different regions and epochs were brought into contact in the course of preparing editions of atlases, so too were technical texts brought together in certain physicians' and astronomers' libraries." (*The Printing Press as an Agent of Change: Communications and Cultural Transformations in Early-Modern Europe*, Cambridge: Cambridge University Press, 1979, vol. I, pp. 74 f.) Eisenstein puts a special emphasis on *maps*. Maps, plans, are in fact the most fundamental carriers of visual knowledge. From the perspective of our present topic, it is not by chance that location-dependent maps soon came to be offered by mobile telephone network operators (cf. the still very readable collection "A Survey of the Mobile Internet", *The Economist*, Oct. 13, 2001, p. 16).

ment and communication... [M]any of the most characteristic ideas and abilities of our western civilization have been intimately related to our skill exactly to repeat pictorial statements and communications."[39] Ivins makes the fundamental point that the lack of a proper technology for duplicating *pictures* was a major obstacle to the development of science throughout most of Western history. Prior to printing pictures could not become aids to the communication of knowledge. Since they were inevitably distorted in the copying process, information could not be preserved by them. There are some enlightening passages by Pliny the Elder in his *Natural History*, written in the first century of our era, describing what can only be regarded as the ultimate failure of Greek botany as a science. Let me here quote the dramatic summary of those passages given by Ivins:

> The Greek botanists realized the necessity of visual statements to give their verbal statements intelligibility. They tried to use pictures for the purpose, but their only ways of making pictures were such that they were utterly unable to repeat their visual statements wholly and exactly. The result was such a distortion at the hands of the successive copyists that the copies became not a help but an obstacle to the clarification and the making precise of their verbal descriptions. And so the Greek botanists gave up trying to use illustrations in their treatises and tried to get along as best they could with words. But, with words alone, they were unable to describe their plants in such a way that they could be recognized – for the same things bore different names in different places and the same names meant different things in different places. So, finally, the Greek botanists gave up even trying to describe their plants in words, and contented themselves by giving all the names they knew for each plant and then told what human ailments it was good for. In other words, there was a complete breakdown of scientific description and analysis once it was confined to words without demonstrative pictures.[40]

Picture printing was invented around 1400 A.D. Ivins argues that this was a much more revolutionary invention in the history of communica-

---

[39] William M. Ivins, Jr., *Prints and Visual Communication*, Cambridge, MA: Harvard University Press, 1953, p. 1.

[40] *Ibid.*, p. 15.

tion than that of typography half a century later. Pictures became more or less exactly repeatable. However, they were still a long way from being faithful copies of particular natural objects; indeed the very demand for faithful representations emerged only gradually in the course of the fifteenth century. The so-called *Pseudo-Apuleius*, a printed version of a ninth-century botanical manuscript, published just after 1480 at Rome, contains woodcuts that are careless copies of the manuscript illustrations, and could of course not be of any practical use. But just a few years later the German herbal *Gart der Gesundheit* is printing woodcuts based on expert drawings of the original plants.

"Asparagus agrestis", from the *Pseudo-Apuleius*

"Gladiolus", from the *Gart der Gesundheit*

(After Ivins)

However, neither woodcuts, nor etchings or engravings, could aim at complete faithfulness. Ivins points out that when Lessing wrote his famous treatise on the Laocoon group, he did not, because he could not, have reliable illustrations at his disposal. "Each engraver", writes Ivins, "phrased such information as he conveyed about [the statues] in terms of the net of rationality of his style of engraving. There is such a disparity between the visual statements they made that only by an effort of historical imagination is it possible to realize that all the so dissimilar pictures were supposed to tell the truth about the one identical thing. At

The head of Laocoon. Engraving around 1527, woodcut 1544, etching 1606
(After Ivins)

best there is a family resemblance between them."[41] Until the age of photography, as Ivins stresses, there existed no technology of exactly repeatable pictorial representations of particular objects.

The work of Ivins had an influence on no lesser a figure than Ernst Gombrich, who refers to him in the foreword to his *Art and Illusion*. Gombrich's theories are of obvious relevance to our present topic; clearly I have no space to summarize them here, but let me at least refer to his talk "Pictorial Instructions", first published in 1990 and reprinted in the volume *The Uses of Images*.[42] In the introduction to this volume Gombrich remarks that the invention and spread of *photography* had a dramatic effect on the crafts of pictorial representation, since the requirement of a faithful visual record came to be met more cheaply and efficiently by the camera. From the talk "Pictorial Instructions" let me single out two observations. First, that instructions expressed through images – be they single pictures or a sequence of them, whether still or moving – are much more easily understood when *verbal explanations* are added.[43] (Gombrich compares and analyzes leaflets provided by British

---

[41] *Ibid.*, p. 89.

[42] Ernst Gombrich, *The Uses of Images: Studies in the Social Function of Art and Visual Communication*, London: Phaidon Press, 1999.

[43] This is the insight, too, at which Edward Tufte arrives in the third volume of his celebrated trilogy. (Edward R. Tufte, *The Visual Display of Quantitative Information*, 1982; *Envisioning Information*, 1990; *Visual Explanations: Images and Quantities, Evidence and Narrative*, 1997. Cheshire, CT: Graphics Press.) "My three books on information design", Tufte sums up, "stand in the following relation: *The Visual Display of Quantitative Information* is about *pictures of numbers*, how to depict data and enforce statistical honesty. *Envisioning Information* is about *pictures of nouns* (maps and aerial photographs, for example, consist of

Airways and Lufthansa on what to do when the aircraft comes down on water.) Secondly, that our pictorial representations today employ numerous conventions which to us seem quite natural, but would have been not at all self-evident some centuries ago. Gombrich's example is the arrow, which prior to the eighteenth century had not assumed a "universal significance as a pointer or a vector".[44]

It was perhaps the main discovery of twentieth-century philosophy that *all* knowledge, ultimately, is based on *practical* knowledge. Now pictures are better at teaching practical knowledge than are texts. It was

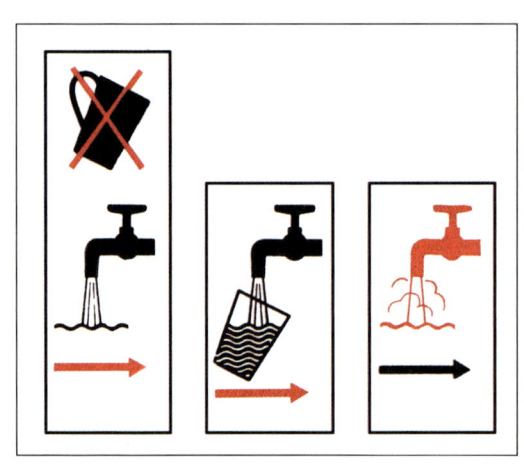

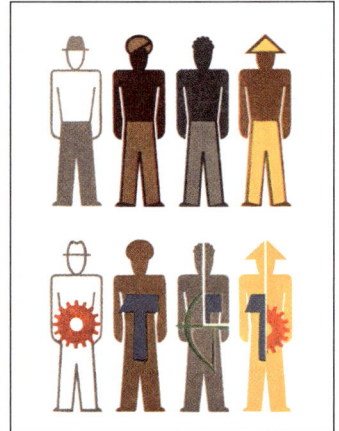

ISOTYPE symbols

not by chance that Otto Neurath, the ardent advocate of the logical positivist thought of a unified science, conceived of the idea of complementing his planned compendia by an *international picture language*. Neurath

---

a great many nouns lying on the ground). ... *Visual Explanations* is about *pictures of verbs*, the representation of mechanism and motion, of process and dynamics, of causes and effects, of explanation and narrative." (*Visual Explanations*, p. 10.) The third volume of the trilogy describes, in particular, "the proper arrangement in space and time of images, words, and numbers" (*ibid.*, p. 9). It is to be noted, too, that in this volume the issue of *animations* occupies a central place. – Both the issue of text and image integration and that of animations is admirably dealt with in the book by Colin Ware referred to above, cf. note 33.

[44] *Ibid.*, pp. 226 ff.

was working towards an "International System Of Typographic Picture Education", abbreviated as *isotype*, an interdependent and interconnected system of images, to be used together with *word languages*, yet having a visual logic of its own. Isotype would be two-dimensional[45], using distinctive conventions, shapes, colours, and so on. "Frequently it is very hard", Neurath wrote, "to say in words what is clear straight away to the eye. It is unnecessary to say in words what we are able to make clear by pictures."[46] Neurath particularly stressed that the elaboration of his picture language was meant to serve a broader task, that of establishing an international encyclopaedia of common, united knowledge.[47]

However, he never even came near to realizing his lofty aims. His experiments, conducted from the 1920s to the 40s, turned out to have beeen technologically premature. The icons elaborated within the framework of the isotype program have served as models for those international picture signs we today daily encounter at airports and railway stations, but – because they are so crude, and so cumbersome to produce – they could not form the basis of a true visual *language*. With the *iconic revolution* we today witness, such a language is clearly becoming feasible.

---

[45] "The writing or talking language is only of 'one expansion' – the sounds come one after the other in time, the word-signs come one after the other on paper, as for example the telegram signs on a long, narrow band of paper. The same is true in books – one word over another in the line under it has no effect on the sense. But there are languages of 'two expansions'... Some of the picture languages in existence are of one expansion, they are made up of long lines of small signs... the ISOTYPE system ... makes use of the connection of parts not only in one direction but in two, and the effect is a language picture." (Otto Neurath, *International Picture Language*, London: 1936, repr. University of Reading: Dept. of Typography & Graphic Communication, 1980, pp. 60 ff.)

[46] *Ibid.*, p. 26. Neurath then adds: "Science gives us accounts of old picture languages in general use, for example, in the first stages of the development of society. The signs used are frequently not very clear to us today, but they were clear when and where they were used. We are not able to take over the old signs as they are. Adjustments have to be made in relation to the forms of today and tomorrow before it is possible for them to come into general use. Giving a sign its fixed form for international use, possibly for a great number of years, is responsible work. ... It will not do to take the taste of the present day as our only guide; we have to take into account the experience of history. The picture-writing of old Egypt and pictures of fights on old military maps ... are of much help in building up a system of signs" (*ibid.*, pp. 40 f.).

[47] *Ibid.*, pp. 65 and 111.

Iconic Languages

The volume *Iconic Communication,* edited by Yazdani und Barker, was published in April 2000.[48] The volume constitutes an important novel beginning in that it heralds the extension, occasionally indeed the replacement, of verbal language by visual languages. The basic idea itself is not new – the volume repeatedly refers for example to Neurath's work. New however – even if not without antecedents – is the investigation of the possibility of iconic languages as viewed against the background of digital graphics and networked communication. The screen, and in particular the small display, has been recognized as a promising new field of application by the architects of visual languages. In the chapter written by Yazdani there emerges the topic of a possible connection between pictorial communication and the *mobile telephone.* This topic, clearly, raises not just technological questions, but psychological, linguistic, and philosophical ones as well.

Of the authors of the volume Colin Beardon has for a number of years argued in favour of the view that ambiguity in pictures can be removed via felicitious animation; that where the still image stands in need of interpretation, the moving image is self-interpreting.

12 icons from Beardon's dictionary
Representing: black, white, house, city, woman, man, telephone, dog, tree, book, car, aeroplane

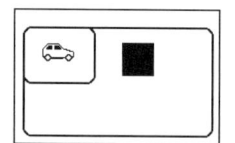

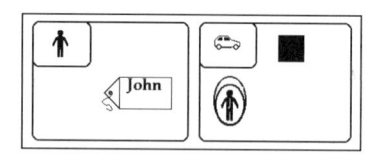

"the black car"   "a man named John" / "a black car owned by John"
Iconic expressions in Beardon's system

---

[48] Masoud Yazdani and Philip Barker (eds.), *Iconic Communication,* Bristol: Intellect Books, 2000.

178

Beardon's system uses picture frames similar to those of a WAP-enabled mobile telephone (though of course no such devices were available at the time when Beardon was writing). Let us look at a frame (an "event window") which carries the meaning "a man goes to a city".[49]

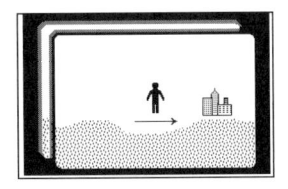

"A man goes to a city."

The fact and the direction of the movement are shown by an arrow. Now we could say that the arrow is not a natural sign: for members of cultures not acquainted with the bow and arrow it means nothing, and it will gain meaning only when its conventional usage is explained – recall Gombrich's point. However, if the arrow is replaced by the actual movement of an icon representing a man, such difficulties are unlikely to arise. Taking up the ideas of Price, Stokoe, and Beardon, I would here venture the following formulation: while still images correspond to the *words* of verbal languages, animations correspond to *sentences*. Animated iconic languages, both in their intuitive and conventional aspects, are rich and dense carriers of meaning, especially well suited to convey large amounts of information on a small display.[50]

---

[49] I here follow Beardon's paper "Discourse Structures in Iconic Communication", *Artificial Intelligence Review* 9/2—3 (1995); the illustrations are reproduced with the author's permission. The paper is accessible at http://www.esad.plym.ac.uk/personal/C-Beardon/papers/9508.html.

[50] In her paper in the present volume Barbara Tversky refers to results of empirical research which seem to disprove the assumption of the cognitive superiority of animations as compared to still pictures. However, she also notes that on the basis of static representations we are capable of conducting as it were mental animations. I believe this is an important point. Static mental images appear to be, generally speaking, merely limiting cases of dynamic ones. With the techniques for creating animations becoming ever easier to employ, it is to be expected that the same situation will come to prevail also in the domain of physical – digital – pictures. The future belongs to moving images as carriers of knowledge. For some detailed arguments to this effect see for instance Mitchell Stephens, *The Rise of the Image and the Fall of the Word*, New York: Oxford University Press, 1998, and especially Colin Ware's book referred to above.

Iconic languages designed for mobile communications should, roughly, meet the following requirements: (1) ease in producing special symbols, and (2) fast recognizability of the symbols employed; (3) pictoriality (icons, as far as possible, should resemble real-world objects); (4) conventions enabling (a) the combinations of icons, and of parts of icons, (b) the generation of complex symbols out of simple ones, (c) the use of symbols standing for abstract concepts, and (d) adding text (written and voiced) to icons; (5) multi-cultural span and historical continuity, as well as (6) dynamic capabilities (allowing for animations). – Requirement 4b should allow for variation, interchangeability, and indeed a measure of free play for spontaneity, while at the same time preserving visual harmony across the whole range of the icon family.[51] – Basic emoticons like :-) , ;-) , :-(satisfy all the above requirements except 6. In particular, they satisfy 4c, since they do not denote some particular object (e.g. "unhappy face"), or class of objects, but permit translations like "I am unhappy", "sad", etc. Indeed they convey a cluster of ideas without there arising the need for any translation into words. Both Neurath's ISOTYPE icons and for instance Aicher's 1972 Olympic Games symbols fulfill 4a and 4b. From the many excellent examples for iconic design fulfilling criterion 5, let me here refer to Paul Honeywill's "Print Belize" logo, juxtaposing patterns of Mayan carvings and Roman letters.[52] – As I have noted above, not all conventions need to be agreed upon explicitly.[53] For instance, in the course of the twentieth century cartoons and comic books contributed significantly to the standardization of a visual language vocabulary.[54] Emoticons, too, as Honeywill puts it, "are a natural progression of language, developed by the users and not by a designed system".[55]

---

[51] Cf. e.g. Rosemary Sassoon and Albertine Gaur, *Signs, Symbols and Icons: Pre-history to the Computer Age*, Exeter: Intellect Books, 1997, pp. 157 f.

[52] Paul Honeywill, *Visual Language for the World Wide Web*, Exeter: Intellect Books, 1999, pp. 96 ff.

[53] See e.g. the useful references to D. K. Lewis, *Convention: A Philosophical Study* (Cambridge, MA: Harvard University Press, 1969) in David Novitz, *Pictures and Their Use in Communication: A Philosophical Essay*, The Hague: Martinus Nijhoff, 1977, pp. 28 ff.

[54] Cf. e.g. Robert E. Horn, *Visual Language: Global Communication for the 21st Century*, pp. 135 ff.

[55] Honeywill, *op. cit.*, p. 123.

MMS Arrives

Ivins recalls that during his time at the Metropolitan Museum he again and again had to experience "how inadequate words are as tools for description, definition, and classification of objects each of which is unique". Words can never, as he puts it, "catch the personality of objects which we know by acquaintance", whereas "pictures or images" can.[56]

Pictorial communication has obvious advantages; but also obvious drawbacks. In his book *The Search for the Perfect Language* Umberto Eco cites with approval all the usual arguments against visual languages – ambiguity, lack of grammar, the need for conventions, limited applicability. "One could say", he writes, "that there is only a single system which can claim the widest range of diffusion and comprehensibility: the images of cinema and television. One is tempted to say that this is certainly a 'language' understood around the earth." However, he adds, "if there is no difficulty involved in receiving cinematic or televised images, it is extremely difficult to produce them. Ease of execution is a notable argument in favour of verbal languages. Anyone who wished to communicate in a strictly visual language would probably have to go about with a camcorder, a portable television set, and a sackful of tapes, resembling Swift's wise men who, having decided that it was necessary to show any object they wanted to designate, were forced to drag enormous sacks behind them."[57]

As I have tried to make clear in the foregoing, I do not advocate communication in a strictly visual language. But I certainly believe that complementing verbal – voiced or written – communication with a pictorial dimension can enhance the effectivity of information exchange. And Swift's wise men are facing a task that is increasingly easy to perform. MMS – multimedia messaging service – in the introduction of which Hungary witnessed pioneering steps early in 2002,[58] constitutes a

---

[56] Ivins, *op. cit.*, pp. 51 and 53.

[57] Umberto Eco, *The Search for the Perfect Language*, Oxford: Blackwell Publishers, 1995, pp. 174 ff.

[58] See http://www.westel900.net/kapcsolat/sajto/sajtokozlemenyek/sajtokozlemeny_20020418_e.html (last visited: Jan. 5, 2003).

significant new phase. MMS allows users of mobile phones to take snapshots with built-in cameras and immediately post them; to create line drawings, edit pictures, add text to graphics, and send the complex messages thus created.

Mobile-phone snapshot received on the way helps to identify the object being looked for.

Drawing created on a mobile phone directing to the place being looked for.

Such capabilities deserve our attentions on at least four counts. Having as it were a drawing block handy all the time, with the continuous possibility of communicating sketches and having them applied to practical tasks at the receiving end, goes at least a small way towards helping to solve the problem Price complained about, namely that *few people know how to draw*. The collection and combination of those mobile and at the same time immutable objects of cognition Latour regards as the foundation of Western intellectual superiority will cease to be the exclusive prerogative of "power centres of knowledge" once they really become mobile, and once "imaging craftmanship"[59] becomes a widespread art. Being able to take photos and send them away on the spot surely alleviates the predicament Ivins pointed at when he wrote that mere words cannot capture the unique characteristics of particular objects. And the disequilibrium Eco alludes to, that producing images is so much more cumbersome than viewing them, will be less marked once the creating and disseminating of images becomes a common everyday skill.

Pictorial Communication and Mobile Communities

At the beginning of my paper I have quoted Neurath's memorable phrase: "Words make division, pictures make connection".[60] Pictures connect people who are otherwise divided by speaking different languages. But let us observe that even among those who share the same tongue pictures have a greater potential to create common bonds than do words. The reason for this has been known since ancient times. Saint Bonaventure in the thirteenth century summed up a millennium of argument about the institution of images in the Church when he said, first, that the illiterate might learn from sculptures and from pictures as if from books, and second, that people who are not excited to devotion when they hear of Christ's deeds might at least be excited when they see them in figures and pictures.[61] The essential fact behind both observations of course is that understanding images, thinking in images, having feelings in connection with images, and even communicating in images – namely in mimetic patterns – is more basic to human nature than thinking and communicating in words. Again, this is not to say that words are dispensable. The significance of MMS is precisely that it combines images and words – words spoken and written. Communicat-

---

[59] Latour, *op. cit.*, p. 3.
[60] *International Picture Language*, p. 18.
[61] I here follow David Freedberg, *The Power of Images: Studies in the History and Theory of Response*, Chicago: University of Chicago Press, 1989, pp. 162 ff.

ing synchronously in voice, writing, and graphics has the potential to create and maintain a higher level of human cohesion than could be achieved by any of these dimensions by themselves. It was Karl W. Deutsch who applied the notion of complementarity, originally a concept in communications theory, to the issues of social communication.[62] In my introduction to the present volume I referred to the distinction Deutsch made between society and community. Communities are characterized precisely by patterns of communication that display a high level of complementarity between information conveyed through various channels. Multimedia messaging, the synchronous-complementary transmission of speech, text and pictures seems to me to be not just a social activity but an activity sustaining those very types of human communication that make up genuine communities.

---

[62] See esp. his *Nationalism and Social Communication: An Inquiry into the Foundations of Nationality*, New York: John Wiley & Sons, 1953, pp. 69 ff.

J. Laki – G. Palló: # New Communication Media and Scientific Change

There is already a bulk of literature available analyzing the impact of new communication technologies on scientific research. Most studies focus on the sociological structure of science in the new era, including the role of publication policies, discussion groups, e-mail and the like. However, the computer, the internet and the latest mobile communication systems could also induce changes in the content of knowledge. One element of the latest change might be the growing importance of pictures as opposed to the overwhelming significance of verbal expressions or mathematical formulae that were characteristic of traditional scientific publications. Another aspect could be that the very character of scientific research is undergoing a radical change. These modifications may lead to important epistemological consequences that are directly related to sociological factors. The sociological components of research have already been influenced by electronic communication technology that will continue to grow into an entirely mobile system in the near future.

The change induced by the internet was the second in a row of major changes that occurred in the practice of science during the second half of the twentieth century. The first major change unfolded after World War Two, following the success of the Manhattan Project aimed at developing the nuclear bomb. As a result of this first shift, the role of financing agencies and the goals drawn up for research became more decisive in the work of science than before. The theoretical reflections given to this change strengthened the relativist tendencies in the philosophy of science, which after the 1960s had come to prevail mainly through the works of Michael Polanyi, Thomas Kuhn, or Paul Feyerabend.

As we will attempt to show, the second change, which was brought about by the rapid development of communication technologies in the 1990s, has certain features that make some elements of the relativist picture untenable. Analysis of the work of Big Science in the internet medium may lead to the conclusion that science is progressing in a less fragmented and less relativistic direction than it had been prior to the new communication systems.

Before characterizing this non-relativistic turn, we briefly summarize some of the more recent views on the relativist fragmentation of science that had purportedly existed before the internet impacted the practice of science. We will then demonstrate those new elements that have been introduced by electronic networks, in the case of Big Science, that contrast with established relativist views.

Some recent views

Big Science

The paradoxical success of the nuclear bomb project resulted in many reflections on the changes in the social role of science and scientists. Nevertheless, it took many years after Hiroshima for the experts to conclude that a fundamental change occurred in the organizational system of science. Derek de Solla Price used the term "Big Science" in 1963 to describe the new phenomena.[1] He relied on an article written by the physicist Alvin Weinberg in 1961.[2] Although he conceded their inevitability, Weinberg called "large-scale science" the mammoth projects such as the Manhattan Project, and was very critical about their effects on scientific activity. Both Weinberg and de Solla Price observed that science had arrived at a new stage of its history. This period was characterized by a sharp increase in numerical data related to research such as the value of the funds invested in research, the number of researchers, the number of publications and the like. To both men, one exceptional and visible peculiarity of new science was the extensive use of extremely large instruments: a growth in the size of hardware. According to de Solla Price, "the manifestations of modern scientific hardware [are] so monumental that they have been usefully compared with the pyramids of Egypt and the great cathedrals of medieval Europe."[3]

There is some ambiguity however in the use of the term "Big Science". With Weinberg and de Solla Price, we use "large-scale science" in the sense of fast growth of expenditures, the number of publications and similar factors in science, while the term "Big Science" is meant to denote some very large individual projects with huge hardware. Accord-

---

[1] Derek de Solla Price, *Little Science, Big Science*, New York and London: Columbia University Press, 1963.

[2] A. M. Weinberg, "Impact of Large-Scale Science on the United States", *Science* 134 (1961), pp. 161–165.

[3] Price, *op. cit.*, p. 2.

ingly, "Big Science" is a particular case of "large-scale science". Many research projects, primarily in particle physics, astronomy and biology, can be considered as Big Science.

As a consequence of the emergence of both Big Science and large-scale science, the public image of the scientist working in Little Science is very different from that of the individual working in Big Science. De Solla Price characterized the former as "the lone, long-haired genius, moldering in an attic or basement workshop, despised by society as a nonconformist, existing in a state of near poverty, motivated by the flame burning within him."[4] In stark contrast, a researcher working in the framework of Big Science is perceived as someone who is "honored in Washington, sought after by all research corporations on the 'Boston ring road', part of an intellectual brotherhood of co-workers, arbiters of political as well as technological destiny."[5] As examples of Big Science, de Solla Price mentioned the Manhattan Project, the space programs, the development of radar and the work of computer science. He observed that large-scale science should be measured by the standards of time. In this way, some scientific endeavors of the earlier period of history could also be considered Big Science. As a good example, he mentions the work of Tycho de Brahe's complex institution, Uraniborg, in Denmark, in the sixteenth century.

Accordingly, after World War Two, many research projects, primarily in particle physics, astronomy and biology, can be considered as Big Science because of their scales. These, however, did not eliminate Little Science that worked parallel with them in other areas. Yet, some special features of Big Science, particularly its organization of research, science policy and also the way research is conducted, differ from those of Little Science. Therefore, it appears fruitful to consider Big Science as an archetype of the modern scientific system.

In the early 1990s, some authors proposed that Big Science was something more than traditional research carried out with tools that were huge in size and expense. While these latter features would remain decisive, others would became more emphatic, such as an increasing accuracy in the work of the measuring equipment, followed by an increasing accuracy in collecting and analyzing data received. Meanwhile, new institutions, political and social organizations had been set up. Accordingly, three criteria could now be used to define Big Science. First, Big Science is characterized by a large concentration of resources in fewer

---

[4] *Ibid.* p. 3.
[5] *Ibid.*

institutes. Secondly, within these institutes, research projects have an increasingly specialized expertise; in addition to the designers of apparatuses and the theoretician, new participants enter research: the team leader, the laboratory manager, and the business coordinator. Thirdly, in its rhetoric alongside with intellectual relevance, science policy refers to the larger social and political goals, such as health or environmental issues, and to economic or military interests, all of which fall outside the scope of traditional science.[6]

The aspect of a possible impact of communication technology on Big Science was omitted from these investigations. This might be due to the fact that the internet had not yet been widespread in the periods examined.

Industrialized Science

Thomas Kuhn and other philosophers published the results of their relativist epistemological investigations at about the same time as Weinberg and de Solla Price had their writings on large-scale science published. In their argumentation, those philosophers relied on historical examples rather than on contemporary scientific activity. Kuhn considered the works of Copernicus, Lavoisier, and Einstein as paradigms without mentioning the Manhattan Project.[7] It was Jerome Ravetz who in the early 1970s drew theoretical conclusions from the analysis of large-scale science.[8]

According to Ravetz, the rapid growth experienced in many of the relevant quantitative indicators of research resulted in a radical change of the character of science. While in the past science could be considered as "the pursuit of Truth", a most effective device in the warfare against theology and metaphysics, recently it has become something like an industrial enterprise.

Industrialized science is a "large organization", Ravetz wrote, "with labor force directed to specialized tasks, producing the sorts of results for which directors have been able to obtain contracts from agencies which

---

[6] Bruce Hevly, "Reflections on Big Science and Big History", in Peter Galison and Bruce Hevly (eds.), *The Growth of Large-Scale Research*, Stanford: Stanford University Press, 1992, pp. 356–357.

[7] Thomas Kuhn, *The Structure of Scientific Revolutions*, Chicago and London: The University of Chicago Press, 1962.

[8] Jerome M. Ravetz, *Scientific Knowledge and Its Social Problems*, Oxford: Clarendon Press, 1971.

invest in such production". The earlier period, lasting until about World War II, is called the period of "academic science" because the informal network of researchers that existed in the Renaissance evolved into a formal institution called "academia". Academia was established to regulate the cooperation between scientists. It remained largely an informal community of a handful of gentlemen, though, as Ravetz noted, it was far from being an ideal "primitive-communist priesthood". The members of academia, apart from their institutionalized relationships, were bound together by "the personal ties of shared endeavor and a common loyalty to an ideal". According to this ideal, knowledge and scientific research (the pursuit of Truth) is good in itself as it contributes to the power of mankind and to the greatness of a nation. Academic science was divided into disciplines ruled by theoretical approaches, paradigms, changing from time to time throughout history and providing an important subject for epistemological analyses. However, according to Ravetz, "as the world of science has grown in size and in power, its deepest problems have changed from the epistemological to the social".

In his theory, industrialized science is craftsmen's work. Researchers as craftsmen use special tools that can be physical (e.g., experimental devices) or intellectual (e.g., mathematical representations, theoretical interpretations). The tools may vary in complexity and sophistication. With their tools, researchers manufacture first data, then information, and finally research reports (published or unpublished) that are the product of the industrial process.

In this approach, "the objects of scientific inquiry are of a very special sort: classes of intellectually constructed things and events". For instance, the various sorts of chemical substances, such as the notion of acids, had been defined in different ways in different historical periods depending on the tools available. With these tools, first a sample of a particular acid was produced that to some extent met the definition (disregarding impurities, etc.). Then, the researcher investigated this sample instead of a substance existing in nature, though he knew that "few 'chemicals' can be found in the world of nature, outside the laboratory". Consequently, "even in the production of data the manipulations are with samples which are designed to serve as true representatives of such classes, rather than 'real' objects which can be known independently of an elaborated structure of theory".

Researchers work on intellectually constructed objects in "problem situations". Whether the scientist has solved the problem or not, "the criteria of adequacy are set by his scientific community, not by Nature itself". Since theories, in this framework, should also be considered as tools, their adequacy can be evaluated according to the function for their use towards a given goal, rather than according to adequacy related to Truth. Moreover, in industrialized science where the fields of science and technology overlap, even the problem of research is set by the practical purpose. "We may define a practical problem", wrote Ravetz, "as a statement of a purpose to be achieved, whose means are to be established as the conclusion of an argument, with a plan for its accomplishment." The evaluation of a particular result depends on judgments connected with particular values.

The values and judgments are related to scientific "schools" defined by the objects, tools and methods that they use in their investigations, and also by their research styles, informal networks and institutional bases. Indeed, in Ravetz's approach, the fallible and non-cumulative character of scientific knowledge is expressed in terms of the rising and declining schools. His relativist conclusion: "No single result in science can be proved to be true; and indeed, most are not merely untrue (as assertions about the external world) but are also of a very temporary usefulness and life."[9]

In this constructivist framework, the larger and more dramatic changes in science, which Kuhn described as scientific revolutions, proceed at the social level of research. Related to the industrialized large-scale science, Ravetz analyzed three special social tasks: the protection of property, the management of novelty and quality control. Among these, the management of novelty raises the problem of the choice between competing theories, in other words, between the new and old schools. The choice is represented as a strategic decision because it is related to the assessment of the school's future development influenced by the success of the novelty it supports. The fundamentally new result introduces new objects of inquiries (new samples), and develops new tools and methods of research. Whether in the future this "daring and ruthless" step would bring success to the new strategy cannot be derived from rules. The assessment depends on the judgments of the brave and greatly talented innovators who, initially, have only scant evidence to convince others about the advantages of the novelty that they want to manage. The new school, in a painful process, destroys the intellectual property of the established one. The representatives of the old school, in the struggle for keeping their positions, may consider the novelty as unscientific. Recently, this kind of shift has led to less bitter processes as whole fields become obsolete very rapidly. The result of the production,

---

[9] Ravetz, *Scientific Knowledge*..., pp. 22, 41, 10, 109, 112, 110, 148, 339, 224, 236.

the research report serves mainly the purpose of protecting the intellectual property of scientists. If the results are published in print, the other researchers are allowed to use this property without limitation but, through citation, they should give credit for the original author. Citation, in Ravetz's approach, represents something like a payment for use of the results.

Extending the constructivist treatment, Bruno Latour presented the process of preparing a scientific publication as manufacturing sentences.[10] In industrialized science, Ravetz pointed out, the demarcation line between science and technology is blurred. Therefore, the role of publication changes because property created by the researcher belongs to his employer rather than to himself. Under these circumstances, the research report takes the form of a patent that cannot be used freely by all interested experts.[11] In addition, as Diane Crane pointed out at about the same time as Ravetz published his book, the informal networks or "invisible colleges" of modern science had an increasing impact upon productivity in science. The enhanced productivity is largely due to the intensive informal communication maintained between members. Correspondence, informal exchange of ideas in small workshops, or circulation of preprints in a closed circle of researchers not only stimulates but at the same time also limits open communication to a close network.[12] The system of patents, the unclear ownership of intellectual property in informal communication inside a network, has led to the ramified subject of "public knowledge" that has been widely debated more recently.[13]

Science in a Steady State

When studying large-scale science, de Solla Price relied on the data of scientometrics. He observed a tendency of acceleration in the growth of a cluster of data characteristic of scientific research. In the early 1990s, John Ziman concluded that in principle this growth couldn't continue endlessly.[14] The expenditures spent on research and develop-

---

[10] Bruno Latour and Steven Woolgar, *Laboratory Life: The Social Construction of Scientific Facts*, London: Sage, 1979.

[11] Ravetz, *op. cit.*, p. 331.

[12] Diana Crane, *Invisible Colleges: Diffusion of Knowledge in Scientific Communities*, Chicago and London: The University of Chicago Press, 1972.

[13] John M. Ziman, *Public Knowledge: An Essay Concerning the Social Dimension of Science*, Cambridge: Cambridge University Press, 1968.

[14] John Ziman, *Prometheus Bound. Science in a Dynamic Steady State*, Cambridge: Cambridge University Press, 1994.

ment stopped at around 2 or 3 percent of the national income in most of the developed countries and they were expected to stay at around the same level. As Ziman said: "the likely prospect is that science will have to exist within a fixed or slowly growing envelope of resources. ... there is good reason to refer to it broadly as a 'steady state' situation from a financial point of view, and to attribute many of the structural changes to this factor."

Under these conditions, industrialized large-scale science produces projects that compete against each other for funding. While during the academic period of science funding was generous and almost unconditional, Ziman says, now it becomes the subject of policy debate, producing a new field called science policy. Science policy studies work out and debate the principles of decision making between the research projects competing for the public expenditure. Market forces may optimize the allocation of resources. "The intense competition for resources", Ziman wrote, "was an unintended – often deplored – consequence of the transition of level funding. The market situation ... does not necessarily operate to produce ideal results from a scientific or social point of view."

Science policy decisions required new concepts for the evaluation of research projects. Its new language uses expressions such as "accountability", "input and output indicators", "priority setting", "allocation management" and many others to free decision making of its former ad hoc character. When writing their applications for research grants, scientists consider these criteria. To meet expectations, they must submit proposals containing specific theoretical or practical goals. Ziman calls this "finalization" that is based on the existing paradigms. The paradigm that governs a particular field provides the basis for setting the goals of research.

Researchers themselves can set the goals in academic science, motivated by professional interest. Their problems, considered "basic" or "pure", may comprise the exploration of some phenomena or the analyses of underlying mechanisms. However, the demarcation line between "basic" and "applied" research becames shadowy. Gradually, many, but not all, features of industrial research occur also in pure science. They create a cycle of research, starting from basic research going through several stages of application and returning to basic research.

In this competition, the instruments of science have become increasingly sophisticated. Through this, a cyclic process has been formed between science and technology: scientific development fuels technological progress which in turn fuels scientific development. According to Ziman, Big Science is the highest peak of this process with its "very large, very elaborate and very expensive piece of apparatus". In Big Science, actual research is carried out by many small research teams. In a steady state, sophistication of the apparatus, which will quickly tend to become obsolete, is also an important factor for success in the competition for funding.

Indeed, in Ziman's approach, the increasing scale of research projects fosters an active collaboration of scientists. Teamwork is an important feature of science in a steady state. In Big Science projects sometimes there can be hundreds of researchers participating in the actual research. In addition, as Ziman says, "the economic and political forces that pull basic science towards greater involvement in practical problems inevitably shape the organization of research into multidisciplinary teams". In particular, the crew of large teams in Big Science (and in Little Science also) consists of members belonging to different nations, giving a transnational character to scientific research.

Ziman agreed with Weinberg on the point that in large-scale science, scientific leadership is associated with managerial function. According to Ziman, "if there is a single word that epitomizes the transition to 'steady state' science, it must be 'management'." The organization of the teams working on research projects requires managers who (by now, let us add, increasingly with mobile phones in their hands) play a similar role in the system of science to those working in industry or business.

"The results of research", Ziman writes, "do not become scientific information until they have been communicated to other researchers. Open channels of communication within an attentive community are an essential condition for active scientific discovery and technological invention."[15] Nevertheless, the communication of information in technological fields is not organized in the same way as in pure science. An invention is private property to be held secret. Considering the cyclic character of research in "steady state" science, the issue of public knowledge becomes a serious problem.

From these observations, Ziman concluded that science had arrived at a new stage in its history that he refers to as "post-academic science".[16] In this period, the complexity of research problems and the

---

[15] Ziman, *Prometheus Bound*, pp. 10–11, 126, 23–26, 44, 60, 222–231, 272, 38.

[16] John Ziman, "Post-Academic Science: Constructing Knowledge with Networks and Norms", *Science Studies* 9 (1996), pp. 67–80.

increasing costs of scientific equipment lead to an increasing degree of collectivization. Disciplinary boundaries are blurred. Research is no longer a self-governing system as the problems of research are also set by teams of various experts rather than individual scientists. Ziman, like Ravetz, draws attention to the changing role of the scientists' ethos, in particular to the fact that the Mertonian norms have become obsolete.

Ziman's widely discussed post-academic science differs little from his concept of steady state science: when science arrives at a steady state it becomes post-academic. Ironically, he has focused on state-supported research conducted for the most part in "academia", with regard to which he established that it went through a thorough modification that made it post-academic. Meanwhile, he has largely neglected the fast-growing area of industrial research.[17]

Mode 2

A team of researchers working in collaboration with each other produced an extensively debated and cited theory, called Mode 2, for describing the features of current science.[18] This approach could also be considered complementary to the view of post-academic science as expressed by Ziman: "Indeed, the Mode 2 research that is typical of post-academic science is focused sharply on problems that arise in the context of application."[19]

In terms of the theory of industrialized science, Mode 2 is in fact knowledge production. While the research group referred to the traditional form of science as Mode 1, the changed form they called Mode 2. Science working in Mode 1 generally operates in centrally ruled universities that are organized according to the logic of disciplinary structures. Research is based on individual creativity. The ambitions and curiosity of individual researchers provide the driving force for disciplinary progress. Quality control is also in the hands of individuals, while the scientific community, the collective part, remains hidden behind the

---

[17] Ziman published his most recent analyses in his book: John Ziman, *Real Science: What It Is, and What It Means*, Oxford: Oxford University Press, 2000.

[18] Michael Gibbons, Camille Limoges, Helga Nowotny, Simon Schwartzman, Peter Scott, and Martin Trow, *The New Production of Knowledge: The Dynamics of Science and Research in Contemporary Societies*, London: Sage Publications, 1994.

[19] See John Ziman's inaugural address given at Zurich: "Scientific Guest of the Collegium Helveticum in the Winter Term 2001/2002", http://www.collegium.ethz.ch/guest/former_guests/john_ziman.en.html.

consensual aspect of the operations. Traditionally, Mode 1 has been considered as being identical with science in the areas of production, legitimation and diffusion of knowledge.[20]

According to the authors, the growth of Mode 1 science has been accompanied by an inner differentiation of disciplines into sub-disciplines. This ramification into a complex structure of networks resulted in a new mode of knowledge production. Mode 2 science, although it does not eliminate the Mode 1 work, has recently become the dominant form of knowledge production.

The main attributes of Mode 2 have been summarized in the following five points:

First, knowledge production is carried out in the context of application. This means that knowledge is produced to satisfy particular interests whether they are industrial, governmental or societal. The distinction between pure and applied science disappears. While "Mode 1 is disciplinary-based and carries a distinction between what is fundamental and what is applied", Mode 2 "is characterized by a constant flow between the fundamental and applied". Consequently, Mode 2 rejects the two-step logic prevalent in Mode 1 that connects basic and applied science. In the first step of this logic, basic research (which is motivated either by disciplinary requirements or the curiosity of the individual researcher) gathers knowledge on nature. In the second, other researchers working in a different institutional framework apply this knowledge to specific cases defined by the users. In Mode 2, the goal of research is defined by practical considerations; when some elements of knowledge on nature are missing, they are produced in the framework of the same project without the two-step logic of Mode 1.

Secondly, knowledge production is transdisciplinary. It has a diverse range of specialists working in the teams. The constitution of the teams depends on the complexity of the problems to be solved. Since Mode 2 research is a problem-solving instrument for which the problem is generated in the context of application and not developed first in pure science, the problems are not set within the boundaries of one discipline. Consequently, the knowledge produced by Mode 2 science has no disciplinary character either. Transdisciplinary knowledge develops its own theoretical structures, methods, disregarding the existing disciplinary network. The researchers communicate their results immediately after they have achieved them without the special procedures of diffusion through journals and books as in the case of disciplinary knowledge

---

[20] Gibbons et al., *op. cit.*, pp. 2–3.

production. Transdisciplinarity makes research dynamic. As its adherents think, Mode 2 science is a problem solving capacity on the move. A succession of problem contexts interacts with the knowledge production and this succession transgresses the disciplinary boundaries.

Mode 2 eliminates the disciplinary borders not because it aims at unifying science; rather it supposes that all kinds of unification are a senseless effort. "The development of science", the authors wrote, "has now reached a stage where many scientists lost interest in search for first principles. They believe that the natural world is too complex an entity to fall under a unitary description that is both comprehensive and useful, in the sense of being able to guide further research."

Third, from an organizational point of view, Mode 2 is heterogeneous and its organization is diverse. This means that the sites of knowledge production are no longer only at universities but also in research institutes, industrial laboratories, government agencies, consultancies and other institutions. The sites constitute networks as they are linked together by formal and informal communication. Studies go through a process of differentiation into finer and finer specialties, while knowledge production moves into new societal contexts.

Fourth, the new mode of knowledge production is characterized by social accountability and reflexivity. Science in Mode 2 is aware of the growing concern about social issues such as environment, health, communication, privacy and others. Therefore, in the research teams scientists, engineers, doctors and economists work together with philosophers, anthropologists, sociologists, librarians, lawyers, etc. Their task is to assure reflexivity of the project in socially sensitive matters.

Fifth, quality control in Mode 2 science is fundamentally different from that in traditional science. While in Mode 1 the assessment of quality is carried out by individuals through peer reviews, in Mode 2 it is largely institutionalized. The quality of research is assessed by its competitive advantages in the market, social acceptance, cost effectivity and similar criteria.

In Mode 2, scientific creativity becomes a group phenomenon. The groups rather employ experts with special knowledge in narrow fields than great scientists with broad disciplinary knowledge. Mode 2 snatches knowledge production from the academic framework and places it into broader institutional organizations. Meanwhile, it converts the researchers into entrepreneurs: "By adopting strategic approach to their careers, many scientists have become entrepreneurs and have had to loosen their disciplinary affiliations while contributing to the blurring of subject boundaries." Researchers develop new career patterns characterized by enhanced mobility. Regulated by the demand of their expertise, they often jump from one laboratory to another and from one country or continent to another.

In Mode 1, paradigm rules research. The term *paradigm*, as the authors expressed, "denotes a way of seeing things, of defining and giving priority to certain problem sets." A paradigm is the result of a particular organizational pattern. On the other hand, when practicing Mode 2, scientists leave the rule of paradigm. They behave as realists, believing that "some kind of reality exists out there, with which they have established a suitable form of communication not only verbally or conceptually, but in a robust, technical sense as well."

Because knowledge production in Mode 2 is carried out in different sites, networking and communication between the team members and between the various teams is vitally important. The internet and mobile phones can be considered as the most effective technical apparatuses of mobility between the sites. This is why the authors have said that "the computer itself has become the new and powerful tool in science which generates a new language and images". Then, they continue: "Through the inclusion of images and other modes of representing data, an entirely artificial world of representation continues to be created, attesting to the creativity of these new forms of scientific communication."[21]

Triple Helix

In the late 1990s Henry Etzkowitz and Loet Leydesdorff worked out a new science policy approach that has gained increasing popularity.[22] Their model is in stark contrast to many of the points in the above-examined theories. A distinctive feature of this new approach is that it relies on the results of research done on a broad international sample and, to some extent, it provides a mathematical model.

Etzkowitz and Leydesdorff believe that the work of current science can be described by the communication between three main actors: university, industry, and government. This is why the model is referred to as the triple helix. The relationship between the three actors can be investigated under different conditions resulting in three main forms (I, II, and III) of the model. The spheres of university, industry, and government are interwoven. The actual state of their interactions and their

---

[21] Gibbons et al., *op. cit.*, pp. 3–8, 19, 23, 22, 42, 39.
[22] Henry Etzkowitz and Loet Leydesdorff (eds.), *Universities and the Global Knowledge Economy: A Triple Helix of University–Industry–Government Relations*, London: Cassell, 1997.

adjustment to each other defines a particular system of science. ("Negotiations and translations at the interfaces induce adaptation mechanisms in the institutional arrangements."[23]) If only two partners interact, their relationship may stabilize into a rigid form. The interrelationship between three partners, however, creates a spiral movement for the progress of the whole system and for the "co-evolution" of each partner. This model focuses on the roles of institutional partners. Their spheres, though independent, overlap and are continuously shaping and reshaping each other.

The triple helix model is based on the principle of "endless transition". This is a result of complex dynamics, similar to market mechanisms, working between the three partners. The dynamics are influenced by market forces, political power, institutional control, social movements and technological requirements. The partners continuously redefine their own roles and also the meanings of the fundamental terms used for designing the projects, such as "market" or "industry". Trilateral networks and hybrid organizations are created at the intersection of the institutional spheres that can handle new kinds of projects.

According to the supporters of the triple helix theory, the idea of Mode 2 research and, with it, the concept of "post-academic science" are erroneous.[24] Etzkowitz and Leydesdorff think that the phenomena that are usually attributed to Mode 2 production of knowledge actually preceded Mode 1 production and not vice versa. "The so-called Mode 2 is not new", they wrote, "it is the original format of science before its academic institutionalization in the 19th century."[25] The authors' argument begins with the observation that networking has always been an indispensable component of scientific activity. They recall the early emergence of the "context of application" in mining and navigation in the seventeenth century or later in the German pharmaceutical industry. Etzkowitz and Leydesdorff accept that the peer review system has shown some signs of a crisis. However, they observe that it broke down under the circumstances of increasing competition for research funds, while within a moderate level of competition the peer review works satisfactorily. Finally, instead of the reign of transdisciplinarity, they see newly

---

[23] Henry Etzkowitz and Loet Leydesdorff, "The Triple Helix: An Evolutionary Model of Innovations", *Research Policy* 29 (2000), 2, pp. 243–255.

[24] Henry Etzkowitz and Loet Leydesdorff, "The Dynamics of Innovation: From National Systems and 'Mode 2' to a Triple Helix of University–Industry–Government Relations", *Research Policy* 29 (2000), 2, pp. 109–123.

[25] *Ibid.*, p. 116.

created disciplines, such as computer science or material science, that have recently arisen through the syntheses of practical and theoretical interests.

The universities (i.e., academia) with their basic structure and ethos remain the core sites of these new disciplines. According to the triple helix approach, the most recent development in science has proven that the geographical site of knowledge production, whether it is a university or an industrial laboratory, has ceased to play a significant role. In the era of mobile phones and the internet, the flow of information between the sites goes so smoothly that the connection between the sites where knowledge is produced and those where knowledge is utilized does not create any problems. The university's comparative advantage consists in the presence of students. Students are potential inventors, and their "flow-through" makes the universities dynamic as opposed to more static research institutes.

Accordingly, the supporters of the triple helix theory think that, instead of a post-academic period, we witness a "second academic revolution", that has been going on since World War Two, but more visibly since the end of the Cold War. They said: "The university has been transformed from a teaching institution into one which combines teaching with research, a revolution that is still ongoing, not only in the USA, but in many other countries. There is a tension between the two activities but nevertheless they coexist in a more or less compatible relationship with each other because it has been found to be both more productive and cost effective to combine the two functions." [26]

In this approach, the most important site of knowledge production, the university, goes through an important change. It becomes entrepreneurial. This means, on the one hand, that the university (academia) cannot work without the other two factors of the triple helix because in its teaching and research activity, industry and government play the role of an investor. The other side of entrepreneurship is that it starts its own spin-off companies. Therefore, the ownership of knowledge, the production of patents and non-public knowledge that can be sold on the market becomes vitally important to academia. Patenting is considered a form of publication, requiring more disclosure of the technical details than an academic paper. On the other hand, universities purchase a lot from industry, leading to a special trade balance between the two sectors.

---

[26] *Ibid.*, p. 118.

Big Science in the New Communications Era

Both "Mode 2" and "post-academic" descriptions of science emphasize that science has been totally absorbed by the market economy. It became part of the industry and has no choice but conduct itself as such: cost-effectiveness grew to be as important as the trade secret. As a consequence of this change, doing science is not a pure intellectual activity driven by desire for knowledge for its own sake, the dividing line between basic and applied science has been blurred and the knowledge obtained is not public property any more. Science has abandoned its quest for a unified picture of reality and is pursued by isolated teams carrying out strictly expedient projects. The supporters of this view tend to speak indiscriminately about "funding agencies" financing scientific research and deciding on its results. It may, however, be useful to distinguish between the types of fund providing organizations.

It stands to reason that different sponsors have different interests and they set up diverse demands. The results of military research are naturally kept secret and (if at all) they become public knowledge only with a substantial delay. The status of industrial research is a bit more complicated. Evidently, there are serious interests causing information retention; this, however, is not synonymous with a complete loss from a scientific point of view. Scientific knowledge resulting from industry-funded research might be made secret as long as the practical invention based on it is finished. After that, however, it has to be revealed in the application for a patent. In most countries, to obtain a patent entails that the information the invention is based on must be disclosed so as to enable others to use and remake it. Investors having financed the research do not need exclusive rights. What they usually want is to ensure that only they can make financial benefit from the practically useful invention based on the results of scientific research. Patent was introduced just to avoid secrecy. If inventions are patented there is no need to conceal the scientific knowledge in the background.

Large-Scale Science – Big Science

The historical fact that science has developed into a large-scale enterprise has an important consequence with regard to its basic attitude. Science is modeled after the classical market economy: there is a fierce competition for financial resources, publication opportunities and prestige. It is primarily this fiercely competitive character of science that fosters isolation of the research groups: results, methods and data are kept secret; rivals are possibly kept away from vital information and opportunities. Competition for financial funds, prestige and opportunities determine the relationships of relatively small groups. As a consequence of competitive organization, the basic unit of exchange between groups is the relatively well-processed information, i.e. the established, elaborated, published and patented result. The most characteristic attribute of communication between closed groups is that it takes place for the most part subsequently, and is about finished or half-finished research. Data gathering and processing as well as the creation of conceptual tools, launching of hypotheses, testing and elaboration of theories are all worked out in relative isolation and published only when completed. In line with the usual strategy of competition people work independently, even in secrecy, and only the end products of isolated knowledge-producing firms come to the market and start to compete with or reflect on each other. This social setting of knowledge production reinforces the disintegrative and relativizing tendency of thinking. Science falls apart into "scientific schools" or paradigms cultivating distinct, even incommensurable traditions. Relativism stems from the lack of cooperation and communication in the course of work. Isolated communities develop particular practices and conceptual tools, form various consensuses and these differences cannot be dissolved by attempts at subsequent conviction. Diversity of truth, meaning, rightness, values etc. is consequent on closeness and separation. Indeed, besides Mode 1 relativism reflects also Mode 2 operation of science.

In the literature spawned by relativists, the non-relativist position is often called "absolutist" claiming dogmatic infallibility, based on an ethereal logic and leaving historical and sociological facts out of consideration. In the concluding part of our essay we intend to outline a non-relativist picture of science, which is based on historical and sociological considerations (namely recent developments and contemporary changes in the sociological setting of Big Science) and still points to the opposite direction.

Data-Pressure

The projects of Big Science aim at disclosing the fundamental components of reality. They investigate the smallest and the largest. This work requires very large, extremely expensive, purpose-built instruments (accelerators, telescopes etc.) and a huge staff consisting of first-rate scientists, computer experts, engineers, technicians, managers and scores of other people. Although Big Science is a kind of large-scale science, the extraordinary infrastructure must be regarded as a distinguishing feature. It is just the enormous facilities Big Science requires that create a new large-scale phenomenon that was unknown before. Since accountability and cost-effectiveness are regarded as decisive factors, investors seek to make the most of the instruments before they become outdated. That is one of the reasons big instruments have to run round the clock. The other reason comes from the very nature of Big Scientific investigations: satellites orbit the earth and take photos day and night, telescopes send pictures without interruption, the beam in the accelerator cannot be switched on and off at will. The consequence of this constant flow is an explosion of data appearing on CDs, floppies, photos, radiographs and other recording tools.

In order to see what this "data-explosion" means in practice, let us have a quick look at one single experiment: the so-called "BaBar" experiment (executed by Stanford Linear Accelerator Center, SLAC) is a collaboration of 600 physicists from 9 nations. The observation of the collisions of subatomic particles 24 hours a day produces industrial quantities of scientific data. The database grows with 500 Gigabytes a day and from 1999 to the beginning of April 2002 it reached 500,000 Gigabytes. If we wanted to put this quantity of information into print it would take approximately 1 billion books, nearly 60 times the number of books in the Library of Congress.[27] This huge amount of information is almost impossible to manage. Even simple storage and organization is a serious job for the group of experts established especially for this task. Scientific analysis is, however, another and incomparably more complicated mission. The traditional researcher cannot do anything with 500 GB/day of information. If it is stored in printed form it is physically impossible to be processed, to find its relevant points, to generalize etc. Indeed, even if these data are stored on powerful computers equipped with effective searching capabilities it is unimaginable that a traditional scientific community (max. 100 researchers) would be able to keep up with such a rate of data-production.

That is where economic considerations play an important role again. Building and running huge equipment, funding projects designed to gather empirical data costs enormous amounts. If, however, data are not processed, the whole effort is rendered meaningless. Put in plain economic terms it becomes an absurdity. That is why this avalanche of data exerts an irresistible pressure on the organization of Big Science. Data processing needs highly qualified, not rarely first-rate scientists, and

---

[27] See the SLAC press release of April 12, 2002, http://www.slac.stanford.edu.

plenty of them – the separation and secrecy will, hence, lead to the loss of financial and intellectual investment. The only way out is to give up the old competition and open up the databases. Briefly, sheer economic considerations, simple quantity of experimental and observational data will force scientific institutions to cooperate, to make their data available to scientists working for other universities. The necessity of processing the data gained makes concentration of the intellectual capacities unavoidable. This is clearly shown by the fact that research projects in Big Science are most often carried out by several universities in cooperation with each other. In addition to this, data are frequently made available to other researchers as well. No matter whether they are free or a modest fee is charged for using them, the point is that a large scientific community can have access to the data gathered.

This state of affairs has a serious consequence for relativism. One of the longest debates of twentieth-century philosophy of science has been about the relationship between empirical and theoretical levels of science. The question is whether scientists use theory-neutral observational and experimental data, whether they can finally justify or refute their theories by experiences. The relativist answer is "no" because perception is not neutral and separated scientific traditions develop diverse conceptual schemes that select, cut up and organize empirical experience in different, even incommensurable ways. Consequently, each tradition, scientific school or paradigm can rely on its own empirical background; there is no common experiential level that would be able to fulfill a universal epistemological task. In Big Science, however, basic data are produced by huge instruments and then shared by different communities. Big facilities provide basic data that are the same for everybody dealing with science. No matter what scientific tradition or school somebody belongs to, they have no choice but use either the common or none empirical raw material. In this sense, data provided by the basic research of Big Science is universal in spite of the fact that they are not neutral. The huge instruments of Big Science embody basic theories and the results produced by them inherit the theoretical assumptions of the inventors and builders of these facilities. Still, the simple fact that there is equipment producing data for every scientist splits science into two parts. There is a fundamental level that is common to everybody and a secondary level that comes into play by the interpretation of fundamental data. Empirical data produced at the fundamental level might be not neutral but still they are universal, the same for every group irrespective of their secondary level theories, interpretations, concepts, commitments, style or whatever. Although these data are admittedly not neutral in an absolute sense, as they are independent of the assumptions of the secondary-level theories they may still be regarded as quasi-neutral compared to them. Thus fundamental level empirical data provide a common basis for the rational tests and arguments, in this way saving us from the excesses of theoretical and conceptual relativism. Though usually we take perceptual relativism as a consequence of conceptual differences, here we see the opposite: the common empirical data makes possible rational justification or refutation and restores some universal rationality in thinking. Anti-relativism, we could say, is a practical consequence and not a stance based on theoretical arguments.

The quasi-neutral status of empirical data certainly does not ensure that the secondary-level theories built on them are true in an absolute sense. The question of relativism, however, should not be mixed with that of realism. Obviously, if we were able to construct theories that would be true and this could be proven to everyone, then that would abolish relativism. The opposite, however, does not hold. The lack of realism does not entail relativism - at least in the case of simultaneously existing theories. One may assume that data provided by contemporary fundamental-level science can become irrelevant or unscientific in the future and a completely different science comes into being. This kind of historical relativism, however, is independent even of a mild synchronic relativism not to mention an "anything goes"-type anarchism. We may accept and apply one common conceptual scheme and one universally accepted theory even if we are aware of their historically temporal nature. This possibility is offered by the separation of a fundamental, common data-producing level of science. Common empirical data make rational justification or refutation of theories possible and restore a measure of universal rationality in thinking.

Fundamental Science as a "Public Service"

The epistemological recognition that in Big Science we can have a common and quasi-neutral empirical basis has practical consequences too. Sheer quantity of data, we have seen, can have a serious effect on how scientific activity is organized in a society. The substitution of cooperation for wild competition at the basic level is, however, not all. Even the fact that the instruments used and experiments executed by Big Science are very expensive has its epistemological consequences. In the Human Genome Project, for instance, research was carried out by a number of different institutions of 18 countries whose representatives held International Strategy Meetings where they agreed that the results would be made available on the World Wide Web. One of the most important principles endorsed was the rapid data release and free public access to the primary genomic sequence. "Rapid release" was rendered concrete as "assemblies greater than 1 Kb would be released automatically on a daily basis".[28]

The intention behind this generous decision was that the financing states wanted to foster innovative research, to catalyze the biotechnology industry and assist the development of new medical applications. The policy of making the results of the state-financed Big Science available divides the previously unitary process of research into separate stages:

- production of primary data (sequences of DNA),
- further research is based on primary data (individual genes, gene families),
- development of particular goods (medicaments).

Irrespective of the profit private firms can make from such information, financing of the whole project is aimed at the public sector. This financial system was meant as a sort of indirect assistance. The states spent taxpayers' money on basic research without compensation: scientific results were placed at the medical firms' disposal free of charge. This way they promoted the production of medicaments. When there is a lack of state-assistance the necessary basic research might never or only with a significant delay be completed. Even if the pharmaceutical factories had undertaken these reseach tasks at their own cost, taxpayers would have had to repay it in the form of considerably higher prices for the medication. In this "public service" scheme, instead of subsidizing partial applied research projects, governments facilitate the necessary basic research, and its results become public knowledge. In this way they are able to support the taxpayers. In the research cycle, basic research is completed as a kind of public service for the benefit of society as a whole.

This example demonstrates that although its costs are enormous, the results of Big Science are not necessarily kept secret. On the contrary, just because its costs are so high, if we want the usable results of applied research, basic research should be financed by the government. The restoration and maintenance of the dividing line between basic and applied research might sometimes be useful both from an epistemological and a social point of view. Although the description of the work of

---

[28] Cf. http://www.ornl.gov/TechResources/Human_Genome/home.html.

science as modeled after the classical market economy is in several respects right, still, when we take into consideration examples such as the Human Genome Project it seems an exaggeration that science is almost exclusively ruled by interests and market or political forces, that is, that science is just an enterprise producing and selling practically useful knowledge. Competition does often cause isolation and secrecy, but it is characteristic rather of Little Science.

This, of course, does not mean that the dividing line between public and secret knowledge is completely wiped away. Regarding its secrecy knowledge is distributed roughly into three classes:

- the results of military research are naturally kept secret and (if at all) they become public knowledge only after a substantial delay
- knowledge produced in industrial laboratories falls somewhere in between: it is patented, i.e. others are excluded from using and selling the invention for a limited term but the condition of patenting is that it must be fully disclosed
- the results of government-financed Big Scientific research projects are often regarded as public, or if not, they are available for a modest price for scientific, and even industrial laboratories.

Not only the steps of scientific research, but the scientific communities that take them are separated as well. This again presents a situation analogous to that of data-pressure: there is a first line of researchers in Big Science who produce basic data that are universal for those in the second line, at least in the sense they are independent of the second-level theories that are based on them. In this respect is Big Science special when compared to large-scale science in general. Instead of the general competition dominating steady-state large-scale science, for practical reasons, Big Science makes some form of cooperation epistemologically possible and socially necessary.

External Mind

Data-pressure and public usefulness make only the *necessity* of changing competition to collaboration in Big Science manifest. There is, however, a technical condition that makes this new organization *possible* and it is the World Wide Web.

Costs of instruments used by Big Science are describable only in astronomical figures. Consequently, it is hopeless for single universities or even countries on their own, to try to build an accelerator. In recent years the U.S. has concentrated its financial and intellectual capacities on the Fermilab while European countries have operated CERN. Nowadays governments are thinking about the possibility of establishing one intercontinental accelerator (Superconducting Supercollider) that would be used by almost every high-energy physicist in the world. If this plan will be realized (and sooner or later it probably will), the most convenient or even the only way of data-processing will be the online connection among scientists sitting in their offices in faraway cities of the world. Data will not only flash on the monitors of the accelerator's controlling room, but simultaneously on university screens all over the world. In fact, it will not be a revolution from the blue. In astrophysics, the evolution of common instruments has already been in process for a considerable period of time. "Large, elaborate, expensive telescopes, run by international consortia, are sited on high mountains in isolated corners of the globe. But the research scientists in the numerous university groups that study the heavens through these instruments do not have to travel half way round the earth to make their observations. Advanced communication links enable them to do their research by remote control."[29]

There would, however, be a real novelty: as opposed to the data banks available on the internet, such cooperation would involve the scientists into the process of research. Upon flashing the new measurements or the result of the experiment they could offer a first interpretation and could then start to discuss the next step to be taken. That is a tremendous change in making science. The internet not only acts as a usual means of communication. Indeed, "means of communication" is not the proper name. There is no "communication" among these scientists in the old sense that elaborated theories or ready-made ideas would be transported from one place to another. There is one single medium, we should rather say, in which experiences and theoretical reflections turn up, become conscious, get supported or refused. The internet provides an intellectual environment populated with ideas and empirical material, a medium in which thinking and acquisition of knowledge is taking place. That is why Joshua Meyrowitz says that the internet is not simply a very effective means of communication, but rather a new environment for thinking.[30] Meyrowitz claims that the electronic medium differs physically, psychologically and socially from print media and

---

[29] John Ziman, *Prometheus Bound*, pp. 55–56.

[30] Joshua Meyrowitz, "Shifting Worlds of Strangers: Medium Theory and Changes in 'Them' Versus 'Us'", *Sociological Inquiry*, vol. 67, no. 1, February 1997.

face-to-face interaction as well. As he puts it, media are not functioning as channels for conveying information, but to provide a social context.

At a certain stage of its development human culture created an external system of memory[31] (namely writing, libraries etc.) and this creation has significantly transformed human thinking. Now we seem to have reached another stage in this development. The stage when an external mind comes into being. This mind is both different and similar to our good old human mind. It is different, because it is essentially collective. And, as far as it can already be seen, it is similar in several respects. Thinking is a process in which rough ideas occur, thoughts are completed, developed further, corrected and varied, new points of view are added, statements refuted and reinforced. If there is a communion of several scientists in the course of research the repository of ideas, consequently the chance of association or completion, is incomparably greater, thinking is naturally more effective. From the point of view of scientific thinking the internet's essential contribution is not that it transfers theories and hypotheses created in isolation, but that it brings about collective thinking, mental cooperation. There are evident signs that scientific research is becoming communal. Investigating the role of digital libraries in scientific research, Michael Lesk presents statistics showing that the number of papers written by several authors working for different universities radically increased in the nineties.[32] Lubanski and Matthew who examined the impact of e-mail on science found already in 1998 such multi-authored papers whose authors had never met in person.[33]

Conclusion

In the light of the peculiar features of Big Science it may come as no surprise that some people speak about the obsolescence of Diana Crane's "invisible college" as an informal communicational network. "Invisible college" has developed, been extended and moved to cyberspace. In John Gresham's opinion the unrestricted communicational opportunities provided by the internet have extended the "invisible college" so radi-

---

[31] Cf. Merlin Donald, *Origins of the Modern Mind*, Cambridge, MA: Harvard University Press, 1991.

[32] Michael Lesk, „Digital Libraries. A Unifying or Distributing Force?", in R. Ekman and R. Q. Quandt (eds.), *Technology and Scholarly Communication*, Berkeley: University of California Press, 1999, pp. 360–61.

[33] A. Lubanski and L. Matthew, "Socio-economic Impact of the Internet in the Academic Research Environment", http://www.sosig.ac.uk/iriss/papers/paper18.htm.

cally that the differences between scientific "centers" and "peripheries" have been wiped away, at least the traditional phase delay of the scientists working on peripheries has been radically diminished.[34] Referring to the Los Alamos preprint archive, Dr. Susskind from Stanford University says that the whole scientific world has turned into one single seminar room by now. For the time being we experience that first-rate physicists browse the papers displayed on this site just like undergraduates. The researchers who profit from it in the highest degree are those who could not (or could only with a heavy delay) get the expensive hard-copy physical journals, thus losing the chance to contribute to the discussions going on in the first line of physics about the most recent questions.[35]

All those who want to make use of the basic empirical data produced by Big Science, who want to get the information on the internet and want to contribute to the international conversation are enforced to use a common language, to apply universally understandable concepts and standards. Anti-relativism, we could say, is a practical consequence and not a stance based on theoretical arguments. Having one common source of data and thinking together in the same mental environment, scientists are induced to take a cooperative strategy. While competitive practice invites "strategic rationality": means-ends calculation and secrecy, cooperative practice supports Habermas' "communicative rationality" aiming at a common understanding of our common world. The worldwide medium of scientific communication counteracts the fragmentation of reason caused by the existence of different scientific schools and traditions and decreases the chance of the development of radically different (not to mention "incommensurable") conceptual schemes, methodological norms and empirical bases. Referring to these epistemological and communicational developments concerning Big Science we feel entitled to speak about a new period of scientific thinking.

---

[34] J. L. Gresham, Jr., "From Invisible College to Cyberspace College: Computer Conferencing and the Transformation of Informal Scholarly Communication Networks", in *Interpersonal Computing and Technology: An Electronic Journal for the 21st Century*, vol. 2, no. 4, pp. 37–52 (http://helsinki.fi/science/optek/1994/n4/ gresham.txt).

[35] J. Glanz, "Web Archive Opens a New Realm of Research", *The New York Times*, May 1, 2001, http://www.nytimes.com/2001/05/01/college/01ARCH.html.

M. Sükösd – E. Dányi: M-Politics
in the Making

SMS and E-mail in the 2002
Hungarian Election Campaign

Introduction

The public sphere exists and functions, for the most part, within the institutional framework of the communications media. Accordingly, changes in media technology affect the structure of the public sphere as well as democratic institutions themselves. The widespread use of new communication technologies like the internet and cellular phones are changing the political communication of democratic systems – as did radio and television a few decades ago.

According to the major approaches in the field, new communication technologies can be seen as having different roles in the transformation of the communication patterns of democratic regimes. On the one hand, the optimistic approach focuses on technologies that make decentralized and interactive communication possible.[1] Cyber-optimists foresee a radical change in the structure of political communication established in the 20th centrury, the loss of importance of one-way communication that characterizes traditional mass media (television, radio, press) as well as a major reform of democratic political institutions, even the increasing role of direct democracy.

On the other hand, the realist approach assumes that the use of new technologies can make existing democratic institutions better, stronger, more efficient and transparent. The use of new communication technologies can thus support a higher quality of repersantative democracy.[2]

---

[1] Nicholas Negroponte, *Being Digital*, New York: Knopf, 1995; Pierre Lévy, *Collective Intelligence: Mankind's Emerging World in Cyberspace*, New York: Plenum, 1997.

[2] Stephen Coleman, "E-Politics: Democracy or Marketing?", *Voxpolitics.com*, http://www.voxpolitics.com/news/voxfpub/story266.shtml, 2001; Pippa Norris, *Digital Divide? Civic Engagement, Information Poverty and the Internet in Democratic Societie*s, New York: Cambridge University Press, 2001. – Cyber-pessimists, opposing both optimists and realists, emphasize inherent dangers in the use of new communications media. They suggest that the internet may reinforce and deepen existing global and social inequalities, and contribute to alienation. Cf. Norman H. Nie and Lutz Erbring, *Internet and Society*, Stan-

Whether it is the optimistic or the realist approach that we embrace, information technologies could definitely play an important part in strengthening the institutions of democratic government and civil society. A decentralized global communication network can help the international activity of civil organizations with similar interests; help citizens and journalists to gain access to official documents and information easier and faster; parties and other political organizations can communicate more effectively with their members, supporters, and the undecided voters.

In this paper we will analyze the changes in political communication, caused by the mass use of new media, focusing on the 2002 Hungarian parliamentary election campaign. We will put emphasis on the use of interactive communication methods – namely e-mail and SMS. We would like to answer the following questions:

1. How can one differentiate between two functions of online media: online content provision and interactive communication techniques?
2. How and toward what goals did parties and their supporters use these interactive techniques during the 2002 election campaign? Based on this experience, what kind of theoretical concept can we develop to understand and analyze the interactive political campaign?
3. How could we evaluate interactive political communication from the normative perpective of the concept of the public sphere?[3]

Content Provision versus Interactivity

Postmodern Campaign Techniques

The distinction made by Norris between pre-modern, modern and postmodern campaign techniques, based on examples of Western Euro-

---

ford Institute for the Quantitative Study of Society, 2000, http://www.stanford.edu/group/siqss/Press_Release/internetStudy.html; Robert D. Putnam, *Bowling Alone*, New York: Free Press, 2000. Cyber-pessimists claim that those enjoying high positions in information networks (the *information-have*) will even increase their lead by the use of new communications technology – putting *the information-have-not* into a sustained disadvantaged position.

[3] Cf. Jürgen Habermas, *The Structural Transformation of the Public Sphere: An Inquiry into a Category of Bourgeois Society*, Cambridge, MA: MIT Press, 1999.

[4] Pippa Norris, "Political Communications and Democratic Politics", in John Bartle and Dylan Griffiths (eds.), *Political Communications Transformed: From Morrison to Mandelson*, Basingstoke: Macmillan, 2000.

pean and American election campaign history,[4] may provide a good starting point for understanding the relevance of interactive media in current election campaigns. In the 19th century, *pre-modern* campaigns were based on personal interaction between candidates and potential voters. The role of party newspapers gradually increased, but campaign events and rallies were organized occasionally. In the 1920's, radio addresses started to dominate over personal campaigns, but partisan newspapers remained the most important channels of political communication. Specific voter groups held close ties to their preferred parties.

Modern campaigns (from the late 1950's to the end of the 1980's) were characterized by centralized press activity on the national level. Campaign teams included party leaders, press officers, a few independent advisers and some public opinion experts. Election campaigns were built around well-planned political events. The most important goal became setting the agenda for the media. In contrast to former traditions, the campaigns of different parties became more similar in terms of the tools they used.

With this (and partly due to this), voters' party affiliation declined. In the mid-1990's *postmodern* campaigns started to dominate elections. Marketing techniques and public opinion polls became main elements of the parties' proactive communication strategies. Professional communication advisers and advertising experts today play just as important a part in campaign planning as politicians themselves. Creating a political strategy thus already requires assessing the marketing aspects of political messages and the agenda itself. The multimedia era, the use of new communication technologies have created a very complex relationship between parties, the media and the public. Alongside modern mass campaign tools, personal interaction has also reappeared in postmodern campaigns. However, in the age of new communication technologies, the role of direct, personal contact of pre-modern campaigns has been taken over by technology mediated communication, by the use of the internet and cellular phones.

The 2002 parliamentary elections were the first in Hungarian history when new communication technologies played a significant part.[5] Politi-

---

[5] This was shown by the fact that the most popular internet portals (those with own political news services) recorded significant increases in traffic during the election campaign. News portals had a larger audience than most of the printed media. According to Hungarian Net market analyst Medián WebAudit, "due to the exceptionally high interest in the elections, Hungarian news service providers recorded outstanding traffic.

cal parties used their websites differently in their campaigns; however, the rules and traditions of offline campaigns seldom seemed to change in an online environment. Websites were basically used as a new outlet of traditional party papers. Neither were small parties able to take advantage of the new technology in increasing their popularity, nor could the larger parties that had major resources and rich websites make better use of their sites than as large bulletin boards.[6]

Online content provision is difficult and risky for political parties. Quality content is expensive to produce, the target group is relatively hard to define and reach (especially in countries with low internet penetration), and effectiveness is difficult to measure. And, most importantly, one-way content provision cannot take advantage of the interaction of users, and the political capital that lies in active, multilateral network communication.[7] However, before one could get the feeling that the use of information technology would not influence traditional campaign strategies, in the Hungarian elections interpersonal communication tools such as e-mail and SMS came to the forefront between the two rounds of the elections (April 7 and 21, respectively). The growth of SMS traffic volume is shown by the sheer numbers. According to our estimates, cell phone users sent around 4-5 million text messages daily between the two rounds of the election, roughly a 20 percent increase over average non-election periods.[8] This increase in traffic, however, is unusual only because it was a product of political activity. Otherwise it cannot be regarded as exceptionally high, as similar numbers can be found on several other occasions during the year, such as Mothers' Day

---

The number of downloads recorded by the news portal Origo had almost reached a previously unthinkable 4 million in the days before the elections, and the 5.1 million downloads and over 680 000 visitors on the day after the first round will doubtless become a long-standing record in Hungarian internet history." ("Kimagasló látogatottság a választások idején", Medián WebAudit, 2002, http://webaudit.hu/.) Hungary's population is ca. 10 million.

[6] Endre Dányi, "A faliújság visszaszól. Politikai kommunikáció és kampány az Interneten", *Médiakutató*, 7, Summer 2002.

[7] Endre Dányi and Miklós Sükösd, "szavazzram.hu – Párthonlapok a választási kampányban", *Népszabadság*, March 25, 2002.

[8] According to the sources of Hungarian daily *Magyar Hírlap*, SMS-traffic between the two rounds grew 20–30 percent (*Magyar Hírlap*, April 16, 2002). Between the two rounds of the elections the estimation of 4-5 million SMS daily is realistic. Hírközlési Felügyelet (Communications Authority of Hungary – http://www.hif.hu) reported 5,361,746 mobile phone users (52.6% of the population) in March 2002.

or Valentine's Day. The reason for such a spectacular SMS- and e-mail-campaign as between the two rounds was the fact that this time it was not only young people who took part in sending and receiving electronic messages. Those mobile phone and internet users who never or very rarely write SMS or e-mail, also joined campaign-related electronic political communication.

Centralized Communication: Party Websites in the Campaign

As for the internet, as a postmodern campaign tool, in the past years many Western politicians and parties have realized that their websites offer a perfect channel for one-to-many communication, that is, for key political players to introduce themselves. This process was greatly enhanced by the qualities of graphic interface on the internet.[9] Hence, the worldwide web fits well into the traditional campaign strategies of political parties. Coleman and Hall analyzed the internet strategies of political parties in the 2001 election campaign in Britain.[10] In their study they listed four reasons why it is worth for parties to maintain a website:

• *Multimedia* – the internet offers the capacity to combine the visual, audio, print and video qualities of other media, and can distribute text via e-mail for much less than the price of a postal mail-out.
• *Personalisation* – the internet provides targeted information at any level of depth for individuals and interest groups; it can adapt delivery according to users' preferences via personalisation of content, e-mail and "narrowcasting".
• *Interactivity* – the internet is dialogical, not monological as is the traditional media. Interaction, dialogue and feedback between hundreds of users is possible via "clickable" links, e-mail, bulletin boards, discussion forums, chatrooms and newsgroups.
• *Unmediated* – the internet gives the parties direct access to the electorate and vice versa, without the intervention and manipulation of the media. For political parties, this means getting a message across to the electorate without intervention; for citizens this means getting information straight from the horse's mouth.

---

[9] Michael Margolis and David Resnick, "Third Voice: Vox Populi Vox Dei?", in *Firstmonday.org*, vol. 4, no. 10 (1999), http://firstmonday.org/issues/issue4_10/margolis.

[10] Stephen Coleman and Nicola Hall, "2001: CyberSpace Odyssey", http://www.hansardsociety.org.uk/cyberodyssey.htm, 2001.

These arguments for online campaigning, however, only draw attention to technical opportunities and general characteristics, and do not address the attitude change that is required for the realization of opportunities inherent in interactivity. No wonder that even those politicians (and parties) who are open to new media are using their websites only to introduce themselves.

On the internet, all actors, including parties, face the dilemma of *content* vs. *communication*. Odlyzko claims that the future of the internet will be determined rather by interpersonal communication (peer-to-peer, p2p communication) than by content provision.[11] In the field of online political communication, this means the real added value is not a download-version of the party's press releases, but the political information flow on various communication networks. The latter makes it possible for internet and mobile phone users interested in public matters and the party to go from passive consumers to active and interactive participants. This is especially important at the height of an election campaign.

The opposition of content vs. interactive communication applications is bad news for political parties. If Odlyzko is right, it might be too late for politicians to start discovering the web. Future campaigns will include more than web applications, i.e., self-introduction, self-representation and one-to-many communication, in the form of online party journals. The change brought by the interactive transition will demand the rearrangement of external communication, the development of internal communication systems, the creation and effective utilization of new databases and networks of information-sharing and management on the long run. The condition of all of this is the creation of new organizational solutions, the formation of professional working teams in new, previously unseen combinations. Whether parties and politicians like it or not, interactivity will be a dominant factor in the new media, besides online versions party programs and party newspapers.

Decentralized Communication: SMS and E-mail in the Campaign

Until April 7, 2002, the first round of the Hungarian elections, it seemed like new communication technologies would not play a significant role in the election campaign. In the heated atmosphere between the two rounds, however, new media suddenly became important. Their political utilization, though, had more to do with interpersonal commu-

---

[11] Andrew Odlyzko, "Content Is Not King", *Firstmonday.org*, vol. 6, no. 2 (2001), http://www.firstmonday.org/issues/issue6_2/odlyzko/index.html.

nication tools – e-mail and SMS – than with genuine content by the parties.

SMS and e-mail – technologically mediated interpersonal communication – had already had important roles in everyday information consumption well before the 2002 election campaign. According to an empirical survey conducted in an active internet community, both of these communication tools compared well with cellular and traditional telephones in terms of four aspects: speed, reliability, personality and expression of individual style.[12] Krajcsi et al. found that SMS and e-mail ranked nearly the same in all four categories. Cellular phones ranked highest in speed and reliability. Evaluating these result from the perspective of political campaign messages, we can draw two important conclusions. First, one of the greatest virtues of SMS and e-mail is that they deliver messages quickly. Second, these types of messages are considered relatively reliable by their users. Both of these qualities are extraordinarily valuable to political parties.

Discussing the features of various communication technologies and tools, Benczik calls e-mail sequentially interactive.[13] This means that although the message can be sent to several recipients at once, it can only function one-way at a time. The telephone, on the other hand, enables simultaneous interaction. This quality of the e-mail can also be extended to SMS. Both interpersonal communication tools – as different as they are in many respects – function on a similar, sequential basis.

The division of sequential vs. simultaneous interactivity coincides with the theoretical background of Wellman et al.[14] In a similar vein, in a National Geographic Society survey ("Survey 2000"), the factor analysis arranged ten selected online activities[15] into two dimensions. One of them is the *synchronous scale*, which consists of activities in which

---

[12] Attila Krajcsi, Kristóf Kovács, and Csaba Pléh, "Internethasználók kommunikatív szokásai", in Kristóf Nyíri (ed.), *A 21. századi kommunikáció új útjai: Tanulmányok* [New Perspectives on 21st-Century Communications: Essays], Budapest: MTA Filozófiai Kutatóintézete, 2001.

[13] Vilmos Benczik, "Másodlagos szóbeliség és mobil telefónia", in Kristóf Nyíri (ed.), *A 21. századi kommunikáció új útjai*.

[14] Barry Wellman, Annabel Quan Haase, James Witte, and Keith Hampton, "Does the Internet Increase, Decrease, or Supplement Social Capital?", *American Behavioural Scientist*, vol. 45, no. 3, November 2001.

[15] Send/receive e-mail; take part in mailing lists; access digital libraries, newspapers, magazines; take online college courses; purchase products or services; surf the web; participate in usenet newsgroups; engage in chats; visit MUDs, MOOs, other multiuser environments; play multiuser games.

two or more users take part simultaneously (these include chat, participation in MUD, MOO or multiuser games). The other is the *asynchronous scale*, comprising activites that do not require the simultaneous presence of the parties. Asynchronous activites meanwhile facilitate "one-to-many" communication (one person can send a messages to more than one recipient at a time). The study concludes that asynchronous e-mail is the most widely used form of online activity.[16] Just like the concept of sequential interactivity, this asynchronous quality can also be extended to SMS.

Summing up this brief theoretical review, we can state that e-mail and SMS are interpersonal communication tools that only function sequantially, one way at a time, and thus do not require the simultaneous activity of two or more parties. Based on the "one-to-many" model, these tools possess the important quality of enabling a message to be sent to many recipients very quickly and at a low cost. All these characteristics – taking into account the fact that users seem to consider them reliable – make e-mail and SMS outstanding marketing and campaign tools.

In terms of Norris' categories, SMS and e-mail are postmodern campaign techniques, as they enable interaction and decentralized communication. The question remains, however, whether mass distribution of campaign SMS and e-mail really stimulate communication. On the one hand, in fact, they do – we receive, read, exchange, and send messages. On the other, not really, as we rarely answer such messages, we merely forward (or delete) them – and this rarely creates dialogue or multilateral exchange of views.

SMS and e-mail are interpersonal communication tools that function on similar principles, at the same time also showing significant differences. SMS costs money (around 20 HUF = ca. 0.08 USD), the number of characters is maximized (at 160), and for the time being messages are mostly restricted to text format. Although SMS is a form of interpersonal communication, the campaign messages in the Hungarian campaign could rather be seen as personally forwarded leaflets. Since they were usually distributed by friends, this was less of a "nuisance" than flyer distribution or political advertisements in the mailbox.

To those with access, e-mail is available at a very low or no cost. As opposed to SMS, the length of the e-mail message is not maximized, we can attach graphics, pictures, audio and even video files. During the 2002 campaign, serious political arguments, articles, rational discussion, political verses and even long, ironic poems were distributed vie e-mail.

---

[16] Wellman et al., *op. cit.*

E-mail can also be more easily forwarded to large groups, and possibly to strangers, than SMS. All this requires are good databases or virus-like programs – and in the 2002 Hungarian elections both were used.

While analyzing their differences, we must also point out the convergence of these two types of messages and the technologies behind them. Campaign managers in the 2002 campaign also sent impersonal, mass SMS via the internet. Another connection between the world of internet and mobile phones was that copies of popular campaign SMS messages themselves were eventually copied into and repeatedly transmitted in e-mail. The overlap was due to the fact that the active users copied the content into the other medium. The trend of technological convergence also keeps narrowing the gap between SMS and e-mail, as their software backgrounds become more and more compatible and the hardware serving the two also converge. Today we can send e-mail from cellular phones, and SMS from PC's. Moreover, the newest mobile communication appliances – though often still called mobile or cell phones – integrate the functions of a telephone and a palmtop computer (as well as PDAs (Personal Digital Assistants) and cameras. The convergence of formerly separate gadgets indicates that the differences that characterize SMS and e-mail today are only temporary and the borderline between the two can and continue to be crossed, from both sides.

How Were Interactive Tools Used during the 2002 Election Campaign?

Several types of SMS could be distinguished well before the election campaign. Perhaps the most important dimension along which SMS messages can be classified is whether they represent personal or mass communication. Balázs lists the following categories:[17]

- personal (private) SMS
- MMS (multimedia messages)
- download-SMS, operator logo
- circular SMS
- official, service information
- other, specific news or information service
- SMS-wall services
- public SMS chat on teletext

---

[17] Géza Balázs, "Futótűz- vagy pontról pontra-kommunikáció – A választási sms-ek folklorisztikai-szövegtani vizsgálata", Manuscript, eDemokrácia Műhely, July 2002.

- private SMS chat services
- souvenir (keepsake) SMS
- action SMS

Out of these SMS-types, it was the action SMS that received most attention during the election campaign. Action or campaign SMS and e-mail can be subdivided into three further categories, which should be dealt with separately:

1. call for common political action and mobilization for political events;
2. propaganda- and PR-messages (several kinds of these appeared in the campaign);
3. political humor, including online jokes.

Political Mobilization

Communication methods play a key role in direct political mobilization for demonstrations or other events, along with political opportunities, human, symbolic and material resources, framing power, and other factors. An effective communication network represents an important organizational resource for political and other public organizations. The first time in Hungarian history when decentralized communication technologies played a serious part in direct mobilization was in 1990. In October 1990, communicating with their CB-radios, taxi drivers closed all major roads in the country, creating a national blockade, in protest against the unexpected rise of gasoline prices.[18]

Such swift and effective organization of the blockade would not have been possible without the autonomous utilization of horizontal communication methods. As leading Hungarian TV host György Baló said in the television program Napzárta on October 26, 1990: "...it has become clear that communication systems outside reach of the central communication authority of the state create extraordinary possibilities of social organization. This country was blocked with the help of CB and VHF radios. This sort of communication obviously works well and can be operated independently of all central intention and control – this is how

---

[18] We would like to thank Mr. Gábor Halmai and Mr. János Kenedi for their valuable observations concerning the taxi blockade.

[19] Source: *Rendszerváltó évek* – dokumentumfilm-sorozat. XXII/16 rész: *Zaklatott ősz*. (1997). [*The Years of the Regime Change* – a documentary series. Part XXII/16: *The Turbulent Fall*] Director: János Litauszki, editor: Gizella Sóvári, series editor: János Gombár.

far technology has come."[19]

On October 24, 1990, a few taxi drivers disappointed by the radical (65 percent) raise of gasoline prices and the previous denial of this by the government, gathered on Dózsa György square. Through their CB and VHF radios, however, the blockade was quickly organized. Drivers blocked bridges and main roads with their taxi-cabs, vans and trucks. The traffic of Budapest, and soon after the whole country, had been paralyzed. Their decentralized communication proved so effective that during their negotiations with the government, the taxi drivers were able to demonstrate their control by quickly making a bridge free and then close it down again.[20] They also made a promise to make all roads in the country free in only three hours in case of a favorable decision. This indicated that horizontal communication networks, independent of centralized communication, could be suitable, and even more effective than former techniques, in self-organiation, mobilization and coordination of direct actions.

Back in 1990 it seemed unique that the taxi drivers were able to organize themselves so quickly and effectively with their decentralized and independent communication tool, the CB radio. Today, in the age of internet and cell phones, decentralized mobilization with forwarded messages does not look so unusual. In the 2002 campaign in Hungary, both the left- and the right-wing parties and supporters organized crowds for several important demonstrations and public events through SMS and e-mail. Let us present some SMS examples of the mobilizing campaign:[21]

- Mobilization to the demonstration against the hostile tone (a speech by FIDESZ leader Mr. Kövér) of FIDESZ in front of their headquarters (after several smaller events this was the only significant political event before the first round for which people were mobilized through SMS): *"Come and demonstrate against the Kövér speech tomorrow at 5 in front of FIDESZ headquarters! Pass this on to 10*

---

[20] Horváth Pál, "Szóval, ha lehet, akkor soha ne lövöldözzünk egymásra", *Magyar Hírlap*, October 25, 1991, pp. 8–9.

[21] The first conscious SMS campaign move was conducted by SZDSZ. In October 2001 they asked voters' opinions about their healthcare-program. They received over a thousand replies. (*Magyar Hírlap*, November 23, 2001.)

[22] The source of all qoutes is the electronic campaign-letter archives of the Open Society Archives, April 10 – May 10, 2002, http://www.osa.ceu.hu/kampanyarchiv/english.html.

people! Cu."[22] (April 2nd)
- Call to the funeral of comedian Géza Hofi: "*Géza Hofi will be buried Saturday at 12 at Farkasréti cemetary. Come and bring a red carnation. (Forward this!)*" [Red carnation is the party symbol of the socialists.] (April 13th)
- Mobilization to the public meeting of MSZP-SZDSZ in a café at Vörösmarty square. Electronic mass mobilization in this case was carried out independently of the parties: "*Sunday at 4pm on Vörösmarty square anti-government voters are holding a peaceful demonstration to show: WE ARE NOT AFRAID! Pass this on to 10 people*" (April 14th)
- Mobilization to the candlelight demonstration of FIDESZ by the Danube before the second round: "*We are building a bridge of light for a civic future. From 8 pm on the 18th on the riverbanks and bridges of Budapest. Come with a lit candle so we can shine far and bright! Pass this on!*" (April 18th)

Although the taxi blockade can be regarded as a precursor to the SMS and e-mail campaign in terms of horizontal communication technology, it is important to note the differences. The CB radio system of taxi drivers represents a professional communication network, a service radio channel that is closed for outsiders. Thus the only ones who could listen to and join the conversations were members of their own professional community. In that community however, everyone automatically got full access to all messages – they did not need to join a separate information network or become members of another community. By contrast, in the case of SMS and e-mail mobilization, several conditions had to be fulfilled in order to get information about an event. One of them was membership in the adequate technological network. Today over half of Hungary's population (52,6%) have cellular phones whereas the proportion of regular internet users is only around 16%.[23] The other condition was membership in a social group or circle of friends where political campaign messages are spread. At this point, we do not even have estimates on the sizes of such networks.

A further difference between the CB radio used during the taxi blockade and new decentralized technologies is that the latter carries a direct risk of being manipulated. In October 1990, the taxi drivers organized the blockade with an intact professional communication network, which made direct, external influence technically impossible. (Assumptions about political influence at the time were also only of indi-

---

[23] "2002. márciusi gyorsjelentés", Hírközlési Felügyelet, http://www.hif.hu/menu3/m3_2/mobil/2002/marcius.pdf.

rect influence, personal contact or symbolic support.) In the 2002 campaign period however, examples could be found of rallies and direct actions that were probably directly influenced by parties.

Black Propaganda and Viral Political Marketing

The first round results of the 2002 election campaign (April 7, 2002) surprised everyone – the parties as well as the public. On the party lists, the center-left Hungarian Socialist Party (MSZP) received 42% and the joint right wing list of right-wing Young Democrats and conservative Hungarian Democratic Forum (FIDESZ-MDF) received 41%. In light of the extremely tight results on the party lists and the mixed outcome of the individual voting district results, FIDESZ still could have won the elections in the second round (the run-offs in the individual districts), at least theoretically. After the first round, FIDESZ changed strategy and launched a harsh negative campaign against its opponents. Voter alignment suddenly became essential, and the close national and district results now made every single vote count.

As a result of the parties' mobilization, a political activity unprecedented in the twelve-year history of Hungarian democracy appeared: families, workplaces, schools, circles of friends and civil organizations were torn by political discussion. The nearly 2000 campaign e-mails and 300 SMS found at the site of the Open Society Archive (http://www.osa.ceu.hu/kampanyarchiv/english.html) show that electronic communication was a true blueprint (and creator) of the campaign atmosphere between the two rounds of the 2002 parliamentary elections.

In the international literature on propaganda, campaign techniques called whispering or black propaganda are not a new phenomenon; there have been several examples of these in other countries. Aronson and Pratkanis analyzed several techniques of mass-influence.[24] The 2002 campaign was especially characterized by two campaign techniques: *factoids* and the *granfalloon technique*.

Factoids are rumors that are made widely known by the media. A textbook example of factoids in Hungary is the 1979 Bicske earthqueake. News was spread nationwide that in January 1980, Hungary was to be struck by an earthquake with an epicenter around the town

---

[24] Elliot Aronson and Anthony Pratkanis, *Age of Propaganda: The Everyday Use and Abuse of Persuasion*, New York: W. H. Freeman, 1992.

of Bicske. The information proved to be a hoax. This case was researched thoroughly by Endre Hann,[25] who proved that mass media played an essential role in the birth and proliferation of factoids, or rumors. The 1979 case, however, was presumable based on some kind of a misunderstanding, whereas in postmodern election campaigns certain factoids are generated consciously.[26]

It should be mentioned that factoids and rumors are partly overlapping categories. Political rumors are in close relation to celebrity gossip. Fox convincingly argues that cellular phones serve to satisfy the universal human need for gossip. In the alienated, busy world of modern society, mobile phones can provide an oportunity for gossip and what it provides, human feelings, friendly voices and emotions, and social affirmation.[27]

Black propaganda and gossip are similar in that they are spread in situations of personal (direct or technology mediated) communication. The time of distribution is open-ended (unlike in traditional mass media, where direct distribution is practically limited to the time of the TV program or the publication of the newspaper), and the symbolic space is all of society or a certain group. The difference is that black propagandists intentionally spread rumors, whereas gossip spreads spontaneously. In both communication types, the truth content of the news remains secondary. The similarity of these two communicatios types is also indicated by the fact that their common area are intentionally spread, discrediting rumors.

The other typical campaign method used was the granfalloon technique.[28] Political camps, according to the needs of political marketing, were separated and defined on the basis of binary oppositions like "them–us", "good guys–bad guys" or "clean–dirty." Between the two rounds the antagonism between the two main political camps (pro-government conservatives, anti-government socialists and liberals) turned to hostility. Both campaign teams intentionally created requisites of group

---

[25] A main feature of rumor is that it makes no difference whether people believe it or not. The point is that they talk about it and spread it even if they doubt the information is true. Cf. Endre Hann, *Egy "földrengés" hatásai. A tájékoztatási rendszer paradoxonairól egy rémhír kapcsán*, Budapest: Tömegkommunikációs Központ, 1981.

[26] A classic example of media generated factoids is Orson Welles' 1938 radio play, War of the Worlds. It is important to note that this program did not intentionally create a rumors. A Hungarian example is the Postabank panic of 1997.

[27] Kate Fox, "Evolution, Alienation and Gossip – The Role of Mobile Telecommunications in the 21st Century", http://www.sirc.org/publik/gossip.shtml.

[28] Aronson and Pratkanis, *op. cit.*, p. 130.

affiliation: symbols, common character traits and hostility toward the other camp. With the help of these techniques, a leader can "divide and rule", and have the followers' group think and reason in the terms s/he wants them to.

Viral Marketing: From Business to Politics

Black propaganda and conscious rumor spreading have a long history to look back on. Their utilization for business marketing purposes is well illustrated in András B. Vágvölgyi's book, *Tokyo Underground:* "New fads are quickest to catch on with young girls, who have extensive contacts everywhere; a PR-manager at a company specialized in teens' goods says they can reach 300,000 high-school girls in Tokyo alone, through their 2000 registered teenager helpers. The only trick is to make everyone who is told about a new product promise to keep it a secret. Then it spreads like fire after an earthquake. They put [the goods] on the market without advertising, and it sells like hot cakes."[29]

Compared to these clever business marketing tricks, the novelty of the 2002 campaign was the utilization of interactive online technologies.[30] Viral marketing, a term not yet widely known, but ever more popular among marketing and pr-experts, refers to the way viruses spread. Its essence is a strategy that urges people to forward the messages they receive. Like a virus, a message can reach large numbers of people (even millions) very quickly.

The online environment – the communication flow of the network of networks[31] – is especially favorable for intentional infections by viral marketing. Various computer viruses and worms also take advantage of the features of network communication. However, while viruses and worms spread and infect on the network sponging on the software, viral marketing spreads the message in or as legitimate content, with the active co-operation of the users.

A classic example of viral marketing is the growth of popularity of Hotmail.com. A one-line advertisement appears at the bottom of each and every e-mail sent from free e-mail service provider Hotmail.com. The message is seen by everyone who receives mail from friends or colleagues via a Hotmail account. This may not seem so new today, but

---

[29] András B. Vágvölgyi, *Tokyo Underground*, Budapest: Új Mandátum Könyvkiadó, 2000, p. 66.

[30] We would like to thank Zsolt Erdélyi for his useful ideas and comments.

[31] Manuel Castells, *The Rise of the Network Society*, Oxford: Blackwell, 2000.

Hotmail were the first to use this technique. Ralph S. Wilson sums up viral marketing strategy in six steps:

An effective viral marketing strategy:

1. Gives away products or services.
2. Provides for effortless transfer to others.
3. Scales easily from small to very large.
4. Exploits common motivations and behaviors.
5. Utilizes existing communication networks.
6. Takes advantage of others' resources.

In the right conditions, viral marketing can lead to an exponential rise in the number of people reached ("infected"). Even in the simplest case, when one person forwards the message to only two others, a message spread with this method reaches 64 people in seven, and 128 people in just eight steps:

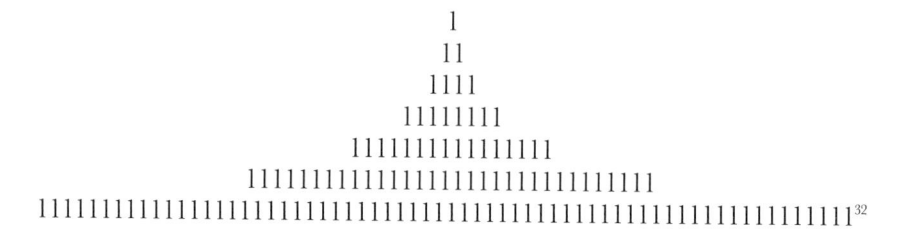

```
                    1
                   11
                  1111
                11111111
              1111111111111111
          11111111111111111111111111111111
  1111111111111111111111111111111111111111111111111111111111111111[32]
```

It is of course vital that participants of horizontal communication actually forward the message. There may be two ways for reaching this. One is to make forwarding impossible to avoid (see the example of Hotmail, where it is not possible to delete the viral message). The other is to motivate participants to forward the message. There are several ways to provide positive incentives: confide a secret to the participants, the spreading of which in the target group gives you high prestige; offer material goods for forwarding the message or even recruiting new members (this is the basis of multi-level marketing systems and pilot games); a great, irresistable offer, where we are actually doing the recipient a favor by forwarding the message; a humorous message that

---

[32] Ralph S. Wilson, "The Six Simple Principles of Viral Marketing", Wilsonweb.com, http://www.wilsonweb.com/wmt5/viral-principles-clean.htm.

spreads just like a joke (forwarding it provokes laughter and community experiences with family, friends, colleagues, which is pleasant for the sender as well as the recipient), etc.

Viral marketing understandably did not remain on the world-wide-web, but appeared also in SMS form. The Brew Crew, an Irish beer delivery company advertised by spreading the text message "Sorry I'm late, the dog ate my...". By completing and sending the message back to the company, one could win free beer.[33] SMS is becoming more and more popular as an advertising tool (although the 160 characters are a strong limiting factor). Thus it is understandable that political messages, jokes and rumors also found their breeding ground in the space created by new technologies.

The thesis of our study is that the technique of viral marketing was used in the 2002 Hungarian election campaign by political parties and their supporters. We created the term political viral marketing in order to conceptualize and understand what happened in the cmpaign and to help differentiate it from viral marketing used for business purposes. In viral political marketing, political actors utilize the technique of viral marketing for political purposes (typically in campaigns), with the use of new interactive media (SMS and e-mail).

Polical viral marketing appeared in the Hungarian campaign partly as the extension of offline black propaganda to the area of the new media.[34] This of course does not mean that several initiatives did not come from voters and party supporters, bottom-up. Voters taking part in the SMS and e-mail campaign became active and occasionally creative participants in campaign communication by creating messages worthy of forwarding, and passing on the ones made up by the parties. This represents a significant change compared to the unidirectional communication pattern of traditional mass media.

Political Humor

The tense political atmosphere of the Hungarian election was un-

---

[33] The idea comes from the advertising firm Rtn2Sndr, see http://www.rtn2sndr.com/home.htm.

[34] For lack of space we must skip the analysis of more examples of viral political marketing messages in the 2002 campaign. Some typical texts can be found at these addresses: http://www.osa.ceu.hu/kampanyarchiv/7.html, http://www.osa.ceu.hu/kampanyarchiv/11.html, http://www.osa.ceu.hu/kampanyarchiv/12.html, http://www.osa.ceu.hu/kampanyarchiv/18.html, http://www.osa.ceu.hu/kampanyarchiv/72.html. Ten messages are also available in English translation at http://www.osa.ceu.hu/kampanyarchiv.

doubtedly favorable for rumors. Factoids further intensified the tension, and conserved the borderlines between the two camps. Political tension was loosened by humor: hundreds of jokes, funny messages and ironic poems appeared in many networks. Coleman and Hall reported similar phenomena in the 2001 elections in the UK, although the leading role there seemes to have been played not by e-mail or SMS, but by funny websites.[35] The authors point out that online humor represents more than just billboard graffiti, or funny (or vulgar) posters.

Virally spread internet jokes often required hard work. A good example is the Star Wars parody: the *Attack of the Reds* bit was a good quality transcription of the official trailer to *Star Wars: Attack of the Clones*, in which the dark side is represented by anti-government forces, while conservative figures appear as heroes such as Obi-Wan Kenobi, Master Yoda or Anakin Skywalker.[36]

Online and SMS humor – just like in traditional, interpersonal situations – play an important role in giving social affirmation and relieving tension. Humor that appeared on interactive technology networks was part of a wider political humor culture. We more or less sent the same jokes in messages that we kept telling each other as well.

Other jokes merely enriched the genres of everyday folklore with motives of the election campaign. Háy published a collection of everyday verbal and children's folklore in 1980: she collected several mocking verses, ditties, parodies and song texts. "Contrary to mass culture and 'high' culture, this is a form of community-forming art, created by the community itself. Although its sources are fresher and more recognizable than those of traditional folklore, this is definitely an independent culture, represented in selection and transformation of [texts]."[37]

The jokes spread during the 2002 campaign resembled these verses in both form and style. Comical and ironic political poetry also appeared on the Net as a strong genre. The line of e-mail folklore contained up-to-date transcriptions and political parodies of János Petőfi, János Arany, and other Hungarian classic poetry of the 19th century.

We should also point out another structural similarity, i.e., with folkloristic canvassing (election) songs. Canvassing songs, related to partisan electioneering, spread in the 19th century in Hungary. Interestigly, they were revitalized in the more recent years of major political changes, in

---

[35] Coleman and Hall, *op. cit.*

[36] See: "Mindenki hozzon magával még egy Jedit" [Everybody should bring yet another Jedi to vote], *Index*, http://index.hu/kultur/showbiz/redalert/.

[37] Ágnes Háy, "Hülye aki elolvassa", *Mozgó Világ*, June 1980, p. 9–17.

1945 (liberation of Hungary from Nazi rule by Red Army, beginning of Soviet occupation and limited democracy), 1956 (the Hungarian revolution), and 1988-90 (democratization).[38]

Canvassing songs, in an updated and often ironic form, resurfaced for the first time in 2002 since the democratic transition in 1990. On the one hand, this was the result of the fact that the campaign turned extremely negative (much more negative than any other democratic campaign before) between the two rounds of the 2002 elections. On the other hand, SMS provided a relevant new medium for the short, sharp, political messages.[39]

A large part of the 2002 SMS-jokes took advantage of the real-time function of the medium, and instantly (within a few hours) reacted to the newest political events. ("I'm Lajos Bokros. I'm packing and coming back!" [Bokros was a former, unpopular Finance Minister during the socialist-liberal government 1994-98] – "young lawyer with experience as prime minister, is looking for a job".) SMS-jokes are tight, offering short rhyming verses, skits, sometimes in graffiti-style. The reason for this is limited character space and restrained form of SMS texts:

- "How many government supporters fit on Kossuth square? All of them."
- "Sunday we are going to solder the red star on to the royal crown."
- "Traffic information: the road is blocked between the House of Parliament and Felcsút by transport vehicles."[40]
- "Don't despair! Napoleon loves you!! Pass this on to 100 true Corsican patriots!!!"
- "Country for sale, in mint condition. Inquiries at Köztársaság square with code-word Gresham."
- "I am convinced that oranges are the healthiest fruit, 'Centrum vitamins' are just some kind of misleading artificial substitute."[41]

---

[38] Balázs, *op. cit.*

[39] *Ibid.*

[40] Viktor Orbán, Prime Minister at the time of the elections, plays in the football team of the village Felcsút (Alcsút being his home village).

[41] Oranges were the party symbol of Fidesz, and Centrum was a small center party.

Postmodern Campaign Techniques and the Public Sphere

Parallel Universes

In the case of e-mail and SMS networks, there was probably little passage between the two large political camps, each group sent and received messages reaffirming their own views. However, it is difficult to find direct proof for this claim. Mobile phone companies provided only total numbers (if any) of their SMS-traffic increase during the elections. Reconstructing the path of the snowball (viral messages) by tracking down forwarded single e-mail or SMS messages, is hardly possible. We do not even know whether it is an urban phenomenon we are dealing with.

Our interviews indicated that several professional mailing lists took on the function of political debate forums during the exceptional fortnight between the two election rounds. These comments, signed with names, included conflicting opinions and argumens, so members of the opposing camps could meet directly, just like in chat forums. On the professional lists, however, the debate was more rational that in chats, because it was colleagues who were taking part, not just anyone under a nickname. Indirect proof the exisiting – however minimal – access between the two camps was that transcriptions of the same joke appeared – like with Kádár, Gorbachev and Reagan-jokes a generation ago – (e.g. "FIDESZ/MSZP want what's best for you – don't let them have it").

Political Spam

An important aspect of viral political marketing is that it may be seen as spam. At times of political peace we would resent receiving many unsolicited messages from friends, online acquaintances or strangers. Sending unwanted messages, or spam, is unpleasant to the recipient, impolite and inadmissible in netiquette, and also considered illegal. In our opinion some of the e-mail and text messages not only violated netiquette, but also broke the law – particularly the Hungarian regulations on e-marketing in the eCommerce Bill – and also violated the statements of the commissioner on data protection.

In the heated, even hysteric two-week runoff campaign, the practice of political spam seemed natural. A significant part of the voters turned into news addicts and politics junkies who needed and rewarded instant opinions, messages (information injections for junkies) by quickly forwarding them. The 2002 campaign caught Hungary in an interesting state of transition: there are *already* masses of people using cell phones and e-mail, but legal protection and self-regulation of the private sphere (especially re spam) are not yet developed.

Interactive Political Marketing

How can we interpret such a drastic growth of political activism in electronic communication and the online activity of voters? On the one hand, we can state that national politics and the public sphere widened, and embraced many thousand, previously passive citizens. Analyzing the effects of the internet on political communication, outstanding theorists – say John Keane[42] – warned that new media will divide the unified public sphere, and create thousands of thematic "public spherecles". People will deal only with their own subjects of interest on thematically specialized debate forums, and important, central questions will get lost in the colorful mosaic. In the last two weeks of the 2002 campaign, however, Hungary witnessed the exact opposite: national political campaigns invaded many other public fora (which may still be favorable) and the private sphere of citizens (which is not acceptable).

On the other hand, there remained few rational elements in the heated debates. All the more were emotional outbreaks, repetitions of party slogans, opinionated statements and manifestations in the interest of the party campaigns. Many party activists communicated as mere puppets of one-to-many political marketing. Increased online political participation is a positive phenomenon, just like high voter turn-out – but it is only valuable if it initiates arguments and multilateral discussion.

The "many-to-many"-type of mass online politics is a previously unknown phenomenon in Hungarian politics. Our research in the framework of the eDemocracy Association included interviewing the campaign teams of political parties before the elections about SMS and e-mail. They answered that these tools were considered marginal in their campaign strategies. They did not expect – and because of the lack of control over such a process, even somewhat feared – that their professional campaign work would be influenced by such mass SMS-es of voters. At the same time, analysis of the interactive campaign and some

---

[42] John Keane, "The Structural Transformations of the Public Sphere", in K. L. Hacker and J. van Dijk (eds.), *Digital Democracy: Issues of Theory and Practice*, London: Sage, pp. 7–89.

written documents of black propaganda show that viral campaigns knowingly became parts of the party strategies on both sides. The interactive campaign focused primarily on the message forwarding activity of those party supporters who were not organized party members. The parties did, however, try to utilize their organizations and activists for sending out internally created messages – at least at the beginning of the diffusion of certain viral messages, in the initial phase of "infection".

Ultimately, the question remains whether this was a one-time, exceptional phenomenon that related to the exceptionally intense runoff campaign of 2002. Virtual communities, linked by interactive technologies, do not necessarily relate to geograpichal areas. Simultaneously, in terms of belonging to a certain community, they are much more homogenous than their offline counterparts. Péter Gedeon makes an important point when he states that "contacts maintained through information technology can be and are used in reinforcing not only virtual but also local community sentiments".[43]

Wellman et al. came to similar conclusions: the role of geographical distance is important in internet communication. Most messages are sent to friends and relatives who live within 50 km of the sender.[44]

In light of the subject of our paper, this aspect is important because the SMS and e-mail that was used to forward political messages represent both homogeneity (in terms of party preference) and locality in the campaign. Although the local dimension was not so accentuated in the interactive parliamentary election campaign, its significance may well increase in political campaigns in the future.

---

[43] Péter Gedeon, "Piac és pénz a mobil információs társadalomban", in *A 21. századi kommunikáció új útjai*.

[44] Wellman et al., *op. cit.*

Notes on Contributors

Wolfgang COY, born in 1947, studied electrical engineering, mathematics, and philosophy at the Technical University of Darmstadt. After working at several universities, among them the University of Dortmund and Paris VI, he was appointed Professor for Informatics at the University of Bremen. He is now head of a research group at the Humboldt University in Berlin. His research areas include digital media, computers and society, theory of informatics, social and cultural history of informatics, as well as the philosophical foundations of the information society. He has authored, co-authored and edited more than one hundred research papers and several books, among them *Industrieroboter – Archäologie der Zweiten Schöpfung*, Berlin: Rotbuch, 1985, and, together with Martin Warnke and Georg Christoph Tholen, *HyperKult: Geschichte, Theorie und Kontext Digitaler Medien*, Basel: Stroemfeld, 1997. Further information: http://waste.informatik.hu-berlin.de/Coy. E-mail: coy@informatik.hu-berlin.de.

Valéria CSÉPE, DSc, is Senior Research Fellow at the Research Institute for Psychology of the Hungarian Academy of Sciences, and Head of the Group for Developmental Psycho-Physiology. Her main research areas are: cognitive psychophysiology, experimental psychology, and developmental neuro-psychology. Some recent publications: Valéria Csépe, Judit Osman-Sági, Márk Molnár, Mária Gósy, "Impaired Speech Perception in Aphasic Patients: Event-Related Potential and Neuropsychological Assessment", *Neuropsychologia*, vol. 39, no. 11 (2001); Valéria Csépe (ed.), *Dyslexia: Different Brain, Different Behavior*, Dordrecht: Kluwer Academic Publishers, 2002. E-mail: csepe@cogpsyphy.hu.

Endre DÁNYI, MA in Sociology and Media Studies (ELTE Institute of Sociology and ELTE Media Centre, 2002) is a sociologist, visiting lecturer at the ELTE Institute of Sociology and at the Social Theory College of the University of Economics in Budapest. He is member of the eDemocracy Association (Hungary) and an MA student at the Department of Political Science of the Central European University. His research and teaching focuses on online political communication, especially online election campaign strategies and digital inequalities. E-mail: danyi.endre@axelero.hu.

Robin DUNBAR graduated in Philosophy and Psychology from Oxford University in 1969, and went on to complete a PhD on the behaviour and ecology of primates at the University of Bristol. He subsequently held Research Fellowships at the Universities of Cambridge and Liverpool, and teaching positions at the University of Stockholm and University College London. He is currently Professor of Evolutionary Psychology at the University of Liverpool, where he leads a large research group working on the behavioural ecology and evolutionary psychology of primates, ungulates and humans. His best-known book is *Grooming, Gossip, and the Evolution of Language*, Cambridge, MA: Harvard University Press, 1996. E-mail: rimd@liverpool.ac.uk.

Péter GEDEON, PhD, born in 1949 in Budapest, is Professor at the Department of Comparative Economics of the Budapest University of Economic Sciences and Public Administration. His research work is in the fields of comparative political economy and social theory. International experience: LSE (UK), Cornell University (USA), Erasmus University (the Netherlands), IWH (Germany). Recent publications: "The Economics of Transition and the Transition of Economics", *Economic Systems*, 1997; "Hungary: Europeanization without EU Leadership?", in J. J. Anderson (ed.), *Regional Integration and Democracy: Expanding on the European Experience*, Oxford: Rowman & Littlefield, 1999; "Racionalitásfogalom és evolúciós elméletek" [The Concept of Rationality and Theories of Evolution], *Világosság*, 1999; and *Piac és demokrácia* [Market and Democracy], Budapest: Aula, 2002. E-mail: pgedeon@bkae.hu.

Nicola GREEN, PhD, is a lecturer in the sociology of new media and new technologies in the Department of Sociology, University of Surrey. Her previous research has included studies of the social production and consumption of virtual reality technologies (during which she was a visiting fellow in the Department of Sociology, UC Berkeley), and more recently studies in the emerging social life of mobile technologies. She is currently working on an Intel funded project examining issues around trust, risk, regulation and surveillance in mobile technologies. Publications include the edited volume *Wireless World: Social and Interactional Aspects of the Mobile Age*, with Barry Brown and Richard Harper (2002); "How Everday Life Became Virtual", *Journal of Consumer Culture*, vol. 1, no. 1 (2001); and "'Strange Yet Stylish Headgear': VR Consumption and the Construction of Gender", in Alison Adam and Eileen Green (eds.), *Virtual Gender: Technology, Consumption and Identity Matters*, 2001; "On the Move: Technology, Mobility, and the Mediation of Social Time and Space", *The Information Society*, vol. 18, no. 4. E-mail. n.green@soc.surrey.ac.uk.

Péter GYÖRGY, PhD, born 1954, lives in Budapest. He is Associate Professor at the University ELTE, Department of Media, Insitute of Theory of Art and Media Research. He is Co-Director of the Media Research Lab at the Technological University of Budapest. Some latest publications: "Between and After Essentialism and Institutionalism", *The Journal of Aesthetics and Art Criticism*, 1999; *Memex*, Budapest: Magvető, 2002; "The Hungarian Neoavantgarde", in Aless Erjavec (ed.), *Postsocialist Art / Postmodern Condition*, California University Press, 2003 (forthcoming).

Herbert HRACHOVEC teaches at the Department of Philosophy, University of Vienna. He has held scholarships and visiting appointments at the universities of Oxford (UK), Münster (Germany), Cambridge, MA (US), Berlin, Essen and Weimar (all Germany). Area of specialization: Analytic Philosophy, Aesthetics and Media Theory. He is currently deputy chairman of the Department of Philosophy, and Visiting Professor at the University of Klagenfurt, Austria. Some main publications: *Drehorte. Arbeiten zu Filmen* (Wien: 1997); *Monist Interactive Issue*, vol. 80, no. 3 (July 1997 – guest editor); "Electronic Texts are Computations are Electronic Texts", in N. Blake and P. Standish (eds.), *Enquiries at the Interface: Philosophical Problems of Online Education*, Oxford: 2000. For further information see: http://hrachovec.philo.at. E-mail: hrachoh3@univie.ac.at.

János LAKI is Senior Research Fellow at the Institute for Philosophical Research of the Hungarian Academy of Sciences. His primary interest is in topics in epistemology and the philosophy of science. His publications include: J. Laki (ed.): *Tudományfilozófia* [Philosophy of Science], Budapest: Osiris, 1998; "Gulliver's Return: On the Concept of Rigid Designation", 'S' *European Journal for Semiotic Studies*, 1991; "Words of Worlds: Conceptual Schemes Once Again", in K. Neumer (ed.), *Sprache und Verstehen: Transdisziplinäre Ansätze*, Vienna: IMGS-ISSS, 1998; "The Fall of the 'Two-Steps Model': Wittgenstein on Seeing and Meaning", in O. Gianluigi (ed.), *From the Tractatus to the Tractatus*, *Wittgenstein-Studien*, vol. 2, Frankfurt: Peter Lang, 2001. E-mail: j.laki@ella.hu.

Kristóf [J. C.] NYÍRI, born 1944, is Member of the Hungarian Academy of Sciences, and Director of the Institute for Philosophical Research of the Academy. He studied mathematics and philosophy at the University of Budapest, where he has been Professor of Philosophy since 1986. He was visiting professor in Austria, Finland, and the US. His main fields of research are the history of philosophy in the 19th and 20th centuries, and the impact of communication technologies on the organization of ideas and social and political organization. Some main publications: *Tradition and Individuality*, Dordrecht: Kluwer, 1992; "Electronic Networking and the Unity of Knowledge", in Stephanie Kenna and Seamus Ross (eds.), *Networking in the Humanities*, London: Bowker-Saur, 1995; "The Concept of Knowledge in the Context of Electronic Networking" (*The Monist*, July 1997); "Towards a Philosophy of Virtual Education", in Marilyn Deegan and Harold Short (eds.), *DRH 99*, London: King's College, 2000; "The Picture Theory of Reason", in Berit Brogaard and Barry Smith (eds.), *Rationality and Irrationality*, Wien: öbv-hpt, 2001. For further information see: www.phil-inst.hu/nyiri. E-mail: nyiri@phil-inst.hu.

Gábor PALLÓ (1942), DSc., is Director of Research at the Institute for Philosophical Research of the Hungarian Academy of Sciences. His fields of interest are the history of science, particularly the 20th-century history of natural sciences with special regard to science in Hungary; philosophy of science; history of chemistry and physics, migration of scientists, the relationships between science, politics and philosophy; cognitive and institutional aspects. Books: *Radioaktivitás és a kémiai atomelmélet: az anyagszerkezeti nézetek válsága a magyarországi kémiában* [Radioactivity and the chemical theory of atoms: crisis of the structural concepts in Hungarian chemistry], Budapest: Akadémiai Kiadó, 1992; "Make a Peak on the Plain: The Rockefeller Foundation's Szeged Project", in William H. Schneider (ed.), *Rockefeller Philanthropy and Modern Biomedicine: International Initiatives from World War I to the Cold War*, Bloomington: Indiana University Press, 2002; "Scientific Recency: George de Hevesy's Nobel Prize", in Elisabeth Crawford (ed.), *Historical Studies in the Nobel Archives: The Prizes in Science and Medicine*, Tokyo: Universal Academy Press, 2002. E-mail: pallo@phil-inst.hu.

Csaba PLÉH (1945) has degrees in psychology and in linguistics. He is Member of the Hungarian Academy of Sciences, and Professor of Psychology at the Budapest University of Technology and Economics. His main research interests are history of psychology, language and cognition, and developmental disorders, especially the Williams syndrome. He has traveled widely and had visiting appointments and fellowships at the Center for Advanced Studies in the Behavioral Sciences (Stanford), Vienna University, and the University of Trieste. Some recent publications: "Ernst Mach and Daniel Dennett: Two Evolutionary Models of Cognition", in P. Fleissner and J. C. Nyíri (eds.), *Philosophy of Culture and the Politics of Electronic Networking*, vol. I, Innsbruck: Studien Verlag, 1999; *A lélektan története* [The history of psychology], Budapest: Osiris, 2000; "Modularity and Pragmatics", *Pragmatics* 10 (2000). E-mail: pleh@itm.bme.hu.

Klára SÁNDOR, PhD, Professor of Linguistics at the University of Szeged. Research fields: language and evolution, the biological and cultural embeddedness of linguistic discrimination; theory of language change. Head of the international projects "From Stigmatization to Tolerance" (1998-1999) and "The Cognitive Embeddedness of Folk Linguistic Theories" (2000-2003). Some recent publications: "Amiért a szinkrón elemzés foszladozik" [Why synchronic analyses fail], in Klára Sándor (ed.) *Nyelvi változó – nyelvi változás* [Linguistic variable – linguistic change], Szeged: JGyF Kiadó, 1998; "National Feeling or Responsibility: The Case of the Csángó Language Revitalization", *Multilingua*, vol. 19, nos. 1–2 (2000); "A nyelv 'gyenge pontjai'" [Weak points in language], in L. Károly and É. Kincses Nagy (eds.), *Néptörténet – nyelvtörténet* [Folk history – language history], Szeged: SzTE BTK Altajisztikai Tanszék, 2001. Further information: http://www.jgytf.u-szeged.hu/~sandor. E-mail: sandor@jgytf.u-szeged.hu.

Miklós SÜKÖSD (1960) is Associate Professor at the Department of Political Science of the Central European University. MA in Sociology and Cultural Studies, 1985, ELTE Institute of Sociology; MA in Sociology, 1994, Department of Sociology, Harvard University; PhD in Political Science, 1992, Hungarian Academy of Sciences. His research focuses on political communication, e-democracy, and media policy. He is research director of the eDemocracy Association (Hungary). He has published 12 books, and many book chapters and papers on politics and media in East Central Europe, including "Democratic Transformation and the Mass Media in Hungary: from Stalinism to Democratic Consolidation", in R. Gunther and A. Moughan (eds.), *Democracy and the Media: A Comparative Perspective*, Cambridge: Cambridge University Press, 2000. He is co-editor (with P. Bajomi-Lázár) of *Reinventing Media: Media Policy Reform in East Central Europe*, forthcoming at CEU Press in 2003.

Barbara TVERSKY, Professor of Psychology, Stanford University, Stanford CA. Research Interests: Spatial thinking and language; memory, especially retellings of the events of one's life; event perception and cognition; knowledge structures and categories, especially in inference; diagrammatic reasoning, especially production, comprehension, inferences, and insights from diagrams, maps, and sketches. Some main publications: B. Tversky and E. Marsh, "Biased Retellings of Events Yield Biased Memories", *Cognitive Psychology* 40 (2000); B. Tversky, J. B. Morrison, and J. Zacks, "On Bodies and Events", in A. Meltzoff and W. Prinz (ed.), *The Imitative Mind: Development, Evolution and Brain Bases* (Cambridge: Cambridge University Press, 2002); B. Tversky, "Functional Significance of Visuospatial Representations", in P. Shah and A. Miyake (eds.), *Handbook of Higher-Level Visuospatial Thinking*, Cambridge: Cambridge University Press (in press). E-mail: bt@psych.stanford.edu.

Index

Aakhus, Mark, 12 f., 17, 44
abstract concepts, 16, 157, 162, 180, *see also* meaning
animation, 154, 171, 176, 178 ff.
  mental, 154, 179
anonymity, 34 f., 37, 45, 65
archive, 101 ff., 209, 221
Aristotle, 158
Arnheim, Rudolf, 162 f.
arrow, 132, 146, 152 ff., 176, 179

Balázs, Béla, 18 f.
basic science, 193
Baudrillard, Jean, 107
Beardon, Colin, 178 f.
Benczik, Vilmos, 217
Berger, A. A., 168
Big Science, 185 ff., 193, 200 ff., 208 f.
Bonaventure, 183
Borges, J. L., 144
Brahe, Tycho, 191
brain, 57, 60, 72, 119, 131 f.
  social brain hypothesis, 57 ff., 66
broadcasting, 17, 88, 90, 93, 98 f., 101, 111 f., 114

campaign techniques, modern, 212 f.
  factoids, 223 f., 227
  granfalloon technique, 223 f.
campaign techniques, postmodern, 212 f.
  black propaganda, 223 ff., 227, 232
  viral political marketing, 223, 225 ff., 230, 232
  online humor, 228 f.
campaign techniques, pre-modern, 212 f.

CB radio, 220 ff.
chat, 63, 80, 91, 94, 110, 136, 139 f., 215, 217 ff., 230
children, 22, 74, 94, 117, 119 ff., 137, 143 ff., 171, 228
Chomsky, Noam, 76
cognitive constraints, 57, 59, 127, 139
cognitive (mental) architecture, 119 f., 124, 127, 131, 135, 163
Coleman, Stephen, 211, 215, 228
colonialism, 98
communication, *passim*
  centralized and decentralized, 211 ff., 215 f., 218, 220 ff.
  complementarity in, 20, 184
  digital, 165
  graphic, 23, 154
  interpersonal, 214, 216 ff.
  means of, 17, 111, 207
  mobile, 13, 20, 22 f., 55, 157, 168, 180, 185, 219
  networks of, 41, 46, 88 f., 212, 216, 220 ff., 226
  nonverbal, 80, 164 ff.
  patterns of, 140, 211, 227
  pictorial, 157, 178, 181, 183
  systems of, 63, 185, 216, 220
  technologies of, 46, 79 f., 94, 185, 188, 211, 213, 216 f., 220, 222
  and society, 13 f., 17, 20, 46, 73, 79 f., 94, 158, 184
community, *passim*
  mobile, 55, 183
  of knowledge, 11, 23
  scientific, 135, 189, 194, 202 f., 206

241

and accountability, 43, 45
and reciprocity, 14, 43 ff., 50 ff., 55, 66
computer, *passim*
   as a "General Purpose" machine, 87
   as a "number cruncher", 83 f.
computer games, 89, 123
computer science, 187, 199
computing revolution, 83
consciousness, 14, 133
   planetary, 97 f., 100 f.
conversation, 60 ff., 69, 73, 76, 81, 94, 111, 209, 222
Cooley, Charles Horton, 17
cooperation, 17, 31, 65, 101, 189, 201, 204, 206 ff.
cortex, 57 ff., 119, 159
Coy, Wolfgang, 16, 83, 235
Crane, Diana, 191, 208
Critchley, Macdonald, 165 f.
Csépe, Valéria, 22, 117, 235
culture, 15 f., 20, 51, 59, 74 ff., 78, 93, 95, 98, 102, 106, 112, 127, 129 f., 133, 139, 143 f., 164, 171, 179, 208
   episodic, 130
   mimetic, 130 ff., 163 f.
   mythical, 72, 130, 132
   oral-linguistic, 19, 101, 164
   theoretical, 130, 132
   and civilization, 18
   political humor culture, 228
cyberspace, 36, 100 f., 105, 208

Damasio, Antonio, 158
Dányi, Endre, 23, 211, 214, 235
data, 22, 46, 52, 55, 84, 113, 172, 175, 187, 189
   anthropological, 72 f.
   data pressure, 201 ff., 206
   data protection, 230
   demographic, 29
   digital, 85 ff., 90
   empirical, 79, 124, 136, 202, 204
   numerical, 186
   quasi-neutral status, 201 f.
   scientific data today, 197, 200–209
   scientometrical, 191
   sociolinguistic, 73

mobile and SMS traffic, 44, 46, 48
databases, 30, 44, 101, 202 f., 207, 216, 219
data communication, mobile, 88
data subject, 44, 46, 48 ff.
De Solla Price, J. D., *see* Price
Deutsch, Karl W., 20, 184
Dewey, John, 14, 17
diagrams, 143 ff., 152 ff., 160, 162
dialects, 15, 64 f., 74, 76 ff., 81
digital technology, 85, 106
discrimination, linguistic, 71, 77
distance, 40, 44, 63, 88, 93, 97 ff., 105 ff., 109 f., 114 f., 143, 145 f., 151 f., 158, 232
   virtual, 97, 100 ff.
Donald, Merlin, 23, 72 f., 129 ff., 163 f., 208
Douglas, Mary, 50
drawing, 95, 97, 154, 160 ff., 171, 174, 182
   drawing block handy all the time, 182
   some people incapable of, 160
Dunbar, Robin, 14 f., 57, 72 f., 78, 139 f., 163, 236
Durkheim, Emile, 54

Eco, Umberto, 181, 183
Edison, Thomas Alva, 90 f., 94
Eibl-Eibesfeldt, Irenäus, 164
Einstein, Albert, 188
Eisenstein, Elisabeth, 172
Ekman, Paul, 164 f.
election campaign, 23, 211 ff., 215 ff., 219 f., 223 f., 227 f., 232
electronic money, *see* money
Eliot, T. S., 20
e-mail, 63, 79 f., 88, 91, 94 f., 101, 103, 117, 136, 138, 140, 185, 208, 211 f., 214–223, 225, 227 f., 230 ff.
emoticons, 180
emotional bonding, 58
epistemology, 107 ff., 132, 185, 188 f., 203 ff., 209
evolution, 14 f., 23, 68, 98, 102, 115, 128 f., 132 ff., 139, 163, 198, 207
   of language, 72
   of money, 34 f.
   of the social brain, 57

facial cues, 63
Feyerabend, Paul, 185
figures of depiction, 146, 154
flaming, 63
Fodor, Jerry A., 129
Fox, Kate, 81, 224
freeriders, 64 f.
Freud, Sigmund, 118

Gedeon, Péter, 14, 25, 50, 232, 236
Gemeinschaft and *Gesellschaft*, 13, 53
Gestalt psychology, 162
Gestalt, 111, 146 f., 154, 162
gestures, 14, 17 f., 92, 117, 131, 144, 157, 161 f., 164–169
　language of gestures, 18, 157, 161, 165 ff.
Giddens, Anthony, 45
globalization, 97, 103
Gombrich, Ernst, 175 f., 179
Goody, Jack, 19, 172
graphics, 23, 85, 92, 143 ff., 148, 154 f., 158, 178, 182, 184, 218
graphs, 143–148, 154
Green, Nicola, 12 f., 30, 33, 43, 45, 52, 106, 236
Gregorian, Vartan, 21
grooming, 58, 60 f., 72
group, 15, 17, 20, 29, 39, 55, 57 f., 61, 63, 65 ff., 72–82
　size of social groups, 15, 58 f., 61 ff.
György, Péter, 17, 97, 237

Hajnal, István, 164, 172
Hann, Endre, 224
Harnad, Stevan, 102
Havelock, Eric, 19
Hayek, F. A. von, 35
Heidegger, Martin, 11–15
Herder, Gottfried, 15, 167
hippocampus, 119
Homo erectus, Homo sapiens, 130, 163
Horton, William, 170
Hrachovec, Herbert, 17, 105, 237

icon, 92, 143, 146, 165 ff., 175 ff.
iconic language, 156, 176 ff.
iconic revolution, 175

identity, 15, 45 ff., 50, 52, 54, 73 f., 78, 80, 82, 100, 103
imagery debate, 158 f.
impersonal intimacy, 28, 40, 50 f.
information, 12 f., 14, 20 ff., 32, 43, 52, 61, 64, 71, 73, 117, 128, 134, 137 ff., 143, 145, 151 f., 155, 173, 179, 184, 189, 202, 212, 217,
　and passim
　scientific, 193, 200 f.
　visual, 159, 173 ff., 179, 181
information overload, 33, 110
information processing, 58, 111, 119 ff.
information society, 11, 26, 28, 82, 114, 134
　mobile, 13, 25, 117
information technology, 26, 28 ff., 34, 38 ff., 44, 46, 71, 128, 212, 214, 232
interaction, 52, 58, 61 ff., 69, 102, 213 ff., 218, *and passim*
　communicative, 47 f.
interactivity, 165, 212, 215 ff.
　sequential, 217 f.
interest
　common, 39, 54
　economical and military, 188
　genetic, 65
　practical and theoretical, 199
　interest groups, 29, 55, 215
internet, *passim*
interpersonal relations, 45 ff., 49 f., 55
invisible college, 191, 208
ISOTYPE, 176 f., 180
Ivins, William M., Jr., 172 ff., 181 ff.

Katz, James E., 12 f., 17, 44
Kennedy, John, 171
knowledge
　contextual, 130 f.
　practical, 176
Kopomaa, Timo, 12
Kuhn, T. S., 185, 188, 190

Laki, János, 23, 40, 185, 237
Lakoff, George, 167 f.
language, *passim*
　natural, 130 f., 135
　nonverbal, 165

Platonic view of, 76 f.
Romantic philosophy of, 14, 128
social function of, 15, 60 f., 72 ff., 78, 80 ff., 133
spoken, 73 f.
standard variant, 77 ff.
visual, 157 f., 161, 168, 176–181, 197
written, 16, 76, 90, 165
large-scale science, 186 ff., 191 ff., 200 f., 206
Latour, Bruno, 171 f., 183, 191
learning, 22 f., 94, 117 ff., 131, 138 f.
implicit and explicit, 120 ff.
probability, 121
procedural, 118 ff.
sequence, 121
Lewicki paradigm, 121 f.
language use, 73–82
"correct", 76
literacy, 15, 34, 75, 77 f., 80, 94, 117, 164
alphabetic, 158, 172
secondary, 94
text traditions, 7
locality, 17, 31 ff., 35 ff., 39 ff., 45, 47, 232
Luria, A. R., 133

Manhattan Project, 185 ff.
maps, 97 f., 101, 143 f., 146, 148–154, 172, 175, 177
sketch maps, 149 ff., 154
market economy, 26, 200, 206
mobile, 14
mass customization, 26 f., 31, 33, 36, 40 f.
mass media, 211, 224, 227
mass production, 26 ff.
McLuhan, Marshall, 19
m-commerce, 31 f.
mobile marketing, 32 f.
meaning
contextual, 131
generic, 160
linguistic, 72
pictorial, 157, 159 ff., 170 f., 179
word meaning, 167
abstract concepts, 16, 157, 162, 180
media, digital, 83, 85 f.
media space, 99 f.

media theory, 105, 110
memory
collective, 53
cultural, 101
explicit and implicit, 118 ff.
external, 23, 71, 163, 208
procedural, 22, 118 ff.
memory system, 118, 123
working memory, 130 ff., 155
metaphor, 98, 143 ff., 165 f.
metonymy, 146, 167
Meyrowitz, Joshua, 207
Milton Keynes, 80
Mithen, Steven, 72, 133
m-money, *see* money
MMS (multimedia messaging), 89, 117, 181 ff., 219
mobile devices, 31 ff., 40 f., 43, 49, 51 f., 55, 117
mobile generation, 125
mobile phone, *passim*
as mate-attraction device, 66
built-in-camera, 182, 219
mobile phone users, 123, 214, 216
mobile technology, 47
money, 26, 28, 30, 34–38, 40, 50
electronic, 33 ff., 41
m-money, 37
private, 35
morphograms, 146, 154
Morse, Samuel, 16, 83, 89, 125
multiculturalism, 103
Musil, Robert, 18
Myerson, George, 11

Naisbitt, John, 20 f.
nation state, 36, 58, 99 f.
Nelson, Ted, 91, 102
net, 85 f., 88, 102, 140
networking, 85 f., 197 f.
networks, *passim*
size of, 59
Neumann, John v., 84
Neurath, Otto, 157, 176 ff., 180, 183
neurophysiology, 129, 158
Nietzsche, Friedrich, 16, 167
Norris, Pippa, 211 f., 218

244

Nyíri, Kristóf, 11 f., 15, 92, 132, 135, 140, 157, 164, 238
Odlyzko, Andrew, 216
Ong, Walter J., 15, 19 f.
orality, 15, 19
  secondary, 15, 19 f., 93 f., 111

Palló, Gábor, 23, 40, 185, 238
paradigm, 107, 121, 121 f., 188 f., 192, 197, 201, 203
parties, political, 212-217, 221 ff., 227, 231 f.
Peirce, Charles Sanders, 167
person, 25, 43 f., 47 ff.
  information personhood, 46
philosophy of language, 14
philosophy of science, 23, 159, 185, 203
photography, 111, 175
pictorial language, 161
pictorial meaning, 157, 171
pictures, 90, 108 ff., 157-164, 168-171, 173-185, 202, 218
  cinematographic, 160, 181
  mental, 158-162, 179
  moving, 92, 218
  static, 179
Plato, 76 f., 158, 165
Pléh, Csaba, 23, 127, 136, 163, 217, 238
Polanyi, Michael, 185
political campaign, 212, 217, 222, 231 f.
Pool, Ithiel de Sola, 99
pragmatics, 152, 154
presence, 17, 46, 74, 105, 107 ff., 113 ff., 160, 218
price discrimination, 29
Price, Derek de Solla, 186 ff., 191
Price, H. H., 159 f., 162, 165, 171, 179, 183
primates, 15, 57 f., 60 f., 64, 72, 130 f., 163
printing, 17, 19, 76 ff., 89, 101, 111, 130, 172 ff.
private sphere, 36, 231
Proust, Marcel, 118
psychoanalysis, 118
psychology, cognitive, 120, 123, 134,

radio, 17, 19, 88 ff., 93 f., 99 f., 109, 111 ff., 211, 213, 220 ff., 224
  digital, 112 f.
Ravetz, Jerome, 188 ff., 194
reaction time, 121 f.
relationships, personal and impersonal, 25-28, 30 f., 33, 38, 40, 50, 58, 158, 189
relativism, 129, 201, 203 f., 209
representation
  artificial, 197
  cognitive, 18, 72, 119, 130 ff., 135, 148, 160 ff., 167, 171 f.
  graphical, 143 ff., 151 ff.
  handshapes representing, 167
  mathematical, 189
  pictorial, 113, 157, 172, 174 ff., 178 f., 197
  systems of, 133
  verbal, 113, 152
Rheingold, Howard, 12
risk, 45, 48-53, 55, 65, 222, 236
Roesler, Alexander, 11 f.
Rötzer, Florian, 106
Rousseau, Jean-Jacques, 15
rule acquisition and application, 121 ff.
rules, explicit and implicit, 121 ff.
Russell, Bertrand, 159

Sándor, Klára, 15, 71, 74 f., 78, 239
Saussure, Ferdinand de, 76
science, 66, 95, 172 f., 177, 185 f., 188-201, 203 f., 206 ff.
  academic, 189, 192
  applied, 195, 200
  Big Science, Little Science, 185-188, 193, 200-206, 209 f.
  industrialized, 188-191, 194
  "Mode 1", 194-198, 201
  "Mode 2", 194-198, 200 f.
  modern, 89, 107, 171 f., 191
  post-academic, 193 f., 198 ff.
  pure, 192 f., 195
  schools and traditions, 190, 201, 203, 209
  scientific revolution, 190
  steady state, 191-194, 206
  unified, 176, 196

search
    costs of, 29 f.
    Internet search, 28, 135 f.
    location as a parameter, 30
self and community, 43, 45 ff., 50, 52
    individualized subject, 53
    mobile subject, 49 ff., 55
semantics, 130, 152, 166
semiotics, 108 f.
signs
    conventional, 169, 171
    iconic, 167
    indexical, 77, 167 ff.
    natural, 157, 170 f., 179
    symbolic, 22, 78, 167, 169
    verbal and nonverbal, 63
    sign system, 108, 177
sign language, natural, 165
Simmel, Georg, 53 f.
skills, 118 ff., 125, 127, 138 f., 173, 183
    motor, 121
slang, 79
SMS, 40, 91, 95, 103, 117, 138, 140, 157, 211 f., 214–223, 227–232
society, 13 f., 17 f., 20, 26, 53, 164, 184
    oral, 19
    industrial, 26
    modern, 67, 89, 134, 224
    post-industrial, 53, 61
    traditional, 25, 67
software technology, 48
space, 47, 81, 97, 106 ff., 114 f., 117, 224
    geographic, 36
    graphic, 143–146, 154
    media, 99 f.
    planetary, 110
    social, 98 ff.
    virtual, 100, 110
speech bubble, 170
spread spectrum, 112 f.
Stokoe, William C., 166 f., 169, 179
storage capacity, 92
strategies
    cooperative, 65, 209
    explicit, 125
    implicit, 121 f., 124 f.
    in campaigns, 214 f., 231

product differentiation, 29
    social, 58
    viral marketing, 225 f.
Sükösd, Miklós, 23, 211, 214, 239
synechdoche, 146
syntax, 152, 154, 166 f.

teenager, *see* children
telecommunication, 62 f., 89, 98, 106, 109, 111, 113
telegraph, 16 f., 34, 89 f., 93, 97 ff.
telephone, 13, 17, 19, 43, 45, 63, 83, 85 ff., 91, 93 f., 99, 109, 111 f., 114, 217, 219
tele-presence, 105 ff., 109 ff., 113 ff.
text, 75 f., 83, 85 f., 89-93, 95, 108, 111, 176, 180, 182, 184, 215, 218
thinking, 57, 128, 135, 161, 167, 172, 207 ff.
    animal, 163
    community the agent of, 14, 23, 208
    imageless, 160
    in absence, 160
    pictorial, 23, 135, 158 ff., 162 f., 183
    productive, 163
    rational, 204
    verbal, 160
    scientific styles of, 94, *see also* paradigm
Tompa, Ferenc, 22
Tönnies, Ferdinand, 13 f., 20, 53
tools
    cognitive, 155
    computer as tool for the mind, 83, 197
    graphic kits, 151 f.
    language as a tool, 14, 73, 75
    mobile phone as a tool, 41, 119
    postmodern campaign tools, 215, 221
    SMS as an advertising tool, 227
    tool acquisition and manipulation, 120
    tool vs. machine, 11
triple helix, 197 ff.
trust, 14, 25 f., 31, 34, 39, 43, 45, 50 ff., 55, 58 ff., 64
    personal and impersonal, 26 ff., 34, 40
Tufte, Edward R., 144, 175
Turing, Alan M., 84
Tversky, Barbara, 23, 143 ff., 147 ff., 153 f., 179, 240

value
    commodity and exchange value, 49 f.
    signal value, 68
viral marketing, 225 ff.
Virilio, Paul, 106
visual images, 157 ff.
voice recording, 90
voice, 40, 47, 83, 86, 88–95, 117, 164, 180 f., 184
Vygotsky, L. S., 133

Wagner, Richard, 15
Ware, Colin, 171, 176, 179
Weber, Max, 54
Weinberg, Alvin, 186, 188, 193

Wellman, Barry, 13, 39 f., 79, 140, 217 f., 232
Wittgenstein, Ludwig, 15, 160 f., 164, 169 ff.
word languages, 157, 161, 164, 166 f., 177 ff., 181
working memory, *see* memory
World Wide Web, 71, 88, 205 f., 227
writing, phonetic, 75 f.

Yazdani, Masoud, 178

Ziman, John, 191–194, 207
Zuse, Konrad, 83 f.